THE EUNUCH

A Novel

Jonathan Kos-Read

The Eunuch

By Jonathan Kos-Read

ISBN-13: 978-988-8769-21-6

© 2021 Jonathan Kos-Read

This book has been reset in 10pt Book Antiqua. Spellings and punctuations are left as in the original edition.

FICTION / Mystery & Detective

EB141

All rights reserved. No part of this book may be reproduced in material form, by any means, whether graphic, electronic, mechanical or other, including photocopying or information storage, in whole or in part. May not be used to prepare other publications without written permission from the publisher except in the case of brief quotations embodied in critical articles or reviews. For information contact info@earnshawbooks.com

Published by Earnshaw Books Ltd. (Hong Kong)

For

Li Zhiyin

List of Characters

Enchenkei Gett — Eunuch, ex-spy for the Jin Empire, now Chief Investigator of the Bureau of Palace Investigations in the Jin Court. Jurchen.

Sulo — Adventurer working as Chief of the Bureau of Enforcement for the Jin Emperor. Italian.

Han Zongcheng — Minister of Espionage for the Jin Emperor. Runs the Imperial Examination once every two years. Chinese.

Kob Meke — Chief of 2nd Class Surveillance Squads for the Jin Emperor. Jurchen.

Arigh — Chief of the Bureau of Interrogations for the Jin Emperor. Jurchen.

Curdeger — Once a high official, now simply the lowly Head of the Sub-Bureau of Evidence Analysis. Jurchen.

Imperial Mother — The power behind the throne. Jurchen.

Emperor — 17 years old. Has been Jin Emperor for three years. Jurchen.

Lao Kou — Palace Librarian and ex-assassin. Jurchen.

Diao Ju — the murdered Concubine Third Class. Chinese.

Ech Un — a boy from a high family. Jurchen.

Gogoro Shen — Jurchen eunuch, Head of The Imperial Harem.

Be empty, still and idle, and from your place of darkness observe the defects of others.
—**Han Feizi, Legalist Essays, (BC 231)**

The City

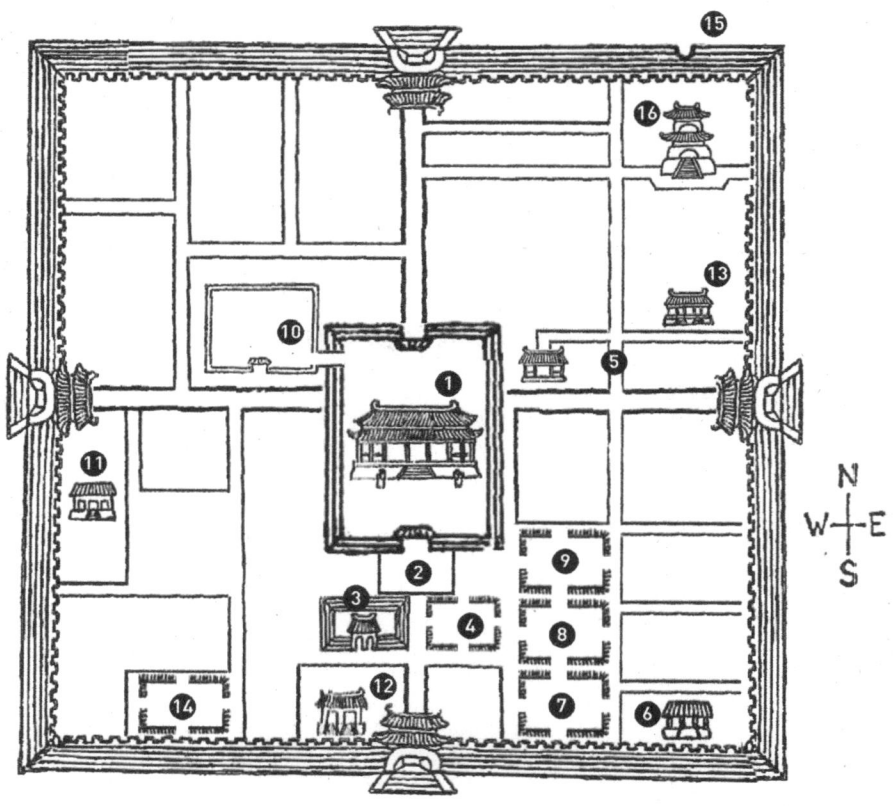

1. Imperial Palace
2. Palace Square
3. Royal Deer Park
4. Steaming District
5. Curdeger's residence
6. Gett residence
7. Huihui brothel district
8. Jurchen brothel district
9. Chinese brothel district
10. Examination Hall
11. Orphanage
12. Eternal Spring Guest House
13. Kob Meke residence
14. Medicine shops district
15. Secret tunnel
16. The Iron Pagoda

The Palace

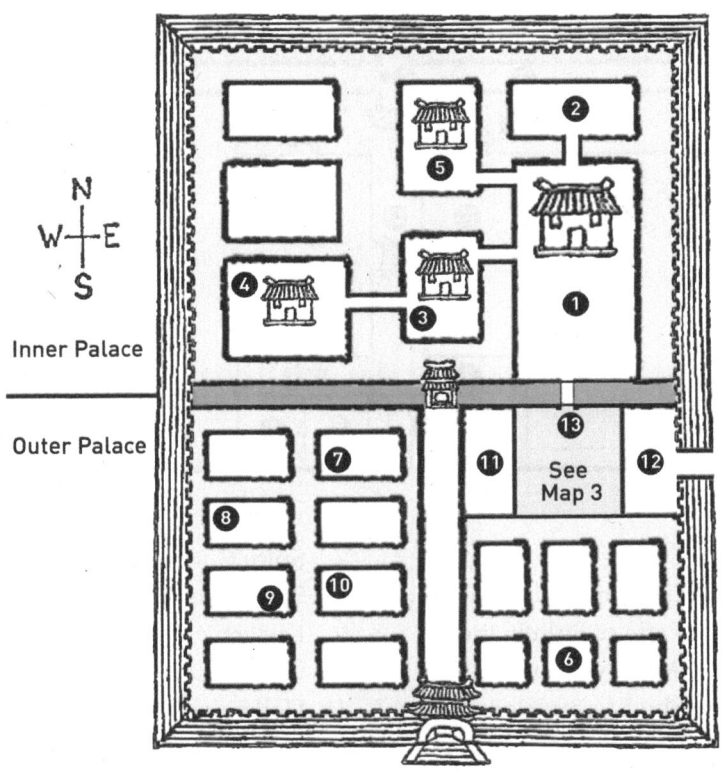

1. Emperor's Residence
2. Harem
3. Throne Room
4. Imperial Mother's Residence
5. Heir-Producing Room
6. Library
7. Sulo office
8. Curdeger office
9. Interrogations
10. Ministry of Espionage
11. Servant Dormitory
12. Subsidiary Victualing Bay
13. Hallway of Everlasting Spring

The Antechamber & Environs

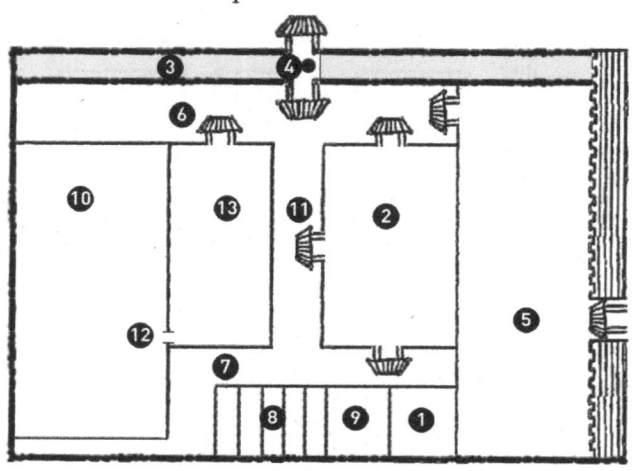

1. Dining Hall
2. Garden of Blissful Respite
3. Patio of Fulmination
4. Antechamber of Shuddering Hooves (location of Concubine body)
5. Subsidiary Victualing Hall
6. Wardrobe Corridor
7. Spice Corridor
8. Spice Rooms
9. Kitchen
10. Servant Dormitory
11. Hallway of Everlasting Spring
12. Unmapped door
13. Wardrobe Rooms

THE DEAD CONCUBINE, Third Class, was pointing at her vagina.

It wasn't intentional. Simply that her body had fallen in such a way that it appeared so. But in the final analysis, perhaps she was not pointing at it, instead through it. Since it is the passageway for all energy in the universe. And thus, ultimately, the key to this strange and complex case.

She was found in the late morning by a tile polisher in the middle of the Hour of the Snake. It was still snowing outside, a light dusting that speckled the stone ground and blew in quiet, turbulent eddies down the long-walled avenues that surrounded the Palace. But this anteroom far inside was warm, and the polisher had set herself in a shaft of sunlight. She was on her knees scraping red dust out of tile grooves when she saw a fly, noticed it because they were rarely seen this far into the Palace. A team was employed to make sure of it. Yet, here one was. Assuming, rightly, that blame would be assigned to her if the fly were discovered, she stood to kill it. It was then that she saw the body.

She began to scream, out of surprise, but also instinctual fear, again prescient, that she might be blamed.

The nearest Palace guards entered through the locked doors on either end of the antechamber. They immediately came to the same conclusion and rushed back to their command stations. Their commanders listened, then ran to the barracks. From there,

THE EUNUCH

in moments, an Alert was issued. A coup, a Chinese assassin, the Southern General, all were considered. The Palace entered a state of emergency.

Runners arrived at the dormitory of the Imperial Bodyguards who then raced down the dim, carved-wood halls to the weapons storehouse where battle machines sat in silent, coiled darkness. They sealed off the Palace, the largest of the men locked outside the gates, the rest barricaded within, stretching the war machines into readiness, close-fighting swords drawn.

The fastest Palace horses were saddled and their riders drove them to the outer passageways, hooves leaving dark, clearly defined prints on the snow-dusted stone. Each exited the Palace by a separate gate, did not slow even as they bore down on the morning crowd along the wide avenues leading to the city wall. The teakwood gates of the city were swung open, and the riders disappeared.

The land surrounding the Capital, despite the name given it by the Great Emperor, was not beautiful. It was flat and drab, and on those parts of it not covered in gray, struggling farms were strewn with ragged, wind-etched poplars.

Each rider had about one hundred *li* to cover; an hour of hard riding. Their horses arrived, swerving outside the fortified gate of army emplacements, snow and dust blooming to mix with the mist coalescing off their bodies. The couriers showed Imperial seals, were ushered into the presence of army commanders and handed over identical messages: "Deploy Immediately. Possible Coup in Progress."

One final deployment occurred, swift but unnoticed: nondescript men excused themselves, some eunuchs, some teachers, even a floor sweeper of the Imperial Examination Hall (busily being cleaned for the arrival of the candidates). They trickled out into the city and disappeared into the cold bustle of the morning, through the steam of hot horse's milk and cooking meat buns, along the uneven, grey brickwork of the city's twisting narrow streets, through and beyond the city gates until, dusty and cold, they too arrived at the same military units. They slipped in: side gates left unlocked, trenches whose guards had temporarily left their posts, a momentarily open stretch of dry and trampled crop field.

The message, when passed in hushed tones in small disused corners of the camps, amidst the chaos of deployment, was different: "If commander moves toward city, eliminate, reorganize, ensure loyalty to Emperor."

These commanders, who hadn't reached their positions through stupidity, redoubled their efforts to display loyalty. In the end, only one was killed. But no action was recommended against the assassin for his mistake. He was judged to have acted within the bounds of his mandate; a salutary reminder to other unit commanders that the Emperor, while far away, had a hand at their throats and could tighten it at will.

Thus, in under an hour, a vast storm had spread out from that one small room, and was still expanding. If one were now to move in reverse, to slide out of the military units, back down the frozen roads through the bleak countryside to the red walls of the city, down the crowded streets, through the massive doors of the Palace, along the whispering corridors and back to the small antechamber from which it had begun, we would see, standing over the body of the dead concubine, the Chief Imperial Investigator, the eunuch, Enchenkei Gett.

He was tall, a Jurchen, and extraordinarily thin. His sunken cheeks and wind-burned face made him an old forty. He was chewing sourly on a betel nut, which (as this species of nut does) had stained his teeth a reddish brown and his saliva bright crimson, as if his mouth were full of blood.

THE EUNUCH

He was thinking about the dead concubine, thinking about the enormous maelstrom that was spreading from this central point.

"The flow of energy," he decided, "is not good."

二

FOR EVERYONE in the room, Gett knew, the problem was the same — time. They had very little of it to make a decision about *one* fact. Not who had killed the girl, but who had *not*. Gett looked around the antechamber. He'd never been here before — it was restricted to harem officials and concubines. It was narrow, Gett estimated about two arms' width, but long, maybe four times its width, a hallway wishing to be a room. Rugs on stone-tiled floor, paintings on walls, high slit paper-covered windows. A small inlaid dark red table in one far corner. Under it, the dead concubine. Around her, filling the room, Palace technicians and their bureau heads, about twenty people in the tight space. Gett walked over and stood in the spot where the tile cleaner had been working and bent down. He looked over to where the dead concubine was. Couldn't see her. Stood up, a little hunched so he was the tile cleaner's height. Now he could see the concubine. So that checked out.

He saw the Minister of Espionage step away from his followers, move towards him. Han Zongcheng, the Chinese traitor. Age scored face. Watching the room through thin black eyes. Nothing obvious in his expression, but then there never was with bureau heads, and especially Chinese ones who could survive at this level. A preparer, he was already in his red phoenix Audience Robe, knew what was coming.

Gett took the required pose — back straight, hands clasped in

THE EUNUCH

front but with head un-bowed, in mandated recognition of his own racial superiority even though he was lower rank.

"She is Chinese," said Han in his slightly raspy voice.

Gett nodded.

"Relevant?"

"It is never neutral," said Gett.

Han said nothing. Gett waited.

"The Examination is in three days," continued Han.

"It is."

"Who do you think killed her?"

"I don't know yet," said Gett.

"Who do you suspect?"

"Like you, I just arrived."

"Does it look like an assassination attempt?"

"No, I don't think it does."

"Why?"

"Well." Gett paused and considered. "It's not messy enough. An assassination and 1st class three concubine gets killed? I don't see it."

"In your experience?"

"In my experience."

Han was silent again, then asked, "Do Curdeger and Arigh have any theories?"

"They think what you think."

"Which is?"

Gett shrugged his shoulders, chewed his betel nut. "You know."

"What do you think?" asked Han.

"I'm not sure, but I don't think so."

"Why?"

Again, Gett thought about it. "Same reason, it doesn't feel like that."

"Specifically what?"

"It's late morning. What would she have been doing there? At this time, she would be gone already. If she wasn't, then what? It doesn't taste right."

"Thank you, Chief Investigator. I will speak to Technician Curdeger and Questioner Arigh." Han turned and walked back to his followers while Gett returned to the dead girl on the other side of the narrow room. Slowly and carefully (because he had the extremely long legs and arms of a teenage castrate), he knelt down to begin his examination.

She had a deep stab in the abdomen and a large laceration along the inside of her forearm. Dark blood had leaked out of these wounds and stained the carpets on the stone floor. Her clothes were made from thick, red silk from loom factories in Hangzhou. No staining except with blood, probably new. Headgear marked her as a Concubine Third Class, relatively low level, but still with potential monthly access to the Emperor and defined by protocol as capable of bearing an Imperial prince. One of the top two hundred women of the thirty million in the empire.

Gett examined her face and neck for signs of choking. Nothing obvious. He decided she was southern, clearly Chinese, not Jurchen, dark arching eyebrows and a bridge on her nose. Different from the softer, flatter faces of Jurchen girls. About nineteen.

Oddly, she was beautiful.

This was surprising. Most subjects believed the Emperor enjoyed a vast harem of beautiful wives. This was incorrect. Wife and concubine-choosing for the Emperor was a complex, ritualized, *scientific* process.

There were two criteria. First, she had to be intelligent. There was understanding that this was inherited. Much investigation had gone into discovering the mechanism. It had not been found, but the fact was recognized.

Second, she had to be lucky. There was a small set of families from whom an Imperial wife or concubine could be chosen. She was a bargaining chip in the complex power dynamics of the Empire.

So the girl's obvious beauty was an anomaly.

"Who kill the girl?"

Gett looked up. Chief of Enforcement Sulo stood over him, the deep-set, blue eyes of his race suspicious and searching. Gett levered himself to his feet, knees cracking from the fulcruming of his long thin legs. Sulo scratched his thick black beard, watching Gett angrily, speaking in his strange toneless accent and odd grammar.

"We don't know yet," answered Gett.

"Killed by somebody outside or inside?"

"Do you want an opinion?"

"If you got facts, I want facts. If only opinion, also fine."

"I think it was outside, but not political."

"Why?"

"It just feels like that to me."

"You think he didn't do it?"

"No, I don't think so."

Sulo looked at him with a deep well of distrust in his blue eyes.

"You will investigate it, maybe."

"I don't know. Jurisdiction will be decided in about an hour with the Emperor and the Imperial Mother."

"She has jurisdiction?"

"She assigns it."

"But maybe it's your jurisdiction, yeah?"

"You know how these things go."

"Maybe. What will you do?"

"Well, technically we don't know if it is a murder yet."

Sulo, as was his way, didn't bother to respond, just looked at Gett, eyes furious, searching for a lie. Finally he turned back to his guards.

The reason for all this, what all of them were seeking, was *certainty*. This death presented them with a difficult choice. It was an opportunity. Because of the identity of the victim and the location of her body, whoever ran the investigation would have broad powers of expropriation. That appropriated bureaucratic control could be locked down and not relinquished. The investigation was, in experienced hands, a long knife. But it was a slippery one.

Chief Analyst Curdeger was squatting by one of the doors with his technicians, quietly and as unobtrusively as possible examining the locks for signs of tampering. Gett caught his attention and gestured politely for him to come.

Gett straightened respectfully — he outranked Curdeger, but like him, he was a Jurchen — as the huge man lumbered over.

"Crime?" Gett asked.

Curdeger leaned in. "Chief Investigator, the girl has two wounds: one on her abdomen, the other on her arm. The second one appears to be a defense wound. I would say she was stabbed like this…" He stepped back and mimed an under-arm stab at waist height. "The girl probably saw it coming so she pulled to one side and brought her arm down, like this…" He swiped a thick arm down in a flailing defensive movement. "That is how she got the deep laceration on the arm."

"When did she die?"

"Well, Chief Investigator, it is always hard to say, but I would estimate that it was at least six hours ago."

"Why?"

THE EUNUCH

"Her blood has hardened considerably and has darkened in a way that indicates roughly that time period."

Gett took all this in as he slowly chewed. Curdeger's description confirmed that he suspected the same thing as Sulo and Han Zongcheng but had decided that discretion was safer.

"Which way do you think the girl came into the room?" Gett asked.

Curdeger had prepared for this question because he didn't want to answer it.

"Chief Investigator, as you know, security dictates that one of these doors must be locked at all times."

"And?"

"In fact, they both were."

"The cleaner was locked in here?"

"She was not."

"So?"

"The outer door was unlocked to allow her access."

"And?"

"The door to the inner quarters was left locked. So when the tile cleaner arrived, both inner and outer doors were locked."

"The guards see anything?"

"I have not asked, as that is beyond the scope of my mandate."

Gett understood this was all he would get.

"How soon will you be able to get me the physical report on the girl's death?"

"I will begin it as soon as I leave here. You may come by tonight, no matter how late. I will be there."

"Thank you."

"Thank you, Chief Investigator."

And with that, Curdeger turned slowly and moved, almost tiptoeing, back to the body.

Gett walked carefully around the girl, past Curdeger and his technicians who were on the floor examining wood fragments around the outer door (studiously ignoring the inner one) and stepped out into the hall that led to the outer Palace quarters.

The hall was long with a turn. Yurt carpets on a stone floor. Walls of bamboo and silk reinforced by brick. It had six entrances — to a subsidiary victualing bay, to the spice testing rooms, to the Imperial Wardrobes, to a Dining Room and attached kitchen, and was connected to two outdoor areas, a garden and a patio set in the space between the Inner and Outer Palace. It was most importantly meant for defense — hard and narrow. The door from the hallway to the antechamber was thick wood with a massive padlock.

In the hallway, Chief of the Bureau of Interrogations, Questioner Arigh was squatting next to the very unhappy Imperial Guard who had originally sounded the alert. Arigh, as usual, was dressed perfectly — not just well, but literally without flaws. His robe new, his topknot exactly centered. Gett suspected it was his way of subtly insulting those around him. At this moment his face was screwed up in artificial, caustic surprise.

"Come on," Arigh said to the frightened guard, "Don't lie to me. You must be lying to me!"

"N-n-no, I'm r-r-really n-n-not."

"You are. I know you are. I can read people."

"N-n-nobody came through."

"Look, I am an honest person. So listen to me right now. You are a piece of Chinese shit. You came from your little village. Now you're a guard in the Palace! I bet you fuck a lot of girls because of the great job you have. But let me tell you. If you don't give me the truth soon, you will regret it. Look into my eyes and believe what I am saying, I am saying 'soon', because you *will* tell me the truth eventually, but if you make me lose face or slow down this investigation, I will torture you to death and cut off

THE EUNUCH

the penis that you use to fuck these local girls and I will send it to your fucking mother with a note that says, 'This is what happens when you let your dumb son come to the big city.'"

"B-b-but really! P-p-p-lease believe me! Nobody came through!"

"All right, torture for you."

Arigh noticed Gett, hopped up and strutted over. His face wasn't handsome, instead a shadow play of handsomeness, illuminated by the glow of family money and status.

"Stupid kid, unlucky to be on the job tonight," said Arigh.

"He is telling the truth?" Gett asked.

"Probably."

"How many guards on duty?"

"One on each side."

"Where's the other one?"

"He's not available."

"Dead?"

"With Enforcement. With Sulo."

Gett looked over at the guard. If the information extracted through Arigh's interrogation of him matched the essentials of what he was saying now, and if Han Zongcheng and Sulo had asked these same questions (and Gett couldn't imagine a scenario in which they hadn't) then they would have all reached the same conclusion.

What made the coming interview with the Emperor dangerous was their suspicion about who had killed her.

Both had quickly assessed the obvious — her identity, the location of her corpse, the extreme unlikelihood that an assassin could have penetrated into this room — and very quickly begun to suspect that the Emperor, for whatever reason (and whatever reason he had was legally valid) had simply killed one of his concubines. Some of the details — who locked the doors, where the guard for the inner door was, when it happened—were odd, but the assumption was, if investigated, there would be an explanation.

In such a situation, the bureau tasked with the investigation was in grave danger. While there were no legal ramifications for the Emperor, there was a potential grave loss of face for him, especially following the Alert. It was possible for the investigating bureau to emerge from such an endeavor unscathed, or even with distinction, but it was difficult. And the penalty for failure was high.

And so, no more time. Gett watched Sulo and Han Zongcheng slipping out. He saw their retinues padding silently and malevolently after them and he knew that he, too, must go.

二

"THE IMPERIAL I will now decide jurisdiction," said the Emperor.

He was young. Seventeen. He had become Emperor three years before. And he sat in that peculiar way that all sons of powerful fathers do. Arrogant, but with doubt trickling out, like un-found leaks in rain.

Behind him sat his mother, obscured by a bead curtain. Gett did not know her well and did not know the details, but after Emperor Gogt-Ech's death, this wife had come out of the struggle alive and with the alliances she needed to sit in that place behind her son. So, lucky, intelligent, a killer.

She whispered something to her son from behind the curtain that separated and bound them in a symbiotic relationship, one who knew how to use power, the other who was its source.

"Respected Chief Investigator, come forward," said the Emperor.

The room was large and dimly lit. Torches lined the walls. Black-clad attendants had prostrated themselves on the black floor making it seem to undulate. They formed a long corridor along which Gett crawled forward. On the freezing stone below the Emperor, Gett kowtowed seven times.

"Please your August Emperor, possessed of the wisdom of the sage Emperors, Yao and Shun, I, your slave, have come to do your bidding."

Again, the rustling whisper from behind the beads.

"You will give your opinion regarding the disposition of responsibility for this investigation," said the boy Emperor.

Gett couldn't of course look up. But he heard in the young Emperor's voice no fear. There could be no punishment for him in the legal sense. But he was inexperienced. If he had killed the girl he would find himself in a situation for which the details and parameters would be strange. Because it was a knife killing, close up, the impact on him would be very strong. Gett heard none of that in his voice.

So now, a decision. A case like this was investigated not with an eye towards truth, but instead towards survival. As Chief Investigator he was a valuable sacrifice. Better to control it.

"Your August Majesty is humbly requested and begged to grant jurisdiction to the Imperial Investigation Department of the Eighth Secretariat."

More rustling. The soft, inaudible whispering voice of the boy Emperor's mother.

"The Imperial I requires an explanation as to why," said the Emperor.

"I humbly submit the following facts. First, the death occurred in the Palace. The charter of the Bureau of Imperial Investigations, granted by the Sage Emperor's August father, states that such deaths, and all serious crimes committed in the Palace, fall under our jurisdiction. Second, it was a death. All deaths, to avoid politicization, are to be investigated by our bureau whose sole function it is to investigate Palace crimes. Third, the deceased is a member of the Imperial entourage. Fourth, even though she is a Chinese, and so of a lesser race, the Emperor's August Father decreed that such victims are to be treated as equal to Jurchens within the Palace. Thus, I humbly beg and abjectly remonstrate, on behalf of the ministry which I here represent, that jurisdiction be granted to the Imperial Investigation Department of the

THE EUNUCH

Eighth Secretariat."

This, thought Gett, was about right. More, and Han Zongcheng and Sulo would suspect he possessed information they did not. Less, and he would not be granted jurisdiction.

"This will be considered by the Imperial I. You are dismissed."

Gett crawled backwards through the long black corridor of supplicants to his place next to Han Zongcheng and Sulo. He considered what they would think of what he had said. He had the choice to speak first only on this matter. On any other he would be expected to give way. So now they would watch him, but then they would anyway. At best, the lesser of two evils.

The Emperor's reedy voice piped up again. "The Imperial I will hear Enforcer Sulo."

Gett, from low on the floor, watched Sulo crawl forward. Gett watched carefully for a sign of what he would do.

"Please, the August Emperor is like the Emperor Yao and the Emperor Shun. Like a sage. I of the Enforcement Bureau have something to say about jurisdiction." Sulo's Jurchen was good, but the formal Jurchen of these audiences was complex.

"The Imperial I listens," said the Emperor.

"We are the Enforcement Bureau. The responsibility of ours is for the Emperor's safety. We guard him. If something happens, we must work out why. This dead concubine was found dead in the place close to the Emperor. So this is a safety issue of the Emperor."

Gett, listened, waiting for his jump in either direction.

"So I represent the Enforcement Bureau to say the Emperor must grant the Enforcement Bureau jurisdiction in this case."

There it was—Sulo's decision. A *mistake*. Instead of the polite, formal word that carried the meaning of both "hope" and "suggest" he had used the vernacular for "must". This was unacceptable. He would be denied jurisdiction as a matter of etiquette. Tomorrow he would brush out an apology to the Emperor. Horrified at his error of vocabulary, he would beg the Emperor to consider his foreign origins and grant clemency. His error would be forgiven as one of ignorance—he was a foreigner after all—but jurisdiction would already have been denied him. Thus would he extricate himself.

Gett thought about this. He knew that Sulo understood killing. Knew he'd done it and seen it done. Knew how it felt. Sulo could see and hear the Emperor—and hear the same things—as well as Gett. And he knew what they meant. But he had removed himself completely.

"Enforcer Sulo," said the Emperor. "Your entreaties have been heard by the Imperial I."

You are dismissed. Minister for the Gathering of Intelligence Within the Empire Han Zongcheng, come forward."

Han crawled across the dark stones, more painful for him because of his age. He kowtowed three times, with full outstretch because of his lower status as a Chinese.

Rustling. Whispers.

"Loyal Chinese servant, Minister Han Zongcheng; the Imperial I wishes to listen to your opinion on the issue of jurisdiction for the matter at hand."

"Honorable Sage King. Equal to the Sage Kings of the Xia and Shang Emperors of old, equal to the great fount of wisdom of Kongzi, Mengzi and Zhuzi, I have carefully examined the evidence and have concluded that a crime has been committed and I have determined by whom."

Gett watched Sulo flick up startled eyes from the floor.

"Who committed that crime?"

"I did, your August Imperial Majesty. As the Minister of Espionage of the Empire, a Ministry whose sole function it is to provide the Emperor with a clear view of all that occurs around

THE EUNUCH

him from the closest to the most distant, I failed in my task to apprehend such a crucial piece of intelligence ahead of time. That oversight—by a bureau composed of thousands of people but ultimately run by me—allowed a death to occur in the very heart of the Emperor's quarters. My fault is so great as to merit great punishment. This investigation will, by necessity, uncover, layer by layer, the depths of my failure. And so of course I must remove myself from consideration as the Minister to lead it. How could I be trusted to run it fairly and impartially when in so doing I would incriminate myself? Even the sage Zhou Yan and Daoist immortal Zhengyang Zushi would be tempted to hide their failure in such a situation. No, I cannot allow myself to be tempted because this would weaken the Empire. Thus I remonstrate to the Emperor that he consider neither I nor the bureau that I lead as suited to handling this investigation. I will rather focus on administering the Examination fairly and speedily."

Gett chewed on his betel nut contemplatively as he stared at the floor. Han had made the same choice. So, done.

But then something surprising happened. Han continued talking.

"And so, Your Majesty, I would request that my role be reduced to a supervisory capacity. Whomsoever is granted jurisdiction would be required only to compile daily reports for me to disseminate within my bureau so we can understand both the magnitude of our failure and the details of how to correct them."

This astonished Gett. Not because it was illogical, but because it was irrelevant. If Han wished to extricate himself, he had already succeeded. Now he was drawing himself back in.

"Your plea has been heard by the Imperial I. You are dismissed."

Han kowtowed again and crawled back to his position next to Sulo. He, Gett and Sulo, heads to the ground, waited for the Emperor to speak.

"I will contemplate this matter and issue a decree within hours."

The Emperor stood and walked behind his curtain and away.

The three of them kept their heads to the ground as the Emperor's scribes stood and filed out, their black robes rustling quietly. Gett and Sulo waited (as protocol required) for Han to rise first. Then Sulo rose, and finally, Gett, creakily on his spindly legs.

Han turned to Gett. "Irrespective of the jurisdictional decision the Emperor makes, I will be honored to work with the chosen bureau and its head in uncovering how my Ministry missed this important issue." And then again, to Gett, "I will expect an exchange of secretaries to make the transfer of daily reports efficient and timely and to see that they are prepared in a manner and form that is compatible with the procedures of our bureau."

"Of course."

Han turned to leave. "Bureau Chief Sulo, goodbye."

"Yes. Goodbye."

Han walked out. Sulo waited as long as protocol required, then followed. Gett, alone now, exited the audience hall.

He thought about Han's motivation. What could he want? How was this the way to get it? He had removed himself from the investigation but demanded he be kept informed. There was some aspect he wished to shape. On its own, that meant little. Men like Han, with long complex histories in the Palace, were always involved in equally complex feuds. Any investigation could bump up against them.

Gett, while thinking these thoughts, was walking down a long side corridor that led out of the audience chamber. Because it was poorly lit and dark, it was not surprising that he didn't see

THE EUNUCH

Sulo standing next to a bend in the corridor until he was almost upon him.

"Gett."

"Bureau Chief Sulo."

"Is good have opportunity maybe work to with you on the case."

"Yes," said Gett, "this will be a complex case. It will require cooperation."

"Maybe. I think you don't need."

"No, no, I definitely would."

"Yeah, maybe."

"And if the jurisdiction is assigned to you, I will put my bureau at your disposal."

"Yeah. Maybe you are better anyway. Ha ha."

"That's very generous of you."

"Yeah, maybe."

"Do you have any suggestions for how to start the investigation?"

"I think this case too complicated. Too much politics."

"I see."

"But maybe I can help. We meet with each other, have a meeting, yeah?"

"Where?"

"You come to my office."

"Of course."

"You come alone."

"I can do that."

Again, Sulo fixed him with his deep blue eyes—eyes that searched for betrayal. Then he smiled.

"I go home. Tired. Too much politics."

"Of course."

Sulo turned and heavily (but quietly) made his way down

the hall.

And in the dark Gett stood. Safety was ebbing away like a tide. Failure could mean a painful death, broken by delicate, expert hands. But what was failure in a case where the Emperor was the suspect? He considered whether the investigation was growing complex. He decided it was not. In the end there was him. There was the murderer. There was a path that would lead him there. The rest were just stones on the way. He hurried off down the dark hall on his long legs. His silk robes swished slightly against the stone floor.

It was Arigh's ordinariness that always struck Gett because Gett knew torturers (both as partners and, in the dark moments of his life, as their subject) and they were usually strange people, deeply different in disturbing and unsettling ways. Arigh was not. He had either made peace with it, didn't care, or pretended not to, and (again oddly) Gett couldn't tell which it was. And Gett had survived for a long time on being good at just that.

So when Gett, with a slight buzz on from a fresh nut, walked into the Bureau of Interrogations it was, as always, with a bit of wariness.

A young kid watched Gett enter. He had the brittle pride that comes with being part of a powerful bureau and being too young to have ever been kicked out of it.

"Hello, is your boss here?"

"Who are you?"

"I'm Ecengkei Gett, from the Bureau of Imperial Investigations. Who are you?"

"Ech Un, of the Harug clan," the kid said proudly.

"Then you are from a great family."

"Yes."

"Questioner Arigh is honored to have such an important partner in his work."

"It is I who am honored to have the opportunity to work with the second son of such a great family as Questioner Arigh's."

"I am honored to have the opportunity to work with both of you."

"Yes."

"Is Questioner Arigh available?"

"He is newly involved in an investigation."

"Yes. I am part of it."

"Message boy!" Ech Un yelled back into the bureau. In a few seconds, an old Chinese man hobbled out and prostrated himself in front of Ech Un.

"Boy, take this message to the secretary of Questioner Arigh. Wait for a response then bring it back here."

The old man tottered off. Gett waited quietly, chewing his betel nut. He welcomed the empty moment, thought about Ech Un who knew neither Gett himself nor his bureau. The most dangerous people in any organization were the incompetent ones, the level of their incompetence a watermark for how powerful their families had to be to force the bureaucracy to accept them. He wondered if Ech Un would learn how to deal with the Palace before he was squashed. Gett decided he had even odds. His family would get him a few reprieves from mistakes. He'd learn or...well, he wouldn't.

The old Chinese man came back in, handed Ech Un a message.

"Follow him," Ech Un said to Gett.

The Chinese man led Gett into the Bureau of Interrogations. There were two ways to get from the front entrance of the Bureau to the rear section where the offices of its staff were located. The first, for use by those employed in the Bureau and for guests, skirted the west boundary, well away from the actual interrogation rooms and holding cells. It was recognized that torture was the province of a few special individuals and that it made most men, if not unhappy, at least uneasy. 'That,' they thought, 'is caused by me.' And so the distance served to shield

THE EUNUCH

those who worked in the bureau from the actuality of their work.

The second way to get to the rear offices led, by design, right through the heart of the holding cells and interrogation rooms. The empire was large, crimes were often committed and so interrogations were common. This corridor was a tool. The first in a sequence that gripped a man's body, dug in its claws and worked them ever deeper until they touched his heart and finally crushed it. Gett *knew*.

He was led down the second corridor. Gett wondered if it was a mistake by the old Chinese servant, an insult by Ech Un, or a message from Arigh. He filed the question away as he walked quietly, surrounded by agony and sobbing.

They arrived finally at the door to Questioner Arigh's work room and the old Chinese knocked. They were ushered in by a pale young Chinese secretary. Arigh, who was sitting at his table working, sprang up and hopped over to Gett, smiling, full of camaraderie.

"Questioner Arigh."

"Hey there, Gett!"

"Could I have a moment of your time?"

"Anything for you. Let's talk in the back, come on. You two," he said to his Chinese secretary and the old Chinese man who had brought Gett, "fuck off."

They walked into the inner room of Arigh's work area and sat cross-legged on Questioner Arigh's personal wooden dais, settling into the pillows. Arigh poured hot fermented horse milk into small porcelain cups.

"So how did it go? Who will get jurisdiction?"

"I will."

"Already?"

"It's not official, but I suspect that's how it will go."

"Congratulations."

"I need the guard."

"Sorry Gett, interrogations are our mandate."

"Nevertheless."

"Listen Gett, we can do this better than you. Lots of new tools since your time."

"I want him."

"Why?"

"I need to talk to him."

"What do you think you can you get out of him that we can't?"

"Questioner Arigh, think about the situation. I need him for unspecified reasons of my own. Remember, this is a matter of Imperial security and so knowledge of many aspects of it are now, and will continue to be, denied you. In a few hours I will have an Imperial mandate to take him. I have come here as a courtesy to you. In this way, you can both gain Imperial favor by anticipating his wishes and also avoid a loss of face when I inevitably take him. I am not your enemy. I am here to offer you a solution to a future problem."

Questioner Arigh sat back on his cushion. He lowered his head. He was young but intelligent. He made his decision.

"Listen to me, I am not going to torture you," said Gett to the frightened Chinese guard. One of his eyes was swollen shut. Two of his teeth were gone. Enormous lacerations, deep to the muscle, striped his back. They were back in Gett's office. "I will ask you questions," Gett continued. "You will answer. Hopefully you will tell the truth. I know you think we are playing a game—a white face, red face switch. We are not. I won't threaten you with a return to the custody of Questioner Arigh. I will do what I can, and I can do a lot, to keep you here. After we've talked I will get you to one of the Emperor's doctors and if I have any more

THE EUNUCH

questions, I'll ask them there. I apologize that we have to do this now, but time is critical. Is all of that clear?"

"Y-y-y-eth."

"Good. Take me through the whole day that led up to the cleaning women finding the Honorable Lady's body. Start from the evening previous. Did anything that wasn't ordinary happen?"

"N-n-o."

"Please take me through her movements."

"I-i-in the evening she—"

"By she, you mean the Honorable Lady?"

"Th-th-the Honorable Lady in the evening—"

"Which evening?"

"Y-y-yesterday evening."

"What time?"

"At the end of the Hour of the Monkey. It was early. We signed her out."

"Did you speak with her?"

"Only to ask her to sign out."

"Did she speak to you?"

"N-no. They n-never do."

"Did she seem ill at ease? Different in any way?"

"No."

"Think hard. Was she nervous? Did she look at you differently? Was she dressed in a different way than she normally was?"

The guard thought about this. It seemed like he was about to say something. Then he bit it off.

"What is it?"

"It's just…"

"It's alright, just tell me."

"If I had to say there was a difference, if I h-h-had to because they're all mostly the same. But she seemed, a little…excited."

"Excited?"

"Like she was anticipating something. She was just in a little bit of a hurry, but not in a mean way like they usually are."

Gett paused. He thought about this. No, it didn't make any sense yet.

"And then?"

"She was out for a little over an hour and then signed back later in that evening."

"What time?"

"I don't remember exactly, but it will be in the record. We were on extra duty because of the Examination."

"How does the signing in and out work?"

"W-what?"

"How does it work, what is the procedure?"

"Everyone who c-c-comes in has to sign."

"Comes in means what?"

"C-comes in to anteroom."

"Comes from the outer Palace into the anteroom?"

"Yes."

"Then that anteroom leads to the Emperor's inner quarters?"

"Y-y-yes."

"And they sign when they go in?"

"Yes."

"Sign what?"

"The s-s-scroll."

"I mean what do they write?"

"They... it's their name."

"Where is the scroll?"

"Now?"

"No, in general, on a normal day."

"With us."

"I mean exactly."

THE EUNUCH

"I...we hold it, then put it on a table for them."
"Where do you stand?"
"At the door."
"Inside or outside."
"Outside...we...we stand on the outer Palace side of the door."
"Not in the inner anteroom."
"No...I mean right...not in the anteroom...outside of it."
"Ever go in?"
"No never! It isn't allowed!"
"Why?"
"It isn't allowed."
"I mean why isn't it allowed."
"I-I don't know."
"Ever see the other guards?"
"Yes, when we change shifts."
"No I mean the guards on the other side."
"The ones in the Emperor's quarters?"
"Yes."
"No."
"Why?"
"It...It's two different commanders. We n-n-never see them."
"So you stand outside the door with a scroll. The door is locked?"
"Yes."
"All the time?"
"Of course!"
"What is the procedure for unlocking it?"
"The person who wants to enter must be on the list."
"There is a list?"
"Yes."
"An actual list like written down? You hold it?"
"Yes."

"Same list available to guards on both sides?"
"Yes."
"It changes?"
"Yes, when it does, they send us a new one."
"Had it changed recently?"
"No."
"And the Honorable Lady is on the list?"
"Most of the concubines are on it."
"Not all?"
"No."
"Why not all."
"I don't know."
"And wives?"
"No."
"No?"
"They use the central anteroom."
"Not the one you're stationed at."
"Never!"
"And so one of the concubines arrives, then what?"
"She signs and we unlock the door. She goes through and we lock it again immediately!"
"The lock is on your side?"
"Yes."
"What's on the other side?"
"Of the door?"
"Yes."
"Nothing."
"Nothing?"
"Right."
"Not even a handle?"
"No, just the face of the door."
"So when people are coming out?"

THE EUNUCH

"They knock and we unlock the padlock and open the door."

"And it is the same on the other side? She walks through the anteroom, knocks on the door leading into the Emperor's inner quarters? Then guards outside open it?"

"I don't know."

"You don't know?"

"We aren't allowed there."

"But you have friends, people talk."

"I think...I think it's the same procedure."

"So the doors are locked from outside the anteroom on both ends and there is no way anyone inside can unlock them. Correct?"

"Yes."

"So how would someone get out of the antechamber without you knowing or the guards on the other side knowing?"

"It's impossible!"

Gett leafed through the documents that had been delivered. Pulled out the time records. After a quick search, he found the entry. It appeared she had signed back in in the Hour of the Dog, early evening. Gett paused a moment. He looked through the scroll. He found the earlier entry signing her out at the end of the Hour of the Monkey. He looked at her signature. He flipped back and looked at where she had signed back in. The first was slightly girlish but with flair. The second was very similar. Gett looked at it closely. It seemed just a little bit more tightly controlled. Did that mean anything? Gett couldn't decide. The difference was small.

"In the Hour of the Dog?"

"Yes, I think that sounds right."

"A little under two hours."

"Yes. I think."

"Describe her."

"She was the same."

"Still excited?"

"No, but when she signed out she wasn't really obviously excited. That's not what I meant, it was just a little bit of a feeling I had."

"Sad? Subdued? Happy?"

"No, just...like every other day."

"Clothes? Carrying anything?"

"C-c-clothes?"

"Yes, what was she wearing?"

"I...I...she changed clothes."

"What do you mean?"

"She came back in a different dress."

"Is that unusual?"

"It's—no, they are always changing clothes."

"Who?"

"The Honorable Ladies."

"Describe what she did."

"She walked over to our guard station and signed the scroll."

"Did she say anything."

"No, but that's normal."

"With anybody?"

"No."

"Not even an escort?"

"No."

"Is that uncommon?"

"A little."

"Did you note it?"

"What do you mean?"

"In a report."

"We don't make reports."

"But if you did, how uncommon is it for a concubine to be

unescorted?"

"They're supposed to be, but we see it."

"See them unescorted?"

"Yes. Sometimes."

"Why don't you report it?"

The boy thought about this, frightened. "Our job is to guard the door."

"And then?"

"That's it. That's our job. Their escorts are the harem's responsibility."

"She signed, then what?"

"She walked past us through the door and we locked it."

Gett thought about all of this. Nothing brilliant came to mind.

"I'll have more questions but that's all for now. Sit here and I'll send someone down to take you to a doctor."

He stepped out of his office into the echoing, flame-lit hallways of the Palace. He turned right, then right again at the Hallway of Gilded Mirrors, avoiding the decoration teams for the Examination three days from now, and headed towards the Bureau of Enforcement. A rat scurried across the hallway. The Examination preparations were squeezing every department, even the outer Palace pest catchers.

As his footsteps echoed on the stone, he thought about Sulo. Gett had, when Sulo first insinuated himself into the structure of the Palace bureaucracy, often wondered about his anger. What was its source? How was it sustained? Why was it so vituperative?

Because it was such a central part of Sulo's personality (and because Gett knew he would inevitably be working with him), he had observed Sulo closely over the course of Sulo's first three months in the Palace.

The focus of that observation, the detail of his character that Gett wanted to extract from the blurred collection of his actions was (as was Gett's custom) always the same: what was Sulo trying to achieve and what was stopping him?

Sulo came from the other side of the Western Desert. This was not an origin without precedence but it was rare. Those who shared it were, in general, engaged in trade and did not stay in the Capital long. And they were, for the most part, unobtrusive because their exotic origins were little reflected in their physical features.

Sulo was different; and he claimed to be representative of his tribe. First, and strangest, he was pale, like a corpse or a woman. And that pale skin was covered, over much of his body, in stiff, black hair. His eyes were recessed into his head. His eyebrows hung over them like the eaves of a house. And the eyes were shaped strangely, rounded, instead of flat, with oddly folded eyelids. And, most disconcerting, they were blue.

His language, too, was unlike anything Gett had ever seen (and Gett had seen a lot). Gett once had, in one of the very few times he had been in Sulo's office, asked to see an example of the writing from his tribe. Sulo had brushed out a shape and recited the sounds it represented: *Minichiatto de Solo*, which he had said was his name, written in its original language.

Gett suspected that the anger lay here, in Sulo's strangeness: because he lived in a world without friends.

This was a world Gett knew. It was a world that bred not love, but loyalty.

Gett found that he had arrived at the gates of the Bureau of Enforcement. It was much busier than usual—extra guards and a patrol leaving because of the Alert. He performed the necessary rituals, was ushered in and down its menacing corridors and

THE EUNUCH

found himself, with a minimum of disruption, sitting in front of Sulo—who was glaring at him.

Sulo asked, "You did it for me or for the kid?"

"Did what?"

"Got my guard back."

"Does it matter?"

"Yes."

"I did it for me."

"Ha ha. Yes, of course."

"I need to talk to the inner side guards on duty yesterday from the Hour of the Monkey to the Hour of the Snake the next day."

"Why?"

"That was when the girl should have signed out and then back in to the Imperial quarters and then the time from then to when she was found. I just want to ask them about the two encounters."

"No."

"Why?"

"Arigh gave me no face. He tortured my guard."

"And I brought him back."

"Doesn't matter. Arigh takes my guard. You take my guard. Everybody thinks my guards are easy to take."

Gett weighed this. Sulo was right. That's how it would be interpreted. Gett could request an Imperial rescript. He would be given permission to interview the other two guards. That would satisfy Sulo. But Gett was impatient.

"I'll ask you and you can ask them."

"What you want to ask?"

"How did she look. What was she wearing. Was there anything notable. Was she carrying anything out or in. What was her mood. Were there any differences between when she left and when she returned."

"Ha, I don't know."

"Well, you can ask them."

"They don't know too."

"Why?"

"She never came back."

"What do you mean?"

"She left but she never came back. Sign out, no sign back in. She died in that room."

"Anybody sign out of the Emperor's quarters and enter the anteroom in all that time?"

"No."

"How did you get this information from them?"

"How your mother's cunt do you think?"

"I'll have to talk to them eventually."

"Yes, not now. Now no dog cunt is giving me face."

Gett sat back for a minute. He reconstructed the events: The girl leaves the Imperial Quarters in the evening, signing out first at the inner door, crosses through the anteroom, then signs out at the outer door. There is no escort. Maybe she is excited, maybe not. She comes back a little over an hour later. She is still unescorted. She is fine. But wearing a different dress. She signs in at the outer door. She walks just a few steps into the anteroom between the doors. It is locked behind her. Seven hours later, having never left the room, she is found stabbed to death. Just another few steps away are the guards to the inner quarters. Both doors remain locked the entire time. No one hears anything. No one else signed in or out. There are no other entrances.

No answers that made sense, but keeping the questions in his mind allowed them to grow slowly, like small vines wrapping around his thoughts.

THE EUNUCH

Gett made his way slowly down the dark hallway toward Curdeger's office, the stillness punctuated by the constant, distant murmur of Examination preparations and the occasional rat that skittered by.

He was fascinated by motivation. It was innate in him and had been reinforced by his younger life. He had survived that period, survived his castration, survived his time among the Chinese, because of this skill. And so when something began to take on a form for him, it was not, as he had realized it was for most of his colleagues, a growing map of what had happened, it was instead a map of what those around him wanted.

It was, for Gett, always the same. As if a web grew in his mind. And a light began to shine weakly through it. That web, woven from the hidden desires of others, cast below it pale tenuous shadows of what they actually did. And because those shadows were often so diffuse, Gett realized early in his life that the true web, the one above the shadows through which the light of the truth of their secret desires shone, was always solid, always traceable, and always led, through the reality of what they wanted, to the actuality of what they did.

There were only two ways a man who *desired* to get into the Palace got there. The first was to be castrated, as Gett had been. The second was to pass the Imperial Examination. Held every two years, it was open to anyone. There was a village test then a provincial test then, finally, the culmination of years of deprivation and struggle, the Palace Examination.

Then a vicious reshuffling; some families went home, some vanished and others were invited in to grab hold of new and very real power. To be one of the very few who emerged from that chaos sane and with that power, you needed to want it beyond every other thing that existed in life. So it was a time of murders. *But only after the test.*

Not, and this was the crux of the matter at hand, three days before it.

五

CURDEGER WAS a large man. Large in every way. His voice, his height, his width, his personality. Gett had known him for a long time, since the Gote Reign Period, and it was strange to watch him now. All of his largeness had been compressed. Now, he controlled his voice, walked carefully so that his width wouldn't inconvenience others, hunched over so that when he talked to people he was closer to them. It was a strange and constant appeasement to normality.

Strange because Curdeger had been so powerful, so used to being powerful and so good at it. He had run the Construction Ministry. This was a large ministry, possessed of large budgets, tasked with building the fortifications to keep out the Chinese to the south and the Cousins to the north. And then, suddenly, a few years ago, to everyone's complete surprise (Curdeger's most of all), he lost it. He had engaged in a minuscule struggle over control of research money for something (the details were less important than the principle) and he found himself outmaneuvered and, astonishingly, out.

Now he ran the Sub-Bureau of Analysis. It was a ridiculous job. A job for somebody's smart son. It was humiliating.

But Curdeger (underneath his hugeness, nestled within the heart hidden behind all that fat) was a hard man. And he knew that the only thing, the inevitable thing, that would allow him to ratchet himself back up to where he had been was time. Because the political tides would ebb. Those who didn't see as clearly as Curdeger would be left on empty sand. But he would, and would crush them.

So he waited. Polite, folded in upon himself. Quiet and unobtrusive. The perfect subordinate.

And thus for Gett, all his dealings with Curdeger were fraught with the danger of unintended insult. Curdeger had a long memory. Gett hoped, however (and he concealed this carefully), that Curdeger never did rise again because, while dealing with Curdeger was a constant grinding stress, this was far outweighed by Curdeger's competence.

Gett now stood just outside the cold room to which bodies from the Palace were brought prior to disposal. Fog jetted from his mouth as he breathed.

"Chief Analyst Curdeger," he said. Curdeger was standing off in the corner of the bright, torch-lit room. He turned, saw Gett standing in the doorway and came respectfully over.

"Chief Investigator Gett. It is late but you are looking well."

"Thank you, Chief Analyst. Have you completed your investigation of the room and the body?"

"We have completed aspects of it."

"Can you share the results with me?"

"Have you been granted exclusive jurisdiction?"

"Not yet, but you know how these things go."

Curdeger sat on his bench and thought for a moment. He decided.

"I will inform both Chief Enforcer Sulo and Minister of Espionage Han Zongcheng that I have briefed you and I will brief them as well."

"I have no problems with that."

"It is what protocol dictates, Chief Investigator. I know you understand."

THE EUNUCH

"So take me through it."

Curdeger trod heavily over to a spare desk, upon which sat bits of fabric and tools. Gett followed.

"The room itself offered us very little physical evidence. It is cleaned regularly but is also a main thoroughfare between the inner and outer quarters. Because of this, most of the substances we search for are not absent; instead they are present in too much abundance. Hair is an example. Most that are present we recognize as being from the main occupants of the inner quarters. However, we have six hairs from unknown sources. Unfortunately other than their general length and color we fear they will be of little use in identification."

Gett picked up one of the hairs laid out carefully on paper.

"Can you tell if it is male or female?"

"We cannot."

"These were found in the room or on her body?"

"They were found in the room. We found no hairs on her body."

"How about the doors?"

"Farther investigation confirmed our initial analysis. Both were locked from the outside. The locks had not been tampered with."

"The Honorable Lady?"

"On her body we discovered two troubling pieces of physical evidence."

Curdeger eased his way between two cold wooden slabs over to the body of the dead girl lying on the table. She was naked. Again, Gett was struck by her beauty.

Curdeger held up her hand for Gett to see.

"She has dirt under her fingernails. These girls are bathed every day, so if she's got dirt here, she got it while she was out. We are picking it apart and comparing it with samples from different places in the Palace. If we are lucky it will tell us where she was."

"How long will that take?"

"It is difficult to say. Maybe tomorrow if we are successful, maybe never if we sample the wrong places. Much of it is luck."

"How many locations have you sampled?"

"We find that a useful division is three Palace regions: the gates, which let in much dust, the kitchens which allow soot and burnt oil to infiltrate the dust, and the horse grounds which throw up pulverized horse dung. None of these is definitive but the sources are widely separated and they alter the consistency of the dust in various identifiable ways. We have much data on this."

"Had she had sexual intercourse before she died?"

Curdeger stopped and for a long moment stared at Gett. Then he took the girl's leg and spread them so that her vagina was exposed. Curdeger now slowed down, a large man stepping out onto thin ice.

"It is possible that she did. We found semen inside of her vagina. One possible interpretation is that she engaged in sexual intercourse about two hours before she died. If that is what happened, then it is likely her partner ejaculated inside her."

"Was it consensual?"

Again, Curdeger hesitated.

"If in fact sexual intercourse occurred, then nothing indicates that it was not consensual."

"Based on what?"

"Her death occurred long enough after this event that if it was non-consensual any bruising would have shown up. The only external wounds she has are defensive wounds from the stabbing. She has no bruising on her shoulders or wrists, where she would have been held down and there is also none around her vagina. The inner lining of her vagina also lacks the tearing that is indicative of forced entry."

"The Emperor?"

Again the long pause. "That would be the conclusion an upright person would come to."

Gett looked at the girl spread out on the cold stone. His breath misted in the freezing air. He was cold even in his fur-lined robe. She was naked and white on the stone.

"Have you put all this in the report?"

"I have indicated the possibility based on our analysis of the physical evidence."

"When will you submit it?"

"Protocol requires a three-day period in which to perform re-analysis when there is, as there is in this case, inconclusive evidence. It is my hope that in those three days your investigation will discover evidence that either corroborates or refutes our analysis."

"I see. Is there other pertinent evidence?"

"There is not."

It was now evening. The sun had set on the brittle, dusty cold of the day. The city had settled into an uneasy watchful stillness.

Gett wended his way down the long, arched corridor that led to the streets outside the Palace. A palanquin was waiting. He stepped in. From there, the bearers made their way quietly into the bustle of the Capital. There was an oddly liquid tension to the street. It was always like this just before the Examination. And that was heightened tonight: why had soldiers been in the city? What did it mean for the future? Why just before the Examination? The questions were asked in whispers, in corners, in the privacy of people's minds as Gett's palanquin bobbed silently into a city carefully watching.

In his palanquin, he was higher up than most of those on the street. He could see their heads moving through the torch-lit street like bugs. He could see, too, those following him. Gett had spent much of his life in this sort of situation. He was often the hunter, sometimes the hunted. And so he had developed an acute sense of the flow of crowds. And a memory for not faces but behavior.

There ahead, outside a steamed bun shop, was a shepherd. This man seemed to be buying but he was not arguing about the price. Gett's palanquin carried him with the pack for a bit then turned onto a narrow alley guarded by a steaming pile of horseshit. His carriers padded down this alley, hiking their robes to avoid the dirty water that ran down its center.

From behind his curtain he saw a cabman grunting awkwardly as he made his way down the uneven stone alley. He was a tired and sweating, but Gett knew his alley was not a shortcut to anywhere. He instructed his carriers to use it for precisely this reason.

He was being monitored. He considered whether this had been ordered by someone in the Palace. It was possible. There were many things to be gained from this investigation, especially from influencing it. But Gett's sense of these things — from long experience — told him it was not that. Because the thing all these watchers shared was they were *afraid*. So this was the city, reaching out, monitoring, trying to understand.

He turned another corner and came to a low, anonymous door set into the side of the alley wall. He stepped out of the palanquin, the door was unlocked by a servant, and he stepped in. His servant locked it behind him, and he was home.

THE EUNUCH

Of Gett's three residences, an annex in his Palace office, a protocol-mandated residence within the Palace walls, this small private one tucked into the city he considered his own. The small number of servants knew to keep back and allow him his privacy.

Tonight the moon was almost full, so he had no trouble as he carried his tea pot up the narrow stairs onto the rooftop patio he had made. It sat among the leaves and branches that shaded his courtyard. From here, he could sip carefully at his tea and look out at the city through the twisting shapes of the steam and the trees.

And he could think about the case. Not about the murderer, but about the others.

What did they each desire?

Han wanted to be connected to the case, but solely as an observer. This could only mean there was a tripwire somewhere. There was a discovery that, when made and when Han was informed, would cause him to...what? Pounce on the case like a tiger? Run? Gett suspected the former. It looked to him like Han had done something, had been involved in something that had somehow gone wrong. This investigation might happen upon it. His involvement was sufficiently removed that he could, if he wished, completely disassociate himself from the case, but he was ready and able to swipe his claw through the jugular of the investigation at any time—because as a Chinese and a traitor to his own race, he was always in danger.

Sulo wanted to extricate himself from the case but still wanted to talk. Gett decided he wasn't involved, but knew something. He would step back and allow Gett to follow a trail to...what? Almost certainly the same thing Han did not want him to find. Han was too powerful an enemy and too smart a bureaucrat to confront directly. So Sulo would make sure Gett knew whatever it was he wanted him to know. But he'd dole it out carefully and slowly and through others. And, he probably wouldn't lie about the locked inner door. In a case like this, that would come back to him.

Arigh was a bad man. Gett was secure enough in his experience of these things to not hesitate in making pejorative moral judgments. And Arigh wanted to prove himself. He would be smart enough to hide behind his title in a bureaucratic war through which his family would surely coach him.

Curdeger wanted to shelter himself. This was not his opportunity to return to what he had been. This was not the political ebbing of a tide that he was waiting for. This case was a vortex. So he, too, would efface himself and carefully become the embodiment of his bureau.

And finally, what had the dead girl wanted? Gett sipped at his tea. When confronted with an obviously beautiful woman, Gett always remembered sexual arousal. His castration had occurred late in his adolescence and so great torrents of sexual feeling had welled up in him strongly before it happened. He had masturbated frequently and had had precisely eight sexual encounters with five different women, two of them prostitutes. Since then, he had used sexual arousal as a tool many times, had found it to be a valuable one in the craftsmanship of persuasion, and so possessed a long mental catalogue of its effects. But it was still those early experiences that informed his gut understanding of the subject.

The sexual feelings that he now had were like those he had felt immediately after ejaculation. They were muted, damped down, but not absent.

The most striking thing he remembered about ejaculation was how disinterested he was in sex right after it occurred, how immediately he thought: why did I expend so much effort? Was it worth it?

THE EUNUCH

Behind this emptiness was the enormous power of the feelings that would slowly but inexorably, over the following hour, pour back in to infiltrate each crack in his soul and control him like a man lost in the waters of a storm. The difference now was that this enormous return never occurred. But strangely, Gett still felt its presence beside him, looming in the darkness of his mind.

And it had taught him an important lesson: Men are driven to women. Sexual arousal is a tool that the body uses. But absent that, others also exist. Most of these drives are stimulated by beauty.

There was an obvious hypothesis to be drawn from this and from the evidence that she'd had sex before she died. Gett however felt, in that same tentative way, as faint tendrils of her motives twisted in front of him like disturbances in mist, that there was more to it than that.

And so Gett, who had been a spy for a long, long time, who had run a ring of agents within the court of the southern Chinese enemies for almost ten years and survived it precisely because his only confidante was his own mind, who, when he returned had arranged to slip quietly into the position of Palace investigator, ultimately a job that allowed him to shape his environment into one of *safety and predictability*, now realized that today's events were tipping him ever so gently back into the chaos of his old life. He could sense it. Like an old man and rain.

He sat there drinking his tea for a long time, watching the shifting lights of the city, almost like, looking back at him, were a million flickering eyes.

It was the Hour of the Rat, the exact middle of the night, as he stepped into the audience room. And surprisingly it was empty. Gett had expected a replay of the earlier scene — kneeling officials and Sulo and Han, but instead, nothing. Just the light of the torches and the muttering of their shaky, curling fire.

Even more surprising, the Emperor was not present. Only his mother, still sitting behind her bead curtain, the torches casting a weird crosshatched shadow over her immobile face.

Gett kowtowed, keeping his head low.

"Any news?" she asked.

Gett had, in the years after which this woman had been elevated first to Chief Wife and then to Imperial Mother, had five meetings with her in the absence of other officials. Each time she had begun with this question. It was probably the reason she was still alive.

It is a question of the powerful. Those who ask it can demand an answer. She asks him "Any news?", and he must scrape out his mind and hand it to her, no detail left hanging by a sinewy thread, because that tiny piece could be the one given to her by someone else. And when that happens, when someone else tells her something that *she knows he knows,* then the thought forms in her head, "Gett holds back on me. Why? Is he plotting? Is that detail important? Is it not? Is it a ruse?" But the most important fact has been made clear: Gett is not to be trusted. And inevitably a time will come when she is threatened, then she must gather around her those who do not deceive her, and destroy those who do.

So Gett told her everything: He told her his suspicions about Han Zongcheng. He told her about Sulo's desire to talk to him and their discussion. He told her about the guard's story. He told her what Curdeger had found.

She listened quietly and when he had finished she remained silent, waiting to see if he had anything to add.

"I am granting you jurisdiction in this case."

"Thank you, noble and August Imperial Mother."

THE EUNUCH

"But there is a stipulation."

"I am your servant and will obey."

"You will provide reports to both Minister of Espionage Han Zongcheng and Enforcer Sulo."

"Yes, your August Imperial Mother."

"But first you will report to me."

"Yes, it will be my honor."

"I am outside the reporting channel."

"Yes."

"But I speak for the August Emperor. His will is law and he wishes me to be informed."

"Of course."

"You are dismissed."

"Please, Imperial Mother, I have a request."

"What is it?"

"Having been granted jurisdiction in this case, I wish to investigate it to the fullest of my ability."

"Of course."

"I wish to search this Imperial audience hall."

"For what?"

"For evidence."

There was a long silence behind the curtain. Finally she spoke.

"Search now."

"May I stand?"

"You may."

"May I turn my back to you?"

"For the duration of the search, you may."

Gett stood and looked around the audience chamber, turned and looked behind him. It was a strange feeling, turning his back on the Imperial Mother. He was sure this was the only opportunity he would have in his life to do it. Secretly, he allowed himself a few moments to savor it.

The audience hall was not large. It was stone-floored like the rest of the Palace. High ceilings were supported by thick red pillars around which dragons curled. The Emperor's throne sat on a platform above the floor, at about hip level, accessible by three short stairways, one on either side and one in the middle. The Imperial Mother sat just behind.

By design, there were not many places to conceal objects in this room and so, before the Hour of the Ox had arrived, well under an hour, Gett had found what he had been searching for. Wrapped in cloth and placed carefully in the mouth of a dragon and so concealed from all but the tallest, was a knife. Its hilt was covered in finely-wrought gold filigree and encrusted with rubies and sapphires, clearly a knife from the Emperor's personal collection.

And its blade was covered in crusted and flaking blood.

Gett padded over to the center of the Throne Room. He knelt and put his head to the floor. He put the knife in front of him.

"I have found an object which may have relevance to this case."

"What is it?"

"It is a knife."

"Come forward and place it near me."

Gett shuffled forward on his knees. He placed the knife outside the beaded curtain in a small, twisting patch of light. He shuffled backwards. A long thin hand slid out from behind the curtain and picked up the knife. It slid back and the beads swayed in the firelight. There was a long silence. Gett stayed on his knees, his head to the floor. Finally the Imperial mother spoke.

"You may go. Continue your investigation."

The torches flickered slightly as the Imperial Mother stood and exited. It was clear now. Failure was chaos. And chaos was death. For him and many others. Gett, his head to the floor, finally allowed himself to ponder his theory. Something he had not allowed himself to do in detail before this meeting.

Why frame the Emperor for a murder?

LAO KOU had been an assassin and enforcer for ten violent years near the beginning of the dynasty. Now he was a librarian. He oversaw the enormous and always growing records of the Central Secretariat. Gett knew him only as a very quiet, very circumspect man of great stillness; a listener.

It is hard to kill a man—some men can do it, others cannot. Lao Kou—a man who could—had now run this library for ten years. He had retired into this obscurity with an enigmatic complacency. Settled into it so completely that the sight of him, deep into the night, shuffling quietly through the stacks, no longer elicited any comment. The only reminder of his former life was a twisted left arm, stiff and clenched as if it were holding the reins of a phantom horse.

But Gett also knew, because Lao Kou sat quietly, day after day behind his desk, because he listened patiently and intelligently to all the men who came to his dusty, backroom empire and because he efficiently gathered for them the information they requested, that Lao Kou had slowly and unprepossessingly built up a detailed and massive repository of knowledge about what every powerful person in the Capital *wanted to know*.

Gett found him, as always, at any time of the day or night, hunched over a table lit by a cheap candle, absorbed in a scroll.

"Hello, Gett," said Lao Kou, his long drooping mustache making him look dour but intelligent. "Killing people again?"

THE EUNUCH

"Only bad ones."

"As it should be."

"How've you been?" asked Gett.

"You know, digging into other people's secrets."

"Anything interesting?"

"There always is."

"I have some research to do."

"The dead girl?"

"Yes."

"Any theories?"

"Many."

"This will be a difficult winter," Lao Kou said as he picked at his long mustache.

"It's possible. Long anyway"

"They always are. Who's in charge?"

"I am."

"Well, that's good."

"For who?"

"Ha, not for you I suppose," Lao Kou laughed.

"I need records on the girl."

"What kind?"

"All of them."

"They'll take a while to find. Which ones do you want first?"

"What have you got?"

Lao Kou stood for a moment pulling on his mustache and thinking, collating the information in his mind.

"Intelligence reports, personnel files, odds and ends."

"Get me the intelligence first and I'll start on those while you look for the rest."

Lao Kou padded off back into the darkness. His candle had guttered down another finger's width before he came back. He carefully placed an armload of scrolls in front of Gett then shuffled back off into the stacks to find the other records on the girl.

Gett felt a gentle tug in his mind. It was time again. He reached into his pocket. Felt around. Empty. His supply of nuts, not prepared for a day like today, had run out. Bad luck.

But the problem was some ways off, hours, now just a gentle tugging. Reminding him. Feed me. Feed me. Gett, in the sputtering light of a candle, deep in the Capital night, began to read.

It took him almost until dawn to slowly and carefully make his way through the records. It was a large task — marriage records of the family, land transfer deeds, multiple intelligence reports, test results, hundreds of interviews. But finally, in the coldest part of the night that just precedes morning, he rolled up the last dusty scroll, hands a little shaky, head dully aching.

He had by this time formed a picture, though sketched and incomplete, of who this girl was, what she had wanted in life, and the shadowy, nebulous goals of those who surrounded and wished to use her.

The large mess in front of him could be reduced, in its essence, to the following five documents:

Summary Report
Security
See appended data for sources and supplementary addenda.
Prepared by the Office of Intelligence of the Great Jin Emperor in the reign year Qu'er, Eighth Month-
The girl Diao Ju is of Chinese descent. She was born in a large estate that covers roughly 5,000 mu in the northern county administered by the Capital. Her family is locally powerful. That power

THE EUNUCH

is based on their alliances with collectors of grain in Kaifeng and their ability to supply it from their holdings. That monopoly market position bought their loyalty through three crises during the Time of Disorganization.

The family has five significant males in positions of local power—a police commissioner in the Capital, a grain collection official in the Capital, a salt merchant on the Southern Border, a cavalry officer in the Army of the Left and a yamen advisor in their county.

However, they have no strong presence in the government in the Capital. They recognize this deficiency and have been actively [see appendix] attempting to gain a foothold for the past six years. This marriage is an opportunity for them to both gain local power and secure access to the Capital. The girl should be allowed yearly visits to her home to extend this relationship.

Verdict: The girl's family is incentivized to maintain their relationship with the Capital through this union. No known ties to the Southern Chinese. They can serve as a conduit for Imperial control in the grain producing region surrounding Kaifeng.

{Approved}

For Data and full listing of reports and source documents refer to appendices—Chopped—Minister of Espionage Han Zongcheng

———

Office of Fecundity

Patrilineal Research Report (matrilineal influence integrated)

The Diao family's history of fecundity is a positive one. The parents of Diao Ju, Diao An and Li Xumei, produced four sons over a period of six years. All sons lived into adulthood. Diao Ju's father-side uncles all engaged in marriages that produced at least one son. Farther, her mother is also the single female offspring of a marriage resulting in five sons. Based on this fecund history she seems an excellent candidate for inclusion as a Class Two Concubine with monthly access to the Emperor. We predict at least one male child over six years will result from her elevation.

[full data appended]

[approved]

Personal Memo

Gogoro Shen, Head of the Imperial Harem, Eunuch of Standing

Personal impressions: Concubine Diao Ju is a welcome addition to the Imperial Harem. She is talented in the fields she enjoys. She is intelligent. Her family related to me an example of her precociousness [appendix #126]. Her intelligence has been noted by all of those who have interviewed her. [see attached transcription appendices #29–31] This leads me to one aspect of her personality that is praiseworthy and should be monitored. Her thinking about court relationships is nuanced and subtle. Also, as we all should be, she is drawn to the Emperor's wisdom and goodness. This has

obvious relevance to the future harmony of the Imperial household. I believe that her talents are obvious and I would advise the harem eunuchs to pay close attention to those talents in this regard and to carefully nurture them to develop in harmonious ways. Taken as a whole, I would rate her highly. Her skill in entertaining, her high intelligence and her motivation make her an excellent candidate for a concubine for the Emperor.
Ministry of the Secretariat
Second Secretary, Harem Affairs

So that order under Heaven is preserved and the harmony of the Palace is unremitting, so that the Emperor may produce a son of heaven, it is imperative that discord be kept to a minimum. Thus the personality and temperament of Diao Ju is of great importance as related to her ability to live in gracious and happy harmony with the other wives and her ability to entertain and please the Emperor.
Training: Diao Ju, since youth, has trained in dance, singing and acting. She has excelled at each and has performed many times for the local elite.
Natural Skills: She has been tested by the recruitment staff in her skills at weaving, dancing and impromptu poetry creation. Her weaving skills are judged to be poor. Her dancing is considered adequate and tends to be imbued with aesthetic hints of clouds and rain. She excels in poetry

creation. **This makes her a good match for the Emperor as this is one of his chief interests.**
Character: She seems to be highly intelligent. Her conversation is erudite with a tendency toward word games. In several interviews over the course of three months, we have been impressed by her ability to understand complex concepts.
Physical Appearance: She is very beautiful. The Emperor, as a sage, will view this as unimportant.

Transcription Appendix #30
Related by mother
/question omitted/
When she was thirteen we were having a dinner for guests from the city. They were coming to see the grain harvest ceremony and they were like us, very aware of the best things and so we used our best table settings. When our guests came, they were of course very impressed with our estate and commented on the artistry of our food and setting. They were surprised that estates like ours in the country could have such things!
[transcriber's note: potential patrons of the family in Kaifeng.]
While we were eating, one of our servants noticed that the third son of our guests had taken a set of chopsticks and put them in his robe. He was trying to steal them! Isn't that just so like city people. To pretend they have so much culture but to steal from the very table of their hosts! We see all the time these poor city people like this! Of course we couldn't stand for this.

THE EUNUCH

These were our guests! We couldn't stand for them coming to our home and stealing our things. But they cared very much about face. Their standing in the city depended on it. So we couldn't just accuse their third son of theft. My husband and I stepped out to discuss it. To decide how we could make their third son return the chopsticks; they were solid silver! First we thought maybe we could pull him aside and tell him we saw him stealing. But he could deny it. Then what would we do? We could discuss it with his mother. But she could deny it too. We even considered hiring a pickpocket or a thief! Our face was involved too! But we saw that this could lead to even more trouble. Then our daughter came out and begged us to know what was going on. She was always interested in people. We didn't want to tell her but she is very strong-willed and finally we relented and told her what had happened. She thought hard about it and then told us she had an idea. What is it we asked her. She told us and, oh, it was so clever! We knew that we could solve the problem. We sent a runner into town to find the right person. And then we continued our dinner with our guests. At the end of the dinner, my husband stood up. And he was so proud! His daughter had thought of such a clever solution! He said how happy he was that our guests had come and how happy he was about the great relationship between our two families and then he said that he wanted to end the night with a special entertainment. Then he called in, guess what, a magician. Do you know what the magician did? Can you guess?
/Response omitted/
He did a bunch of tricks and then for his finale he

took a set of chopsticks from my husband's plate and made them disappear. He said, oh my where are the chopsticks?! I've made them disappear! And then he walked over to the third son and pulled the stolen chopsticks out of his robe! We got our chopsticks back! And everybody thought it was a magic trick! That was my daughter's idea. She's so clever! And then she said the funniest thing. She said to the third son, "From my family to yours and back again." Oh she's so naughty. I know the Emperor will fall in love with her.
/Transcript ends}

There was a code in these reports. None of these memos of course would be critical; as an Imperial Concubine, she would have access to them. But the writers could employ a bureaucratic language with which Gett was familiar; a code common to intelligence reports. And this (whatever else these documents might be called) is exactly what they were.

The reports, reduced to their essence, said the following: **Danger. Intelligent. Driven to power. Schemer. Value of family's local alliances of overriding importance but watch her carefully.**

Gett stretched. His joints ached. His mind was tripping on its own thoughts. And he was feeling much more uncomfortable. An addiction to betel nut is not like other addictions. Opium was a strong addiction and Gett steered clear of it. It slowed his mind and was tough to quit. To end a betel nut addiction was a week of discomfort. No more. It was a hard gristly fibrous thing. When you chewed it juice filtered out of the fibers. Soon a lump would develop in your throat, but that would disappear and then the flood of energy would come. It was this which allowed him to make it through these nights.

THE EUNUCH

And while going off it wasn't so bad, still, it was an addiction. And his head was now steadily aching. He looked at Lao Kou, still engrossed in his scrolls, yellow eyes locked on the dusty paper, the guttering candle burnt down to a nub that now cast strange dancing shadows of his long mustache on the ceiling.

Gett thought about sleep. Whether he should return to his villa. Fall into oblivion. And sitting there in the pale yellow light of his candle, a silent Lao Kou next to him and a girl's life laid out before him, he decided he should not.

Because as tired as he was, he knew something most people did not: now, the cold brittle hour before dawn, was the hour of interrogations. If a man is settled in his dreams and you wake him, he is enveloped by a sense of doom and foreboding. And that dread, like a wraith, reaches into his soul and begins to scratch.

But even more, if a man has not slept, has forced his mind to focus when it should be insensate, the doors of the mind open, the crowded thoughts of the day dissipate, and along these empty echoing corridors energy can flow unimpeded. Then he thinks, not in a haze of dreadful half-dreams but instead too clearly, too sharply, the hard outlines of reality ringing, bell-like in his body. And the truth leaks into his mind.

Gett quietly left the library. He made his way through the maze of dark corridors that was the Palace. He headed finally towards the best guarded, most secret, most restricted location in the empire, and possibly on earth.

The Imperial Harem.

七

Gett stood off to one side of the blazingly-lit Harem Medical Room while, in its center, Imperial Wife Second Class Kekolo lay on the large inspection table, eyes watching Gett, legs spread while a grey old Chinese doctor carefully examined her vagina. Nervous ceremonial eunuchs in dark red robes were carefully kneeling, heads to the ground — like a wall of rustling blood.

Standing beside Gett — and ignoring him — was the head of the Imperial Harem, the eunuch Gogoro Shen.

He was a strangely shaped man. Most eunuchs whose castration occurs before puberty grow to be fat. Clearly, this had been true of Gogoro, but now skin hung off him in folds. As if suddenly, one day, all his weight had vanished, as if he himself had vanished and a tiny man had taken his place in the drooping bag of his flesh.

His large, watery eyes monitored every step of the medical inspection. They didn't move even when he flicked his hand at an assistant eunuch who brought him a large, brown, sedimented drink. He knocked it back and blanched, color draining out of his face until sweat covered it. Slowly the paleness faded. He turned to Gett, who had been patiently waiting.

"I am very busy," said Gogoro.

"With what?"

"With our internal investigation."

"What are you investigating?"

THE EUNUCH

Gogoro stared at him for a moment. Hard eyes, glaring out of his drooping face.

"We are investigating, internally, how one of the Exalted Imperial Concubines could have been killed."

"Why?"

"Why should be obvious. We are very busy. I can set aside only a very short time to answer your questions. Please ask them now."

"I already am."

"Then please continue."

"What specifically are you investigating internally?"

"That is privileged information."

"Privileged to whom? Who can know it? Specifically."

"I think this is not relevant to your investigation."

"It could be."

The old Chinese doctor bent down and used his clamps to open Imperial Wife Second Class Kekolo's vagina and began to inspect its interior. All of the eunuchs on the floor lowered their heads farther. She twitched from the cold clamps but remained silent.

"Our investigation is much like yours, I suspect. We are recreating her movements on the day, we are interviewing those wives with whom she was close, and we are investigating the sexual state of all of the wives."

"Why?"

"Why what?"

"What about their sexual state?"

"To discover any anomalous behavior."

"You mean sexual acts with men other than the Emperor?"

"The Imperial Wives would neither wish to do that, nor would they be able."

"But you're checking them for it."

Again, the hard, watery stare.

"Yes."

"It seems like it is taking up a lot of your resources."

"It is."

"And the other?"

"We are not you. Our primary responsibility is the safeguarding of the wombs of the two hundred and seventy six women of the Imperial Harem. All else is secondary. How many more questions do you have?"

"A lot."

"Then ask them quickly."

The old Chinese doctor stood up again. Five eunuchs rushed over to Imperial Wife Second Class Kekolo with silk sheets and obscured her from view.

"Who was the victim?" asked Gett.

"She was an Imperial Concubine Third Class."

"Yes. I've seen her fecundity report."

"Of course."

"Well, with a report like that, she should have been at least Second Class."

"What makes you think so?"

"The fecundity report."

"And you think that is all that goes into deciding a woman's status when she enters the Imperial Harem?"

"I'm asking you."

"It is not."

"So what was it then? Why was she only a Class Three instead of something that reflected her fecundity results?"

"These details are secret."

"Why?"

"Because they are valuable."

"To whom?"

THE EUNUCH

"I think you have no idea of what we do here. Think about it. We have two hundred and seventy six women, the full complement of the Emperor's wives and concubines. Each of them has potentially bi-monthly access to the Emperor. That is almost an hour of unmonitored, unregulated contact with the Emperor. Do you know how valuable that is? Do you know what a person can do with that time? That makes these Imperial wives and concubines very valuable. There is not a moment of their lives when those in the court are not pushing *as hard as they can* to have access to them, because they have influence. They have the Emperor's ear. And if they favor you, you will be rich and powerful. Most of what we do is designed to control that."

The Imperial Wife Second Class Kekelo, now dressed in her ceremonial robes — red silk embroidered with horse, dragon and phoenix — stepped from behind the silk sheets. The tiny eunuchs scurried backwards. Her eunuch retainers rushed forward and took her arms and led her out of the chamber. The Chinese doctor lowered himself wheezing to the floor to kowtow until she was gone.

Imperial Wife First Class Nokon Besan was escorted in. There was an immediate tensing of every muscle in the room. The air itself tightened. Real Power had arrived. Her eunuchs brought her to the table and stepped back. The silk-bearing eunuchs rushed forward and obscured her from view.

"How long did it take you to figure out who had been killed?"

"When the alert was issued we knew it was a concubine so we checked everyone. They were in different parts of the Palace so that took a while."

"Roughly."

"About an hour."

"That seems like a long time."

"We had to find two hundred and seventy six people."

"Where exactly do concubines and wives have the right to be within the Palace?"

"That is secret."

"Can they leave the Palace?"

"They cannot."

"Never?"

"It requires an Imperial Guard. Depending on when, about two hundred soldiers."

Gett considered this sourly. It was all completely uncheckable.

"Do you know why she was killed?" asked Gett.

"I do not."

"Any guesses?"

"No."

"Was she liked? Disliked?"

"None of the girls are liked."

"What do you mean?"

"They are in competition with each other. One's loss is another's gain. Whatever they feel when they first meet, it degenerates into mutual hatred."

"Anybody special?"

"No."

"Are you sure?"

"No, but I watch very closely and have a lot of experience."

"Any talk about, hint about, a lover?"

"No."

"Would you have heard?"

"Probably."

"Why?"

"Like I said, the girls hate each other. They have no incentive to keep those secrets. One of them would have betrayed her."

"Could she have kept it a secret?"

"She couldn't have done it. So there could be no secret to keep."

"Chinese hate Jurchens? Jurchens hate Chinese? That sort of thing?"
"Of course."
"And?"
"And what?"
"And this causes conflict?"
"Of course."
"Anything bad?"
"What do you mean by bad?"
"Fights?"
"Yes."
"Violent ones?"
"Sometimes."
"Killing?"
"It hasn't yet."
"Until this time?"
"I think its unlikely."
"Why?"
"My feeling."
"Yes but where does the feeling come from?"
"I told you, I've been doing it for a long time. The wives and concubines fight, but only the ones at the top seriously. She wasn't at that level."
"Everybody is sure until somebody dies."
"True, I suppose."
"So?"
"So then it becomes your job."
"How are relations between Jurchens and Chinese structured?"
"It's complicated."
"Explain it in a simple way."
"There are no Chinese wives. Jurchen concubines have higher

status than Chinese concubines."

"What exactly does higher status mean?"

"They are above them in all matters of status."

"But in the concrete day-to-day running of the harem?"

"The Jurchen concubines have more access to the Emperor."

"Why?"

"Because they are Jurchen."

"No, I mean how does it occur? It's mandated or there is a thumb on the scale of the calculations?"

"There is never a thumb."

"Then what is it?"

"Their superiority is factored in to their availability cycle."

"And the Chinese concubines don't like it."

"What do you think."

"What do they do?"

"They suffer silently."

"Why silently."

"There aren't enough of them to make a difference."

"Why?"

"Why can't they make a difference?"

"No, why is there a small number?"

"Their number is the minimum decreed by the previous Glorious Emperor."

"You don't go over that?"

"We do not."

"Why?"

"For the reasons we are discussing."

"Why was Diao Ju scheduled to be with the Emperor last night?"

"Her slot had come up."

"No, I mean, why was she scheduled in that slot?"

"That is secret."

THE EUNUCH

"Why?"

"For the same reason. If people at court knew the procedure we used to determine the schedules for wives and concubines, they would attempt to manipulate it. We will investigate internally and submit a report to your bureau."

"And if you discover a lapse in your own bureau?"

"We will report it and correct it."

The assistant rushed up with more of Gogoro Shen's drink. Gogoro paused, then with difficulty drank half. Again, paling. "I know that this makes your job difficult. That's life. Think about this more deeply. Think about what is at stake. An Imperial companion has died. This is a tragedy of the first order. All of these wives will engage in mourning for three months. I myself will mourn for a full year. There remain, however, the facts of the situation. These wives, because of the information they have and their influence, are the most valuable resource in the Palace. They are the focus of every minister and bureau chief in the Empire. These are not arbitrary rules invented by a crazy person to make your job more difficult. They are real and valuable solutions to a genuine and pernicious problem. Don't make the mistake of thinking you are the only good and pure man. We all have things we protect. This is mine."

The silk sheets fell back with the eunuchs. Imperial Wife First Class Nokon Besan lay on the inspection table, legs straight, feet hanging over the edge of the table. The Chinese doctor stood and approached her. Head down, he spoke to her eunuch retainer. The retainer in turn whispered into Nokon Besan's ear.

Her head rolled around and a look of lidded hatred spat out of her face at the doctor. He started to shake. She spread her legs open and propped her feet up on the table. She said something to the eunuch. He indicated for the doctor to begin.

Gett wondered why she allowed herself that look. Of course

it was understandable. This was one of the most deeply insulting moments of her life. But she was an Imperial wife. And like every person who survived in the claustrophobic and ever narrowing space at the top of the Palace hierarchy, she would have learned to control herself.

But then, Gett thought, sometimes it is difficult to control. As it had been for him.

Penis, vagina, sex. Starkly out in the open in the mind. So vivid. The visceral images, the concepts of the things disassociated from the awkward words describing them. Lashed to the core of the mind.

The old man leaned in and began to examine her vagina. She raised her head and, eyes hard, watched him do it.

Gogoro Shen took another drink from his cup, grimaced.

"Did you like her?" asked Gett.

Gogoro thought about this question for a bit. He took another long drink of his dark, sandy medicine.

"Awful, disgusting stuff."

"What is it?"

"Medicine. Why do you ask?"

"It looks terrible."

"No, why do you ask whether I liked her?"

"I don't yet have a sense of who she was."

"It's not really relevant to what I do whether I like the girls or not."

"Why?"

"My job is to make sure that the girls get to the Emperor at the right times, on the right schedules in the right state. Whether I like them is irrelevant to that."

"How do you determine the schedules for the girls?"

"It's important for the Emperor to produce a male heir. We calculate the schedule that will make that happen."

THE EUNUCH

"Does it work?"

"We think it does."

"What are the variables that you take into account?"

"The variables we calculate to determine the Emperor's monthly schedule are secret."

"Why?"

"The same reason; If people knew how we make the schedules they'd find ways to manipulate the process."

"What's the protocol for getting the Imperial consorts to and from the Emperor's quarters?"

"Secret."

"Why?"

"Security."

"What are the security procedures surrounding the girls?"

"Secret."

"You do know that as the Chief Investigator I can approach the Emperor and request that the information be turned over to me?"

"You can, but we still wouldn't give them to you."

"Why?"

"The protocol exists because the process is circular. If a person can convince the Emperor to hand over this information, he has power. He can make sure his people are scheduled. Thus he will have even more influence over the Emperor. The Emperor can demand I hand over the information but I won't do it and his entire secretariat will support me."

Gett thought about this. Gogoro Shen stood in front of him, tired, eyes bloodshot. He took another drink.

The Chinese doctor stepped back, hand shaking, head down. He mumbled something to Nokan Besan's retainer. Eunuchs rushed up to cover her with silk. The last things to disappear were her eyes, as, legs propped up on the table and spread wide, she stared out at the room with hatred.

※

Again darkness. The blazing light and panic of the harem now far away, Gett again slid down quiet corridors.

In the darkness he found the passageway that led to Sulo's sleeping office. He padded along it, the document he had just prepared tucked under his arm.

Sulo's guards stopped him then brought him into a dimly-lit waiting room. He stood waiting.

About half an hour later, Sulo, eyes bleary with sleep, walked in.

Gett said, "I am here to report on the progress of the investigation."

"It's early."

"In fact it is late."

"Ha. Give to me."

Get pulled out the report he had written detailing his interview in the Harem.

"What is it?"

"It is the record of a friendly interrogation of the Head of the Imperial Harem, Eunuch of Standing, Gogoro Shen."

"What did he say?"

Gett thought about how to answer this question.

"Very little."

"Why?"

"He's worried that one of the concubines was slutting around."

"He didn't say this."

"No, but that's what he's worried about."

"You think it's true?"

"I don't know."

THE EUNUCH

"He kill the girl?"

"Without more information, it's hard to say."

"What do you think?"

"I doubt it."

"Why?"

"It is difficult to think of a motive that would cause him to."

"You give to Old Han?"

"I have not yet submitted this to Minister of Espionage Han."

"Why?"

"He doesn't like being disturbed at night. I'll submit it in the morning."

"When?"

"Possibly not before the Hour of the Dragon."

Gett watched Sulo as Sulo calculated how much time this gave him.

"I need surveillance on Eunuch of Standing Gogoro Shen," said Gett.

"Yes, can do. Anybody else?"

"How many can you run concurrently?"

"One or two. Three maybe miss things."

"Just him for now."

"Yes. Daily report?"

"Yes."

"You go now. I go back to sleep."

"Thank you," said Gett.

Sulo stood and walked out. Gett was again alone in the dim light. Sulo would not get any more sleep this night. What Sulo did with these extra waking hours would tell Gett a lot about Sulo's place in this strange case. It was time to go.

Gett left Sulo's sleeping office and emerged into the hall connecting to the official Palace. High windows had begun to glow with the deep blue of an impending dawn.

Gett knew he had to sleep. If he continued, he would make an error of judgment, an error of speech; dangerous — often fatal. But he did not yet wish to leave.

Caught in indecision, he stood in the hall. The glow in the high windows above him slowly brightened.

Gett's mind, awash with the noise that comes after a night of no sleep began, again, to go over the facts of the case as he so far knew them:

During her selection, the concubine Diao Ju is judged to be clever. There is fear that she will involve herself in Palace matters — or involve herself more often and more successfully than others. Several bureaus express this reservation to her entering the Palace. Based on her natural fecundity, she should be a high level concubine but instead enters the Palace and is degraded several levels. She stays in the Palace for one year. What happens? Unknown. The records are not available yet and Gett has yet to interview the other wives and concubines, a difficult process. Gogoro Shen, in his interview gives away little. But the sense, clearly, is that she had inserted herself in Palace politics in the way the vetting bureaus had feared. At the time she is murdered she leaves the inner Palace for an hour. She returns to an antechamber between two sets of guards. For some reason she spends several hours in this tiny room waiting for...something. Then she is killed by someone who no one saw enter or exit this tiny room. A very thorough inspection shows that there are no other exits. A bloody knife is found in a place that suggests the Emperor killed her, but there is no way he could have been at the place of the crime. Gett knew that a second interrogation of the Eunuch Gogoro Shen would begin to illuminate the year she spent in the Palace. Interviews with the other wives would clarify it even more. But, motives aside, the physical circumstances of the murder still made no sense. He couldn't think his way through it. His head was throbbing now. He needed to leave.

There came a point with a headache when, even if he killed its cause, it continued, orphaned and sullen. It might not get worse, but it wouldn't get better. Now he was approaching that point so he needed to get to his stash of betel nuts. He could see them in his mind, in their jar, sitting up above his desk, within easy reach for when he was writing. This thought propelled him down the hallway. Finally he arrived at his office. He loudly opened the padlock, both irritated by the grating sound but accepting it as quicker. He made his way across the dark office, reached up pulled down the jar. Surprisingly, it was open. He had forgotten to close it. He reached inside. It was a mess. He took the jar to the hallway and held it under a torch. He looked. His betel nuts had been chewed into a shredded ruined stew.

A rat. It had to have been a rat. Climbing in after Gett had forgotten to close the jar. He was furious. His temples throbbed with pain. The rat wouldn't be far, in darkness, away from the torch. Gett stepped down the stone hallway, searching the shadows. And there the rat was, only about thirty steps down, wheezing and dragging itself slowly forward.

Betel nut isn't poisonous *per se*, but what for Gett was a potent dose, for a rat would be a horrible death. So it lay now in agony. Near the terminus of its flight as it ran back to its hole but couldn't make it. Here, still angry, and with that anger exacerbated by his headache and his — still existing — lack of access to his drug, Gett stood to kick the rat, give it a vicious final send off. And then, as his foot was descending, as the rat's eyes turned up toward him, milky and close to death, the noise that fatigue and manic alertness created in his mind, the by-product of the energy that kept him awake and alert, coalesced into clarity, silence and one thought—a way it could have happened.

It could explain why she had been in the room so long. How her killer had not been seen entering or exiting. And it would make her hazy motives (or the parameters of the many motives she could possibly have had) clearer and more structured.

He hurried down the twisting, carpet-draped halls to Curdeger's morgue. He stepped into the cold and now dark room. He brushed his way silently past the stone tables.

The Concubine Third Class Diao Ju lay, still naked, on the fourth table on the left. Her open eyes stared into the darkness. Gett padded his way to the back of the room where there was a wooden door set into the wall. He knocked.

As he had expected, after a pause, Curdeger opened the door. He had not been asleep. A candle burned on a table strewn with minute pieces of evidence.

"Gett."

"You are up late, Curdeger."

"There is much to analyze."

"I need you to do something. I wanted to get to you before I went back to sleep."

"What is it?"

"I want you to redo your inspection of how she was killed."

"She was stabbed."

"She was stabbed, but we haven't actually checked whether it killed her."

八

CURDEGER STARED at Gett, and as he did, Gett imagined himself in Curdeger's mind; why was Gett here just before dawn, at the darkest, coldest hour of the night? What dangers did it hold for him personally and what should he do about Gett's statement: "...we haven't actually checked whether it killed her."

If in fact the knife wound had killed her, then Curdeger was relatively safe (or at least not in immediately foreseeable danger); he hadn't made a mistake and hadn't exposed himself to be used or sacrificed. If he was wrong, then he faced difficulties.

Curdeger spoke slowly, so as not to make any errors of haste. "Why do you think that something else might have killed her?"

"Mostly because if she was killed by the knife then I can't get the case to make any sense."

Gett watched Curdeger think about this. Finally Curdeger spoke. "Why?"

"She was in that room for seven hours. What was she doing there? I can't think of anything. How did somebody else get in and then out again? I can't think of any way either. It all hangs on her being stabbed in that room and dying from it."

"I see," said Curdeger after a pause.

Gett stood framed in the doorway, his spindly gaunt frame caught by the flickering light from Curdeger's candle. His jaw moving slowly as he rolled his betel nut across his tongue. He understood Curdeger's reluctance but, well, this was the Palace.

"So I need to know if she died from something else."

He waited. Curdeger nodded. Gett understood. Curdeger wasn't playing a game. There was a deep reluctance in him to continue.

"So I want you to cut the girl open and look at the wound."

"I have already written my report."

"But you haven't submitted it."

"That is true."

"This is a concubine who you suspect, who Chief of Harem Gogoro Shen suspects, was out of harem with a man. You know what will happen if you're wrong."

Gett, leaning against Curdeger's doorframe, his breath misting in front of him in the dead, deep silence of pre-dawn, could almost hear the complex gears grinding in Curdeger's mind as he thought about how to come out of this. Finally Curdeger gathered himself up to his full prodigious height and said in his whisper:

"Of course, Chief Investigator. When would you like to begin?"

As it happened, the death inspection took less time to complete than Gett (and clearly Curdeger) had anticipated.

With Gett standing beside him, Curdeger hacked into Diao Ju's chest with a large semicircular metal bone cutter. Gett chewed his (rat-gnawed) betel nut faster to cover up the grinding noise and reflected on how many of these inspections he had attended. Five, he calculated. He didn't like the bone cutters. It was the shape, he had decided. They looked like larger versions of the execution halberds that the Chinese pacification squads used. Even though here, their size and serrations were for practical rather than psychological effect, they still bothered Gett because they were (and Gett had groped for the right word each of the five times he had witnessed it) very...evil.

After the victims were opened and cut up, somehow it was less difficult.

Her flesh, already beginning to putrefy (but slowly in the cold), shredded under the teeth of the cutter as it ground into the thick hard bone of her central rib cage. It took Curdeger a good portion of an hour to saw through, steam beginning to rise off of his body as he generated heat from within his thick robe.

Finally Curdeger laid the cutter down and picked up a hammer. He whacked Diao Ju's ribcage and with a crack, the two halves separated. Curdeger reached in and pulled them apart.

Gett was always struck by this moment in an inspection. Suddenly a corpse seemed to push out its chest and stomach, as the spine was ratcheted forward by the back rotation of the ribcage. Like a last moment of pride against this invasion and the surprising and insulting fact of its own death.

Curdeger picked up a long set of inspection sticks and probed at the wound, tracing its trajectory through skin, muscle and into the lower organ cavity. Curdeger pulled the skin and muscle back, then closed it and looked at the entry wound again, then again back underneath to look at the point of exit from the muscle into the body cavity.

He laid the flap of skin and muscle down and stood back up, looking at Diao Ju's body, in thought. People like Curdeger did not, in the exact sense, betray their emotions. In an interrogation, or even in conversation, most people reveal to a skilled spotter what, or at least the categories about which, they were thinking. But here too (even with what he knew, beyond a shadow of a doubt, he was now facing) he did not. He simply turned to Gett.

"I believe I have made a mistake."

Gett nodded.

"Please look here," said Curdeger.

Curdeger pulled back the muscle; there was the puncture, about two finger widths wide, clearly an assassination knife, but on the underside of the muscle, only a tiny point. And that tiny point was offset by a full two hand widths from the entry wound.

"Do you see this entry wound?"

"Yes."

"And the exit?"

"Yes."

"It is an oblique wound. Either the attacker was clumsy or he did this deliberately. The result is that, from the front, the attacker stabbed her abdomen with a sideways thrust like this—"

Curdeger stepped back and made a low roundhouse against Gett's stomach.

"The knife entered her abdomen here, cut through the muscle, but transversely so that just the end of the tip penetrated into her body cavity. The organ of spitefulness was nicked here—"

Curdeger pointed to a tiny slice on the small organ.

"But the organ of bravery was missed entirely. Had the knife thrust been straight, the knife would have entered the organ of bravery here—"

Curdeger pointed to the large, heavily ensanguinated organ.

"And the bleeding and release of organ poison would have killed her very quickly—say two minutes. But as it is, this is not a fatal wound."

"Definitively not?"

"Definitively not."

"Could the knife have been poisoned?"

Curdeger pulled open the knife wound with two fingers. "Look at the interior of the wound."

Curdeger peeled it back and Gett peered closely at the cut flesh.

THE EUNUCH

"Most contact poisons discolor these wounds. There are a few that do not, but they leave other signs, none of which she has."

So here they were. Two men. A fallen bureaucrat, and an Ex-spy standing in a dark room over a dead girl in the cold just before dawn. To the surprise of both of them, a new and disquieting structure had settled down upon their relationship, unannounced and unexpected: Curdeger had made a *mistake*. That mistake would not enter the official record because the report was sitting in his office, finished but not yet submitted. It was officially due at the Hour of the Snake: original copies mandated to go to Gett, Sulo, Han Zongcheng, the Imperial Mother and the Emperor's secretary.

Gett, however, through a guess, had interrupted that process. Curdeger now had just enough time now to amend the report to include this finding, namely that Diao Ju had died, not from a penetrating stab wound but instead from causes as yet undetermined.

The problem was this: Curdeger's mistake, almost without question, would have been, in the course of this investigation, fraught as it was with political ramifications, eventually discovered. So Gett had inadvertently done for Curdeger something important. However:

Gett knew.

Curdeger could amend the existing report, he could erase all records of its existence. But still Gett knew that it had existed. *Only* Gett knew.

If this version of it and the larger case became a weapon in one of the struggles that would result from the murder, and at some point it inevitably would, Curdeger was in danger.

Curdeger unquestionably recognized he owed Gett (and this was not a trivial recognition on his part), but Curdeger was a hard man.

Gett spoke. "How long will it take you to complete the analysis of what killed her?"

"That is difficult to say. It depends on what actually did kill her."

"What are the parameters?"

"There are two possibilities. The first is that she was killed by poison. If we are successful in discovering which poison it will take between one day and one week, depending on the type. Some of the tests are complex, others simple. But most likely we will not be able to detect anything even if it is there. That is the nature of poisons. The other possibility is that she was killed by a small weapon that has left a small wound, one that we haven't found yet."

"What kind?"

"It is hard to say."

"What kind would kill her slowly, I mean one where she would be fine for at least a few minutes but it would kill her quickly later."

"That would likely be a poison. We have catalogued six mixtures that will cause symptoms that mimic heart death. Each takes under an hour to take effect and depends on dosage."

"Any weapons?"

Curdeger thought about it. "They are rare and used only by assassins. A hot metal splinter inserted up through the back of the neck into the skull. Similarly into the heart. But because of the circumstances of course I have checked and those wounds are not present on her body."

Gett chewed on his betel nut, looked for a place to spit out his red sticky saliva. Finding none, he swallowed it.

There was no use pretending that the situation was not what it was—Curdeger would be careful. But he would begin to delve into Gett's past. He would look at Gett's behavior and he would

THE EUNUCH

begin to build up a picture of what he thought Gett would do with his information. And if his conclusion was — danger — then Gett would be eliminated. Not right away but soon enough.

This was a function of fatigue. Had Gett not been walking on that edge that sharpens as a man stretches far beyond when he should be asleep, he would sooner have seen the ramifications of his request. But he had simply not thought clearly. He had gotten his answer but he too had made a mistake.

"I will wait for your results, Chief Analyst. Thank you for your time."

"I will perform these analyses as fast as I can, Chief Investigator. I look forward to working with you on this."

九

"Morning," said Gett as he walked into the library.

Lao Kou looked up from his scrolls with his bloodshot yellow eyes and a smile of conspiracy stretched up and across his face. It was a smile Gett liked — clearly natural to Lao Kou and he had kept it (so there must have been some reward in it) throughout his life. It was a truly remarkable smile. His whole mouth stretched out, yellow teeth jutting forward, eyes narrowing to slits. All in enjoyment of the secret he was about to hear, and the camaraderie it would engender.

Gett had decided, after long thought about it, that the smile made Lao Kou look like the perfect friend. Someone who enjoyed you, recognized in a deep and true way your value, saw in you an ally — and was devious and intelligent enough to be useful to you.

Gett eased himself onto one of the reading stools and took out another rat chewed betel nut. It was damp and disgusting. Gett put it in his mouth anyway. Because he was so hopped up on the energy that flooded his body when he lacked sleep, the high hit him sharp and hard.

Lao Kou lit up and took a long contemplative drag on his pipe, the sticky smell of the hemp filling the room waiting for Gett to make his request. The two of them sat in the yellow, flickering darkness, not speaking.

THE EUNUCH

Gett was at the reading desk. Lao Kou had brought him an extra candle so the light cast over the table was strange and flickering. Double shadows, twining around each other as the candles guttered and wavered at their own unpredictable, internally determined rates. Like the people in this case, Gett thought.

Illuminated by these candles, spread out over the reading table, was a heavy cache of documents.

Gett had organized them so that on the left were, in chronological order, the records detailing the movements of all ministries through the parts of the Palace surrounding the Antechamber of Shuddering Hooves. They covered a full day time window bracketing Diao Ju's death. On the right side of the table, Gett had lain cracked and yellowing maps that showed, in great detail, the geography of the Palace.

Lao Kou, after delivering this mass of documentation and looking over Gett's shoulder for a while, sucking on his long pipe, had ambled off into another room, possibly to sleep but more likely to read copies of the same documents to prise out what Gett was trying learn.

So Gett was now alone. And he went to work.

If she wasn't stabbed in the antechamber, then where? The Antechamber of Shuddering Hooves, where Diao Ju had been found by the cleaning girl, was about ten paces wide by twenty long and, as the map showed, it had a southern entrance leading to the inner quarters and an outer, wider entrance that opened into a corridor with the ponderous name The Hallway of Everlasting Spring. Gett knew the corridor as long and dark. Tiled with black stone and without windows.

Gett looked at the movement records. Diao Ju was the only person to be signed in and out of the Antechamber into the

Hallway that entire day. But they showed heavy traffic in the Hallway of Everlasting Spring.

The schedule looked like this:

> **Hour of the Monkey:** Planting rites held on the Patio of Fulmination with the Hallway the main route between the Patio and the seed storage rooms. Also Chefs for Wife Second Class Avowed Constancy scheduled to shuttle dishes between kitchen and the Dining Hall of Golden Radiance through the Hallway.
>
> **Hour of the Rooster:** Banquet due to end in the first quarter of the hour, and guests to disperse through the Hallway. Towards the end of the Hour, there is a period of about a quarter hour when the Hallway should be empty.
>
> **Hour of the Dog:** Examination Rites begin in the Garden of Blissful Respite and many scholars use the Hallway as a shortcut, resulting in heavy traffic for the whole hour.

This accorded with Diao Ju's sign-in time on the guards' register outside the Antechamber—recorded during the third quarter of the Hour of the Dog.

Gett sat back to think: So she arrives, presumably near the end of the hour, at the entrance to the Hallway of Everlasting Spring. What is in her mind? What does she see as the problem for the immediate future?

By now, she should be calming down. She is almost back. She has somehow made her way, without being seen, from wherever she was stabbed, through the Palace and all the way

THE EUNUCH

to this point; the last stage in a frightening journey that now maybe, just maybe, she has begun to believe will not end badly for her. Farther, the fact that she is still alive is heartening to her; it has become apparent by now that whatever her wound is, it is not immediately fatal and she has probably begun to believe, recognizing her own lack of experience, that it may not be as serious as it looked.

If the schedules are accurate, she arrives at an entrance into the Hallway sometime near the end of the Hour of the Dog. The corridor is deserted. She makes her way quickly down it to the entrance to the antechamber. She manages to stand up straight in front of the guard and holds herself together long enough to sign in. Somehow she conceals her wound from him and the fact that she is bleeding, even if less so than before. She passes the guard and enters the Antechamber of Shuddering Hooves. Here, she almost certainly pauses to collect herself before she enters the inner quarters. It is possible she even looks for a way that she could have realistically injured herself within the antechamber, because once she enters the inner quarters, again, she puts herself in danger of discovery before she can fake an accident. At some point soon after that—while still in the antechamber—she collapses, loses consciousness, and dies.

If in fact she *was* stabbed outside then this much was relatively clear. But how had she gotten to the Hallway? The maps showed six entrances. The first entrance, furthest from the Antechamber of Shuddering Hooves and around a corner, opened from the spice sorting halls, the second, closer, from a subsidiary victualing bay, the third from a small wardrobe passageway, then the Dining Hall of Golden Radiance and attached kitchen, and finally the Garden of Blissful Respite and the Patio of Fulmination. All usually busy, and all guarded because they were so close to the Inner Palace.

The first of these, the door to the spice sorting halls, Gett knew well. It was a low, arched entrance hung with a wool tapestry and connected the Hallway of Everlasting Spring to the spice sorting warrens in which Chinese girls picked through piles of dry caked dirt to sift out the tiny spices that went into Imperial dishes — and it was close so they could get them there quickly. Gett knew it as a narrow passageway, poorly lit and honeycombed with doors that led off to the spice sorting rooms. (And it was fragrant, the reason Gett knew it well. Passing through it was one of the small pleasures he allowed himself over the course of a day — to walk slowly down it when his route allowed, breathing in the dirty, fraught complexity of the Imperial spices.) The passageway itself was rarely occupied, but it was visible from the sorting rooms so the girls would have seen anybody walking down it, and they would have reported it because of the sensitivity of what they did. The Kitchen and Dining Hall room were on the same eyeline and so also were unlikely.

The records for the day showed a change of shift at the end of the Hour of the Rooster. The rooms should have been empty long enough for Diao Ju to slip through, but the timing was dicey, half an hour off.

The second possible entry point, Gett knew less well. It led into a long, doorless corridor to the victualing bays where camel and horse caravans offloaded the daily supplies specifically for the Emperor and family. This was the least likely of her possible routes. It was very close to the entrance to the inner Palace so was heavily guarded because it was a direct link to the world outside the Palace walls. And it was always occupied — the Emperor and his entourage consumed a great deal over the course of a day. Security was low that day because of the Examination. But the docks were full constantly so it shouldn't have made a difference.

The third entrance to the Hall of Everlasting Spring was

THE EUNUCH

slightly farther down the hallway. It was a corridor that led to the wardrobe fitting rooms for Ceremonies of Extraordinary Significance. If Diao Ju had stolen a dress to hide her wound and blood from the guard, this was the likely place. But both the banquet of Wife Second Class Avowed Constancy and the Imperial Examination had kept it busy for almost the entire time in question — and hallways used by Examination candidates were closely watched to prevent cheating. However the records did show a tiny time window, roughly the time it took the servants to eat a meal, during the Rites of Confluence a quarter way through the Hour of the Dog. Again, possible, but dicey.

The garden around which the Hallway of Everlasting Spring wrapped was simply that, an outdoor space, not a passageway to anywhere and even less likely as a hiding place since it was viewable from all sides. The Patio of Fulmination which sat in the empty space between the inner and outer Palace was similarly exposed, impossible to hide in, and not a pathway to anywhere. And in any case, it had been occupied the entire time.

So again Gett constructed it in his mind — she arrives at one of three possible routes to the Hall of Everlasting Spring. Earlier, immediately after being stabbed, she is probably in shock and numbed. But this point is most likely the height of her fear. Her wound has really starting to bleed. And the fear of death is beginning to creep up her arms and legs, reaching with its greasy claws up her back through her neck and into her mind. And it's starting to hurt. Now about five minutes in, as the numbness is wearing off, a dull throb has started, an ache that comes in waves and increasingly painful beats.

She is consumed by uncertainty. This is a nineteen-year-old girl. She doesn't know how serious her wound is, doesn't know if it's nothing or if she'll collapse and die in minutes.

And finally, she realizes that she is walking wrong. The knife severed almost a hand's length of muscle transversally across her abdomen. What she doesn't know is that the very thing that made it non-fatal is what is making it hard to walk. Those muscles pull on every forward step. But again, even with all this, she is smart enough and clear enough about the consequences that she doesn't call out for help. Instead, she presses forward along one of these paths until she reaches the Hallway of Everlasting Spring.

Gett rubbed his eyes, tired. It was entirely possible that she had been stabbed in, say, the Spice Corridors, or the Fitting Rooms, but Gett felt it was unlikely. It didn't feel right to him, even if he wasn't quite sure why yet. It was also unlikely to have occurred in the Hallway of Everlasting Spring. That would be too close to the guards, too dangerous for the perpetrator. So Gett's money was on somewhere deeper in the Palace, connected to a route through to one of these places.

Gett thought about Diao Ju in the moment just after she was stabbed. In that moment what did she think she was facing? What did she do?

What *does* she do?

She is petrified. It isn't immediately apparent to her that her wound isn't fatal. She almost certainly has no experience with these kinds of wounds (those sorts of things make their way into reports and he hadn't even seen any oblique references to it), so, she is just a kid who has grown up in some rich dad's house and suddenly has watched a knife slide into her belly. The knife comes out and the shock is replaced by real fear as she watches incredibly red blood pouring out of her.

But, and this is important, she *doesn't scream*. If she is stabbed somewhere in the wider Palace, then it is a silent event. So Diao Ju is smart enough even with a knife in her belly, to realize that to scream is to die. She realizes that she's got to get back to the inner

THE EUNUCH

quarters and only then, only when she passes that threshold, can she fake an accident that will explain her wound.

Because if she screams and she is caught out there, then very quickly the parameters of what she might have been doing will become clear. Even more quickly the truth will be extracted. And the most likely truth is: a sexual liaison. She'll die for that, and it will be slow, painful and humiliating and more than likely her entire family will die too. So not only does she instantly realize this, but she is thinking fast enough to control herself. And most importantly, she is almost certainly LET GO by the perpetrator, because the wound looks like a deliberate miss, intentionally non-fatal.

Does he chase her? Does he run first? Hard to say, but the odds are that she leaves, terrified but with a clear goal — get back into the inner quarters WITHOUT BEING SEEN, except of course by the guards signing her through to the Emperor's Quarters. However, from these three rooms, and the corridors which connect them the exits open up essentially to the entire remainder of the Palace, including — if she came through the victualing bay — to the city outside.

But the timing doesn't add up. There are places, like a servants' back hallway, the eunuch entryways to the pantry and numerous others with small time windows during which Diao Ju can slip past. But none of them are contiguous and, with a few exceptions, there is nowhere to hide between them.

So Diao Ju's path from wherever she is in the Palace back to the Antechamber of Shuddering Hooves is irrevocably blocked by the normal ebb and flow of human traffic within the corridors that honeycomb it.

Gett could, if he wished, task either Sulo or an investigation team to search every one of these corridors and rooms. And eventually they would probably find blood or the signs of a struggle. But the Palace was big and it would take a while.

And these things always had a logic to them. Gett had found that if he was clear about what the people involved wanted and what they had at their disposal to get it, usually he could reach down into a tangled mess like this and tease out, with a crooked finger as it were, the one thread that drew him towards the murderer.

But here the problem was not one of goals: he was settling into an idea about what the possible motivations of her killer might have been. Nothing definite, but the parameters were there.

No, the problem here was physical reality. There was no good path through to the Antechamber of Shuddering Hooves that ran out farther than the spice rooms, and if it hadn't happened there (and Gett didn't think it had), and if there was no path back from anywhere farther, then Gett was in a bind.

He sat back in the darkness and chewed his now-stale nut. He looked at the maps; looked back at the schedules. He stood up.

Here too, in the side annex in which Lao Kou was snoring, there was very little light, just a dying candle. Gett sat in a chair next to Lao Kou's cot, took out a fresh nut and then prodded him.

Lao Kou came awake before he opened his eyes; rubbed them in the darkness as he sat up, only finally opening them sleepily and with a smile when he was fully upright.

"Find what you needed?"

"No."

"Hmmm."

"But I suspect I know why," said Gett.

Lao Kou grinned and reached for his pipe. He lit it again and took a long deep drag, the kind that infiltrates deep into the mossy crevices in the mind of the old addict.

THE EUNUCH

"What is it that you need to know?" asked Lao Kou.
"I think there is more than one set of maps to the Palace."
"There might just be."
"How exactly do they differ?"
Lao Kou smiled. He enjoyed precision.
"In accuracy."
"What is inaccurate in one of the sets?"
"What matters to you?"
"Distances, routes and...completeness."
"All of those are inaccurate."
"I would like to see the accurate ones."
"Many people would."

Gett smiled, chewed his betel nut. His red teeth looked black in the flickering candle light. Lao Kou sat quietly on his bed. He took another long pull on his pipe. He smiled in return.

"You are the Chief Investigator. Come on. I'll take you down. Everybody is still asleep."

Lao Kou got up and shuffled out the door. Gett followed. The door led directly to a winding stairway that led down. Very quickly the candlelight disappeared. The one thing the hall of records feared above all was fire. So it was very dark.

Gett made his way by feel down the pitch-black stairway. Strangely, as they reached the bottom it got a quite a bit lighter.

"We have skylights," said Lao Kou as he shuffled away through the stacks.

In the milky dawn light that filtered down from the invisible skylights, Gett could see the piles. They towered over him, reaching up to a ceiling that was obscured by darkness. So, too, did they disappear into the distance. The stacks were arrayed in rows, and the shelves themselves were crammed with scrolls.

Lao Kou stood at the mouth of one of the rows waiting for Gett. Gett stepped off the stairway and followed. They began to move slowly through the labyrinthine paths laid out by the shelves, two tiny figures moving below dark and shrouded cliffs overgrown with dry and heavy paper. After some distance, Lao Kou spoke, his voice flat and strangely un-echoing in the paper-damped claustrophobia.

"So how is it going?"

"It's hard for me to say," said Gett after a pause as they slowly trudged along. "I don't have a handle on it yet."

"Why not?"

"It's a confusing murder. There are aspects of it that I can't tell you about."

"Of course."

"But she was killed in a certain way so as to make it look as though she died in a different way. And the killer tried to frame somebody else for the murder."

"Who?"

"I can't say."

"Why?"

Gett pondered this as they moved their way slowly down the dark aisles. It was important that he not give to Lao Kou any… information Lao Kou was potentially not mandated to know, and soon such distinctions would matter. But he knew also that this was the deal; Lao Kou would lead him on this slow circuit of the stacks until Gett made good on the silent agreement they had struck in Lao Kou's dark annex. So Gett carefully organized his thoughts for precision in his speech.

"It would be dangerous for me to tell you, and dangerous for you to know."

Lao Kou wheezed out a laugh.

More silence as they shuffled down the corridor made by the shelves. Dusty scrolls in square shelves disappearing into the darkness above them.

THE EUNUCH

"Anything to be aware of for today?"

Gett again carefully forced himself to be precise.

"Today it will be important to follow the rules."

Lao Kou took this in. He nodded. He had been a survivor for long enough to know what this meant and know both the parameters and the magnitude of the trade he had just made.

After a few more turns, Lao Kou stopped, stepped back and pulled out two scrolls.

Gett took the maps, moved under one of the skylights, and opened them in the filtered dawn light.

He had, in truth, expected a secret passageway. The Palace was honeycombed with them. He knew where a few were, but most of the Imperial family, including wives and concubines, knew more and used them frequently. His first overlook of the map, though, produced no passage with obvious relevance to Diao Ju's escape route.

And then he saw it. The maps were different, not obviously so, and not just in the clear delineation of secret passageways, but also in the lengths of many corridors and the placement of doors. The Palace produced these inaccurate maps for a variety of purposes but mostly as a precaution against assassination. Anyone with access to a map could trace a route to the Imperial quarters, but upon his arrival in the actual physical space of the Palace would find himself turned down corridors that did not exist on the map, stuck in unmarked dead ends or nonplussed in front of blank walls that his map showed to have (now proven to be imaginary) doors. The differences were subtle and rare, but crucial. Insiders knew the layout they needed to know and they were monitored. Outsiders did not and generally died.

But there it was, in the lower right-hand corner of the map; a door that led directly from a servant dormitory into the back of one of the wardrobe fitting rooms.

JONATHAN KOS-READ

As Gett hurried along, his robes swished just a bit louder than normal in the deserted hallway—it was the time when, for reasons Gett did not understand, sound was somehow sharper and more defined than even silence and emptiness would explain. He moved past the kitchens, the smell of stewing lamb and curdling cheese spreading through the cold hallway. He turned left and entered the wide echoing Courtyard of Sacrifice, padded slippers allowing the deep cold of the stones to absorb into his feet.

It was going to be a cold day. Cold in that clear-sky, no-wind, absolutely still way, as if the universe itself had simply stopped and was now dying away. He could make out all the details of the courtyard now; it was almost fully daylight.

He entered a side door of the open square that led towards the Palace tailors, where small eunuchs with small fingers sewed Palace uniforms. The corridor smelled like dye, the smell fainter than usual in the cold.

He moved down the tailoring corridor, turned a corner and came to a small bend that led in one direction toward the janitorial staff apartments and in the other direction towards the back doors of the poultry delivery station for the eunuch quarters. He stopped. He looked around.

And there it was—obvious if you were looking for it. He knelt down, knees cracking, looking like an awkward insect.

He brought his face very close to it. There was no mistaking it. Dried, but without too much discoloration, so no more than a day old.

On the wall next to the floor, a small spatter of blood.

And here was, encapsulated in this tiny stain, the crux of the matter for Gett. What was Diao Ju's killer trying to achieve? What he had done almost guaranteed that there would be an Imperial

THE EUNUCH

investigation—the killing of an Imperial concubine inside the Palace who dies within the sanctum sanctorum of the Emperor's personal quarters. And the stab looked a lot like the killer knew what he was doing, like it was meant to injure her just enough that she would—and could—run back to the safety of the inner quarters and only then die there from (Curdeger's analysis had not finished yet but Gett couldn't imagine a scenario in which it would not show this) the earlier application of a poison.

Second...and here Gett sat back and allowed his eyes to close, swirling the bitter juice that he crushed out of the little nut in his mouth. He slipped himself into the mind of her killer and then, more difficult, crawled along the delicate structure of what he knew about the case, into the killer's theory of Diao Ju's mind. The records that Gett had carefully picked through had, without ever saying it explicitly, detailed a clever girl.

This was a girl who had had the guts to fuck somebody while concubined to the *Emperor*. To have a liaison *inside* the Palace. Then, bleeding and terrified, be smart enough to realize she had to get back before she was found out, cross a fully-occupied loading bay, sign back in, and somehow conceal the fact that she was bleeding terribly. That wasn't easy.

And it wasn't something you would *expect* somebody to do.

Unless you knew her.

—⎯—

As G℮tt stood in the quiet hallway forcing his tired and scattered mind to extend itself out onto the branches of the meanings this discovery represented, he heard a patter of footsteps ahead in the darkness. He squinted and a figure resolved itself. A Secretariat servant. He walked to Gett, acknowledged him and his rank.

"Inspector Gett."

"Yes."

"I am a messenger from the Central Secretariat."

"Yes, I see that. What message are you delivering?"

He handed a waxed scroll to Gett. Gett opened and read: 'The presence of Inspector Gett required in the Imperial Audience Room'

Gett stood thinking about this until the servant asked quietly, "and what is your reply?"

"My reply?"

"Yes. I was told to wait for one."

Gett thought about that.

"What is the nature of the audience?"

"The Imperial Examination."

"How long were you told to wait?"

"It was not specified to me, but I was told to wait until you had given a reply and to remind you if you had not."

"Tell them of course I will be there and I am deeply grateful for this summons."

THE EUNUCH

"Yes, Honorable Eunuch."

The servant disappeared back into the gloom of the hallway. Why ask for an answer for something that was by its nature an order? Time was tight now. An audience in the Throne Room was not something simply to be attended. There was a meticulous preparation that preceded it. He calculated. He had under an hour.

An approach to the Imperial Throne Room could not be made with errors. And close to a hundred people existed to make sure none were. They lined the hallway that led in, half holding torches, the other half checking Gett's robe, reminding him of protocol and moving him forward.

The question of why he was here was in his mind like a heavy stone, rolling about and crushing his other thoughts. Finally, he passed the threshold and could see past the dragon-carved columns into the room. It was dimly lit as usual, so it was hard to make anything out clearly. But down in front were about fifty Examination candidates. Regulation white robes. In abject kowtows. All Chinese. Possibly — Gett quickly counted — all the Chinese allowed to sit for the Examination. The Jurchen candidates, all four of them, knelt farther back and to the side. Cordoned off away from them were the Examination officials. A quiet feeling began in the back of Gett's mind, like the inexorable but miniscule drip of a water clock. The Chinese and Jurchen candidates shouldn't be here together — the preponderance of Chinese an unacceptable message.

Beyond them, security officials. The bureaucrats of course. They were required at every Imperial audience like this. But in the dark shadows of the walls, the guards. Cramped in, claustrophobic, too many of them. Far too many for an audience like this.

He looked carefully at the Chinese examination candidates. He could see only their backs as they kept their faces pressed to the ground. But just before Gett turned away, he saw one of them, near the rear, raise his head. Just for a moment, but he clearly took in his surroundings, the throne, the officials, those around him. This was often the way with the very arrogant when they first arrived in the Palace. It was the first trait they shed.

Gett saw Han, the Chinese traitor. Hidden among the security bureaucrats, not with the Examination officials. His rank as Minister of Espionage was higher than the rank he held as Bureau Chief of Examinations. Gett checked the throne before moving. Checked the protocol officers. Not yet preparing a general kowtow. Enough time. He threaded his way through the officials. Bending so he did not stick up. There was anonymity in the soft rustling crowd. Finally, he gently edged up next to Han.

Officials shuffled into their places. The lamps were adjusted. Silence incrementally descended onto the room as they prepared for the Emperor's entrance. Then, in the moments just before he arrived, Han finally spoke.

"Gett. Let me ask you a question."

"Of course."

"How will you proceed?"

"With the investigation?"

"Yes."

"That's an odd question."

"I don't think so. How will you carry it out?"

"In the normal way. I will follow the evidence where it leads me."

"And if it leads you here?"

"Here?"

"Here to my Examination."

"Then I will follow it there."

THE EUNUCH

"Follow it to this crucially important event that happens once every two years and is still fragile? This event that will cement the hold of your people on mine? This event that will bring peace to the people your Emperor rules? This is where you will follow it?"

"Is there a reason I should not?"

"There is no reason you should not. You must serve the Emperor faithfully, as I do. Every day giving thanks that your more enlightened people rule over mine."

Get often encountered a practical problem when dealing with people who were smarter or stupider than him—a bit smarter, it was easy to tell. A bit stupider, again, easy. But when someone was too much removed, it was hard to judge. And it took on great importance when the person was powerful.

In the hierarchy of the Palace, Han vastly outranked him. For a Chinese to reach that level, he had to be an incredibly special person. Intelligent and ruthless in the extreme, the things Han said and did were observable but difficult to understand. Often that opacity was the product of distance—he was perched higher, saw more, and pulled deeper levers. That strangeness, strangeness that looked like stupidity in others was, for Gett, always the key that he had missed something—and not just an event or a fact, but a fundamental insight into how the world around him had re-structured itself. Again, Gett looked out at the Chinese scholars. And at their four Jurchen counterparts. Again, the steady drip of a warning in his mind. They shouldn't be here.

The room was now almost completely silent. Just scattered whispering conversations. The arrival of the Emperor was imminent.

"How are the preparations for the Examination progressing?" asked Gett.

"Your investigation has made them difficult."

"In what way?"

"In the ways that you would expect. It is why you are here."

"I was ordered to be here."

"You could have avoided it. You could have stayed on the other side of this room. It's much more comfortable over there. But here you are."

They were silent as Gett chose his words.

"This killing occurred three days before the Imperial Examination."

"Yes."

"What do you think about that?"

"I think it is an unfortunate fact," said Han.

"It seems to me that even if it has nothing to do with the Examination, people will assume that it does."

"I suspect you are right. People will think that."

"What do you think?"

"Gett, you know how it is. After the Examination, this family is losing out. This other family has a new position. It is a tense time. We deal with it. But before the Examination, nothing happens. Nothing can happen. There is only the examination. There is only the question: will the candidate pass, what will he score, what is his final rank? And that is all determined by the examination and *nothing* else. People do kill each other over the Examination, Gett. But after. Not before."

Gett considered this, rolled it around in his mind. It was true. He felt, though, not like this was an answer, but instead, a clarification of something he was missing.

"Gett, do you know how you came to be here?"

"I have been wondering that."

"Of course. Do you know who summoned you?"

"The Office of the Secretariat."

"Yes, correct."

THE EUNUCH

"And thus, the Emperor or the Imperial Mother."

"In general, Gett, that is correct. But not in this case. I arranged for you to be invited."

"Why did you arrange that?"

"The Emperor is here, Gett."

Han nodded toward the throne. At the same time the protocol officer announced a general kowtow. The entire room dropped to its knees as the Emperor walked in. He sat in his throne. Behind him, the bead curtain rustled as the Imperial Mother seated herself.

The Emperor stared out at the crowd, the officials and finally at the scholars. He let the silence sit over them for a long time. He motioned at the head guard and Gett saw at least twenty more soldiers slip into the room and place themselves in the shadows behind the torches. Finally, he began to talk in an almost conversational voice. Slow, quiet, and friendly. Except for the adolescent shine of insecurity in his eyes, he did a remarkable job of controlling his speech.

"The Imperial People have reinstated the Examination. This should be taken as an honor for all Chinese. The Imperial People have shown its respect for your culture. The Imperial People did not have to do this. But the Imperial People did. This is what a great conquering power does. This is *why* the Imperial People are great. But the Imperial I is unhappy. The Imperial I is uncomfortable. And disappointed! A killing has occurred. This can only mean that there is an unbalance in the Palace. An unbalance in energy, as you Chinese say. What is it?"

The Emperor searched the faces of the scholars, hoping for a reaction. The only one he got was fear, as they kept their heads low. Then he did a strange thing. He stood and descended from his dais and began to pace in front of the scholars, carefully looking at them. Bending down even. Finally, he began to speak, but this time, not to the assembled officials. He leaned in and whispered very slowly and quietly to the kneeling scholars. Gett strained but could only catch small hissing fragments of coherence.

"Are you all true scholars of the classics? The Imperial I wonders. The Imperial I thinks that our Imperial People maybe have surpassed Chinese. The Imperial I knows you use your studies only to undermine the Imperial People. It is a known fact. Why should the Imperial People trust you? True knowledge comes from within, when we know a thing is right. The Imperial I has learning as well. The Imperial I knows this. So many Chinese sit for the Examination. More than the Jurchen. Why is this? Is the Chinese man superior? No. The Jurchen man, the man of the Imperial People, is obviously superior, so this must be something else. What could it be?"

The Emperor waited. Gett listened, but also watched the shadows. Soldiers were moving, not quickly but they were spreading out, flanking the hall. Gett calculated a path to the exits. Not easy; even if nobody went for the doors, the confusion would block him. Other options? There were no tapestries to slip behind, and anyway the guards lined the walls. Gett continued searching. The dragon columns were thick. The best—far from good but nothing else offered itself—was to lie flat next to a column. They were also climbable, Gett judged, if it came to it. No one would notice; no one ever looked up.

"Could it be the result of cheating. Would you all agree?" asked the Emperor.

Terrified silence. The Emperor asked again.

"Would you all agree that this must be the result of cheating?"

"Yes!" a few of the prostrate Chinese scholars yelled.

"Yes! Yes! Yes!" The rest of them followed.

The guards now surrounded the entire room, having

THE EUNUCH

soundlessly and professionally moved to their positions. Almost imperceptible rustling whispers were starting.

"Of course," the Emperor said, "cheating is wrong. It is an insult to the Imperial I. It is proof you do not deserve your place here. This must be the disbalance in the world that allowed a killing to occur. You took it from a Jurchen who deserved it. Who worked hard but was cheated as always by devious Chinese. The Imperial I is kind. The Imperial I is benevolent. Your sages teach this. But you Chinese clearly do not know your own customs. So the Imperial I must be firm. The Imperial I must show you the clear way. This is the true love the Imperial I shows. You must be punished. But The Imperial I is benevolent! The Imperial I wishes to give you a chance! Because you should be able to prove that you are special and worthy of the term scholar! Therefore the Imperial I has prepared a test. A test only a scholar could pass!"

He motioned toward the shadows next to the throne without looking. He waited. Clearly planned. Nothing happened. He continued to wait. Longer than he expected certainly. The Emperor was not in complete control, someone had made a mistake. This knowledge settled onto the room like a mist. Gett knew someone would die for it.

Finally, six Palace girls moved out of the shadows. Dressed for this occasion—an Imperial audience and even more to cross the throne line—in the special eagle and wolf fur fringe headgear with tasseling. A mark of honor. Each was trying to not make mistakes. They moved gracefully. Then stopped, nervous, staring at the ground.

The Emperor said, "These are Palace girls! But one is the sister of the Imperial I. She is of the Clan of the Left Banner! A true scholar, versed in the classics, would immediately distinguish which are common Palace girls and which is a Bannered Noble!

This is the simplest thing in the world! So-called scholars who can't do this...ridiculous. The Imperial I would be forced to send you all home! You would forfeit the right to even take the examination! It is not what the Imperial I wishes! But it must be! It is unavoidable! So, tell us. Which is the sister of the Imperial I?"

Gett looked at the Palace girls, then at the scholars. The distance from the throne to where they were huddled was about ten arm-spans. So, an impossible task. At least half were afflicted with blurriness of distant things—common among scholars. Second, the Palace was new, strange. Even if they could see clearly, they would have no way to judge.

The Emperor was waiting for them. Was stopping, stooping down. They were taking the Emperor's time by not answering, heartbeat by terrifying heartbeat. The Emperor began to pace slowly in front of them, forcing an acknowledgment of this on them. All sound in the room had ceased, even Gett found himself breathing carefully. And then, finally, just as the Emperor was raising his arm to the guards in the back of the Throne Room, one small, clear voice spoke.

"Exalted Emperor, I can answer this question."

The Emperor paused. Brought his arm back down. Looked over at him. Smiling. Anticipating his failure. Anticipating an opportunity for humiliation. The Palace girls flicked up their eyes nervously to look at what was happening.

"The Imperial I commands you to stand, scholar."

A young thin man near the back stood carefully, the same who had raised his head earlier. He was at the other end of the audience room so Gett could not see him clearly. Scholars ranged from ugly to forgettable usually. This one, though, had an awkward, dark birthmark running from his ear down his neck, like the shadow of a thin hand.

THE EUNUCH

"Exalted Emperor. May I state which of these honorable women is the sister of the Exalted Emperor and which are respected Palace servants?"

"The Imperial I allows it."

It was an impossible task. But the scholar had a one-in-six chance of being right. He might as well guess. Better than certain failure.

"This is a question that those who have not studied the classics of Mengzi, Kongzi and Taoist Immortals would have difficulty with. But under the Exalted Emperor's tutelage, it has been possible to study these texts. And thus, I believe I can answer this question."

The Emperor became still. Not just his pacing ceased, but the small movements as well. His fingers and shoulders and knees slowed down and stopped.

"Speak."

The Palace girls' eyes flicked over to the scholar, now able to locate him.

"It is a well-known fact," the scholar said, "that those related to the Emperor are special. Not just in their moral uprightness and perfection, but even more that this righteousness and proper behavior is a manifestation of the power of the energy that flows through them, an energy so powerful, in fact, that it manifests itself in their bodies."

The room was completely silent, a death watch for the boy.

"All who have studied the classics properly know that this energy causes the air around the head of a true princess, if you really look at it...to glow."

All heads in the room tilted almost imperceptibly to look again at the Palace girls. And finally—it was small, but it was noticeable, even from as far back as the scholar was standing—five of the six Palace girls flicked their eyes up at the head of the third girl, and then quickly down to the floor again.

"And so this knowledge tells me that the glow I see around her head..." the scholar pointed to the third Palace girl, "means she has Imperial blood and is the sister of the Exalted Emperor."

It was as when a cart hurtling down a hill, just as it is reaching its maximum speed, suddenly simply stops. All eyes following it continue in its path and all those in it jam forward. And then over the next few heartbeats the watchers bring their surprised eyes back to it, those inside it separate themselves, and they wrench not just their bodies, but also their minds into this new and unexpected stillness.

The Emperor was silent for an exceptionally long moment. Then finally he said, "That is correct,"

He looked for a moment into the scholar's eyes — genuinely looked, saw him for the first time. The scholar, quite bravely Gett thought, looked back. Gett tried to predict what the Emperor would do. This final game had been simply a diversion for the emperor, a sideshow, a way to falsely present the scholars with a sliver of hope. Even possibly a way for him to justify it to himself.

But the scholar's answer had put them all in danger; to simply be present during a humiliation, even a small one, was to find oneself walking near the river of death. Gett watched the Emperor calculate how much face he would lose by simply killing the scholar immediately. It would be a high price, and Gett — and all assembled — could see the Emperor knew that.

Gett hunched down. He knew what was coming. The Emperor could not now dismiss them all. But he would make it worse for the rest. He gestured to the soldiers in the shadows. "I reprieve half of them. Take the other half. This will restore balance."

Gett had watched many boys sentenced to die in his life. Watched them realize it. Watched them understand this was it. No achievements. No children. No respect. No old age. Nothing

THE EUNUCH

but one more hour. These boys would not be killed. But they had spent their entire short lives preparing for this Examination. They had nothing else. It defined them. And now it was to be snatched away. Never to be re-given. They writhed. Robes tearing. Eyes bulging. Struggling in desperate tortured horrified panic, helpless, thin arms bent backwards or snapped. They screamed. "Please Exalted Emperor no! Please spare me!" "Exalted Emperor I have prepared for ten years!' Some of them sobbed. Spit smeared across their mouths, eyes red, veins breaking. Mucous spraying.

The guards were veterans. Hard men. Strong. They wrenched back the arms of the scholars. Smashed their faces to stun them, armored gloves crushing their lips and noses. Dragged them out. Heavy carpets deadened echoes, but the screams went on until they were far away. Not stopped, just finally too distant to hear.

The Emperor smiled. Gett, from his kneeling position watched him settle back into his throne. He had seen three young Emperors in his life. And each of them shared this smile that did not reach their eyes. Not because they were evil or untruthful in their expressions, but because they could not pull away from the need to watch the world. To test it, to ask it: do you see a boy, or do you see the awesome and frightening man I wish to be?

The other Chinese scholars who had been saved simply by luck trembled on the cold stone ground. Not even daring to weep openly, sucking huge wracking sobs back into their throats.

"You see what happens," the Emperor said, "This is your fault. You should explain this to the other members of your people. The Imperial I did not want to do this, but you *forced* the Imperial I. You are too weak. The Imperial People cannot have you here. This is what happens when a subservient people attempts to gain advantage over the Imperial People. This may be a warning."

Gett looked at the scholar who had answered the question.

He was still standing in the same spot. The birthmark on his neck now looking almost alive in the flickering firelight. Seeming to wrap itself around his throat. He had not moved even when the guards swarmed around him. And they had not touched him. Both because he had not run, and so could not be chased. But also, because Palace guards are careful, and in the absence of a clear order from the Emperor, this scholar was safe for the time being.

A symbol of the failure of honor and bravery. He had demonstrated why the Examination were valuable—they attracted the very smart. But ultimately, it did not matter. The Emperor would quietly send out an order to crush him. And, unless he was extraordinarily clever, he would go the way of all incautious young men.

The Emperor sat, clearly deciding how to exit. Finally, he simply stood up and walked out. There was a wait as protocol officers sent runners to confirm he had left and would not return. After a short, whispered conference they gave the signal that the audience had ended. Officials began to file out in the reverse order in which they had arrived.

Gett looked over at the bead curtain. He could just make out the Imperial Mother. She was still there. Waiting. Motionless. Watching.

Gett waited next to Han, who, just before it was his turn to exit, finally spoke.

"Do you know what this was, Gett?"

"In what sense?"

"This was the Exalted Emperor exercising his wisdom on the Examination."

Gett said nothing.

"Murder investigations such as this one you are involved in, sometimes they are very slow, but sometimes they can be made

THE EUNUCH

to happen more quickly."

Gett waited for more, but there was no more. Han nodded. Then stood, turned, and walked out.

It was time to go leave the Palace and sleep. Sleep because he was stretched to his limit. Leave because it was *safer*—both to be hidden while he slept but also to think carefully through his discovery before telling someone about it. To be *absent* from the Palace when he was vulnerable. And for those same reasons Gett preferred to do it alone, without a retinue to disturb his thoughts and announce his absence. But the mandated palanquin was waiting for him at the gate. His bearers stepped out into the sharp early morning sun. Two extra guards because of the murder. Bun sellers prepared for the day, wreathed in steam that glowed from the hard light, wary and watching the Palace. The dragon was restless.

Immediately he felt it.

Gett had lived for a long time in the dark interstices of other people's habits. And now, he sensed something was wrong—more wrong than just an uneasiness to the city—almost as if the long shadows cast by the sunrise magnified the tiny movements that were out of place—like the huge yawing of a long stick whose base has been nicked.

The surveillance that had attached itself to him the previous evening was just that—something low-level. He was investigating a murder in the Palace and it could have been any number of people; Han Zongcheng, the Imperial Mother, but probably someone from outside the Palace. Worried people watching. Most likely Chinese because they had the most to fear. But it had been surveillance, barely competent, and nonthreatening.

This was different. There was a man near the bun seller,

moving toward the alleyway shortcut that Gett's bearers used to return him to his villa. He was leading a donkey with a cart—a blocking tool. His path would take him right into the mouth of the alley as Gett's palanquin reached its center.

As Gett's bearers moved forward, he saw another peasant, one of the day workers assembling for work on the Palace walls, peel away down a side street. That street would lead him straight to the end of the alley mouth from which Gett would emerge. Two Palace workers were there painting over one of the ubiquitous large painted characters: Southern General Save Us.

So this was not surveillance. This was an assassination.

Gett motioned for his bearers to stop. Through the curtain he checked behind. No one at the gate. So they hadn't circled around him. Soldiers were stationed at the corners of the square, leftovers from the alert. But they wouldn't get to him in time, and might not even try anyway. They were guarding the Palace, not him. He told his bearers to turn back toward the Palace. About a hundred steps, time enough for them to get to him. But would they?

The square was very public, a good thing if they wanted it messy, not so good for escaping.

First, who? Who would want to assassinate him?

Curdeger? It was too fast. It would put Curdeger in too much danger. Gett had been out of his office for just over two hours. Curdeger would have had to make the decision, contact the assassins, formulate a plan. This wasn't Curdeger. He might try later but Curdeger was careful, he wouldn't stake everything on a plan thrown together in an hour.

Sulo? No. Sulo wanted him alive. Sulo had guessed something. He wanted Gett to discover it.

Han Zongcheng? No. He had a secret, but he knew that Sulo had a dagger out for him. Gett's death would allow it to come

THE EUNUCH

fully out of its sheath.

The Imperial Mother? If she had killed Diao Ju, then Gett was a dead man. But Gett doubted it. Diao Ju was clearly not an Imperial favorite. And she wasn't pregnant. Everything pointed towards her status as a minor concubine, on the make but still minor. Gett saw no way she could have been a threat to the Imperial Mother. What was much, much more likely was that the Imperial Mother was desperate. If her son was threatened, she was threatened. Setting aside her maternal instincts which were unknown to Gett, if her son died, her death would follow, at the very latest, within a few months. So Gett judged her, as he had from the beginning, to be incentivized to solve this case — or to be more precise, to remove the threat that its unknowns represented for her.

Who else? Gogoro, Head of the Imperial Harem? They didn't feel right either. He certainly had, at the very least, made a mistake, maybe been involved in something. But he was protected by a lot of layers and the one thing that would slice though them was killing a Chief Investigator.

None of them had an obvious motive or one strong enough to step into the extreme personal danger that killing Gett would place them in.

Who, then? Arigh? Lao Kou?

Gett's palanquin was now about halfway back. He opened the curtain again and saw that donkey man had turned and was now beginning to cross the square in his direction. Anyone else? It would take more than one. He looked out the other side of the palanquin. The day workers were starting to pack up tools.

Gett figured his bearers could get back to the gate in time, that they'd have to move fast to get to him now. And anyway, in a conquered city, Imperial bearers knew how to handle themselves. But even looking at it from a purely professional standpoint, the crucial question still remained: then what? There is a momentum to assassination attempts. If they didn't get him on his way to his villa, they would try again in a few hours inside the Palace, when they would assume he was off his guard, holed up somewhere fighting sleep. But for the same reason, if they failed today, whoever had hired them would wait for a while before trying again — would wait to see if he had noticed, what he would do, if he told anyone about it and what ramifications that would have.

It was why they would try hard to succeed today. By the nature of things, it was their only chance before the case became much more complex — say three days before they could try again, and by then who knew what the situation would be — certainly not them, and they would recognize this.

Gett was now two-thirds of the way back, almost a certainty now that he would make it — unless one of his bearers was in on it, possible but unlikely.

What could he get out of them if he caught an assassin? Who hired them, obviously. But that might or might not be useful. It was likely to be a cutout if they were pros.

Did he want to risk it? His sense told him that it was a two-man team but again, with good ones it was hard to tell. Gett had run teams like this and it might be a decoy, a mark to make him let down his guard in the face of what looked like a poorly planned hit.

It was unknowable. The gate opened. Gett's bearers carried him back into the Palace.

"Any news?"

"There is, Your Imperial Majesty."

"Tell me."

Again she was behind the motionless bead curtain, Gett kneeling in front of her, the room still dimly lit, but empty now, the dragon-curled columns rising up into the dark, smoke-shrouded ceiling, waiting for Gett's answer.

The point had come, as he'd known it would (and as Curdeger, standing over the beautiful sawn up corpse in his frozen inspection room, had known) when Gett had to make a decision. He knew something no one else did: Curdeger had been uncareful. If he told the Imperial Mother now, Curdeger would go down, not now, but later when things became complex, his death or banishment a weapon in some other struggle. But... but... not necessarily. Curdeger was smart, an experienced bloody infighter. He might get out of it. And if he did, then Gett was a dead man.

But if Gett didn't tell her about Curderger's mistake, didn't tell her Curdeger had missed the cause of Concubine Diao Ju's death, she'd still find out eventually. And then, because she knew she couldn't trust Gett, she would kill him.

Gett's mind ground through what he knew. How could the Imperial Mother find out? Could she already know? Curdeger wouldn't keep the draft report; that, without a shadow of a doubt, had been incinerated. But had he possibly preempted Gett, come here immediately after cutting the girl open? Curdeger would know that if the Imperial Mother heard the information from someone else he was a dead man. How long since he had been with Curdeger? Just before sunrise. The sun had now been up for an hour. Enough time. But had he? Because if he had, and Gett held back, again, death.

The moment Gett spent thinking this through was not a long one (Gett could not be seen to pause). But it was a beat nonetheless. There was none of the morning light in this room, and Gett felt, kneeling there, as if all of the darkness was gathering itself up and accreting above him.

"Analyst Curdeger and I have discovered a new interpretation of the evidence."

"Explain."

Gett did — explained the route that the victim had most likely taken, where she had been stabbed, and how finally, based on the analysis Curdeger had made from cutting her open, based on the *correction* of Curdeger's *mistake*, how it must have happened. The Imperial Mother listened quietly and without interruption.

And Gett knew, could feel through the beads, though the thick, smoky air that separated them as he listed the facts of the case, her terror. An hour ago in the audience, now, every muscle in her body, every piece of her, vibrating. Somewhere there was a killer, one whose motives were *opaque*, who was *in the Palace*, and who was — and this was important — *clever*. So again, as it had so many times in her life, the possibility of death from an unforeseen direction was crawling up over the horizon and reaching out for her with its quiet and disgusting hands.

And as he neared the end of his recitation, he could see himself as she saw him: one small official in the long chain of nervous men and women who had knelt here today, quietly telling her secrets. While she built up a picture not only of what had happened but of what those around her were doing about it.

When Gett finished, there was silence. But she was clearly still there. The torches on the wall flickered. Gett waited, head to the floor, knees beginning to hurt. Finally she spoke.

"What do you want?"

"Imperial Mother, I humbly request the use of a Surveillance squad."

"Why?"

"I believe an assassination has been purchased for me."

"Why?"

"I believe someone contracted it because of some specific trigger from the investigation. I believe that it is going to happen today because I saw the assassins as I left the Palace."

"How did you see them?"

"They were moving into position in a way that I recognized from my experience."

"Why do you need a Surveillance squad?"

"I wish to bait the assassins, then capture them so I can interrogate them to find out who hired them and why."

"Do you know where our Surveillance squads come from?"

"I believe they operate as an adjunct authority of the Eighth Secretariat under the Ministry of Espionage, your Imperial Majesty."

"Are they under me?"

"No."

"Exactly. Do you know what else they do?"

"Palace security, your Imperial Majesty."

"That is correct."

In the pause that followed, a freeze crept over Gett. *Anything I give you decreases my own security. A warning.*

The beads swayed. A scratching sound. The long thin hand

slid through and out, manicured and delicate. It placed an Imperial Prescript on the platform. Chopped.

With a rustle of the beads, she was gone.

Gett waited, kneeling on the floor. He was locked in place as his mind scattered itself across the possibilities. She suspected him. Of what? That he was trying to damage her security? That he was part of a subtle plot to decrease her ability to survive an attack?

He reached out and took the prescript.

> Request by Chief Investigator Enchenkei Gett for Imperial Second Class Counter-Espionage Squad:
> Granted
> Chopped: The Imperial Mother.

But if she really suspected him, she wouldn't have said anything. She would pretend she knew nothing. Would she? Was she prodding him, watching him jump?

Who ran the Counter-Espionage Second Class squads? Somebody she trusted. Who? She would keep her people close to her. Would she? Close to him?

Who ran the Counter-Espionage squads?

Kob Meke.

Son of a minor family.

Smart. Stuttered but didn't seem bothered by it—spasmed his way through his surprisingly urbane life. There was something Gett liked about him. What was it? Gett thought back on the nights he had worked with him. He was thoughtful, that was it. Not considerate, not at all, but he thought about things. Good with Chinese people. Without the prejudice that most of Gett's race brought to their interactions. Why a Second Class squad? Why Kob?

THE EUNUCH

And thus Gett felt himself finally now, here at this moment, slide fully back into his old life. Here now everything, his thoughts themselves, was danger. A state of constant bone crushing tension. And it was exactly as he remembered it, an old enemy.

Gett creaked to his feet. He swept quietly out the door.

A wave of blood was swelling, would break soon.

※

Gett and Kob Meke, their footsteps echoing in the arched tunnel, moved quickly towards the doors that led out of the Palace. Kob finally spoke.

"H-h-how's it going?"

"My life or the case?"

"C-c-case."

"I don't have a handle on it."

"Why?"

"It's like bad information from a bad operation."

"What d-d-do you kn-know?"

"That's part of the problem. Everything I know makes the murder seem impossible."

"It's a murder then, not a...?"

"Yes, definitely a murder. Maybe a frame."

"To w-w-w-what end?

"I don't know yet."

"What direction?"

"We're at a dead end on tracing her movements, they don't make any sense. She was probably fucking a guy. Not pregnant though. Harem is giving us trouble."

"How?"

"You know, they have their mandate. But more than that I think."

"Want a s-s-s-suggestion?"

"Sure."

"You could b-b-b-bait G-G-Gogoro into obstructing you. He runs the harem, he'll d-d-d-definitely push back on you. Then send him to Enforcement."

"Ha ha."

"It's still Sulo, right?"

"Yeah."

"You talk to the other wives?"

"Maybe tomorrow. See what happens this morning with Sulo."

"Weapon?"

"Found a knife, but it's a plant."

"Outside job or inside?"

"Inside."

"For?"

"Not political."

"Why not?"

"Doesn't feel like it. It's a frame up, definitely. There's something about the girl. She was a hustler. She got involved in something that killed her."

"What?"

"Don't know yet."

And here Gett came to the point, the unspoken deal. Kob was a player. He knew at some vague point in their conversation, he'd stepped over the line beyond where what he was getting was free.

"I need somebody inside the harem," said Gett.

"W-w-w-why?"

"To explain it to me, to map out the relationships."

"T-t-that's a t-t-t-tough thing to have."

"It is."

THE EUNUCH

"I'll ch-ch-check but I think that probably it will be imp-p-possible."

Which meant, 'I have someone. I'll send her over tomorrow. Never mention this.'

Kob stopped, the Palace gates opened, Gett stepped out into the cold dawn and was alone — shadowed by an invisible army.

THE MASSIVE GATES closed behind him. The outrushing air made a dull thud as they juddered together. His single escort stood behind him as Gett looked at the square. It was full now that the sun was really up and the small Palace gates for exterior business were open. Soldiers still milled about aimlessly near the edges.

Gett parsed the square in his mind. If he were an assassin, watching a thin, weak official step out of the Palace early in the morning, where would he want to make his takedown?

To his left were the supplicants. It was a large group holding numbers that would get them in the door and directly to the Emperor. The Emperor only saw five a day so most had been there for weeks, a little agglomerated village that shifted forward a small distance each day.

No official would go near it, so his assassins wouldn't be there.

On the other side of the square was the gate for the day workers, small filthy peasants conscripted for work in the Palace. The press gang from earlier was gone because the gates were now open. But there was a fitful stream of carriages that dumped loads of workers at the gate. Again, not a place officials would go near. And it too had a shifting population, so no cover.

Across the square and off from the main avenue was the alley Gett usually was carried through to get to his villa and the one where he had first noticed his hitters.

THE EUNUCH

Gett figured Kob Meke's squad was already spread across the square. They were facing what couldn't be more than a three-man hit team. More was unwieldy and expensive. If Gett took anything but his usual route back, the hitters would sniff danger and dissolve into the city. Probably they had picked somewhere on his route and were waiting there, ready.

He paused for just a moment as the fear hit his stomach. It had returned now. Just like he remembered it. A pain in his gut like a hand reaching into his abdomen, spreading its fingers up into his chest and down to his groin, gripping his flesh, and then tightening itself into a fist, pulling his insides into vibrating, taut sinews into a hard, crushed knot at its center.

Someone was trying to kill him, for the first time in a long while.

He stepped off into the square, the sound of his footsteps now no longer echoing in the loud morning bustle of the city, his dour escort trotting behind him.

Very quickly he was in the alley. It was a dirty scratch of a street, muddy water with a thin ice skin lying about in crevices. Reach out and you could touch the buildings on both sides. Fish sellers shuffled and blew out of their red cheeks while slaves haggled with them. Porters pressed through and so to traverse it was to shuffle slowly edgewise down its length. He spat a large red gob of betel nut saliva into a puddle. It split through the brittle ice and spread out to mix with the oily fish blood on the stones. People watched him through upper windows, wary today of Palace officials.

Roughly a hundred and fifty steps later he was through it.

Now he had a choice. About half the time, he made his way through the steaming district. At night when he left the Palace, he would be carried through the flour-dusted streets. Even in the hottest part of the summer it looked like there was snow on the ground. They would be steaming buns for the breakfast sellers the next morning. It was a reassuring smell, and he enjoyed the clouds it generated. In winter, because it was warm, it was like traveling down a whole street heated just for him.

His other choice was the Imperial deer park, a section of the city set aside for the Imperial relatives. As an official he had right of access to it as a thoroughfare (something he had quietly arranged for himself. He enjoyed it immensely and he enjoyed being able to show it off to people).

But it was the long way, and usually empty.

Bad for a hit even if the hitters could get in — and they couldn't.

He turned left into the steaming district. He could see ahead of him the white street. In a few more steps the world began disappearing.

Now he was in real danger. No one, neither he nor his entourage, had expected the hit to come in the side alley. It was too close to the Palace, and the hitters, if they were careful, wouldn't have picked the same assassination point twice.

But here, in this pale wet steam was their first real opportunity. The street itself was wide; it had to be for the carts to get in and out during the morning rush to distribute the buns. It was full of peasants carting bun bags on their backs and also a major thoroughfare for both Chinese and Jurchen merchants. And the steam hid most movement.

A three-man team. Two to create a distraction — get in a fight, throw up, whatever, something that would get people's attention for a few seconds, and then the hitter, already close, would move in, probably with a knife stabbing from behind next to the arm and through the space between the third and fourth rib. It would be a long thin knife, thin enough to slide through the half finger-width gap, long enough to reach the heart and puncture the thick muscle wall. And then he would disappear back into the crowd.

THE EUNUCH

A puncture wound to the heart kills—but it would only take a few slowing heartbeats for the drop in blood pressure to black him out.

Gett continued to walk down the street. Chinese peasants filtered past him, roiling the steam and kicking up flour that coated Gett's feet. Gett forced himself to walk slowly. He tried to spot Kob Meke's team. They would have been pre-stationed. Already looped ahead onto both of Gett's possible routes as soon as he entered the first narrow alley. The Jurchen official haggling with a bun wholesaler was probably one, but a spotter, not an enforcer. Two Chinese peasants were sitting having a hemp smoke on one of the gutters. Probably enforcers; Kob Meke liked to use Chinese especially on operations like this because Jurchens mostly ignored them.

The steaming district was about a hundred and fifty steps long, he'd covered about seventy five, so halfway.

If the hit was going to come, it would come near the end. That's where the steam was thickest and the crowd tightest. The final fifty steps. There were twenty cookers pumping out buns that got immediately loaded onto donkey carts. Each cart was a two-man team, a loader and a driver. Up ahead he could see faintly five carts, but through the drifting steam he couldn't be sure. So at a minimum ten, probably Chinese, plus the bun wholesalers. Another twenty people. But there was always a flow. So that was a concentration of about eighty people in the last stretch at any one time, and they had to filter through the tight spaces created by the carts. Perfect for an attack: the assassins could get close in naturally, they were obscured from view and they could get out quickly from the blocked street.

Gett's stomach tightened. As always happened, Gett had to shit. It pulled at his insides, whispering at him to squat down and shit out all his fear. He still felt nervous in his life now but it was pale, muted. This, as it had always been in the past, was much worse. He walked through the drifting steam towards the carts. He tried to spot Kob Meke's agents but he knew that Kob would have made the same analysis and so his best agents would be stationed here, impossible to spot.

Now Gett was just twenty steps away. The donkeys, stupid eyes and drooping ears, were coming into sharper view through the steam. Two riders sat on their carts waiting quietly to push off, but three more carts were empty. Where were they? Gett searched the steam. There was one, leaning against a bun seller's wall, chewing a betel nut. Where were the other two? He couldn't see them.

He scanned the wholesalers. Next to the carts, they seemed normal. If they had been replaced with agents, then they would be watching. They weren't.

Ten steps now.

Where were the two other drivers? Gett saw one, down on the ground fixing a broken spoke on one of the cart wheels. Where was the other one?

He picked his route; there was a gap between two carts ahead and to his left. Five steps now. No change in activity, but then there wouldn't be until the last moment.

The spoke fixer started to stand up. Gett watched his hands, where would the knife come from, did he have one? Gett couldn't see it. Two steps.

Gett thought he was going to shit his pants. Urine dribbled out of his severed urethra, always a problem for eunuchs and now exacerbated by his fear.

He forced himself through the last two steps and now he was right between the two carts,

The spoke fixer began to turn; Gett tensed himself to hit the ground as Kob Meke's enforcers took him down. The fixer hopped onto his cart. A hawker yelled. Two Chinese threw their buns on to their donkey cart.

Four more steps before he was through, past the tight space between the carts.

A courier made his first step out of the shop to Gett's left. The spoke fixer made no move.

Gett saw him.

The fourth driver.

He was under the cart next to him, lying in dirty flour. Hidden from everybody's view except Gett's.

The driver swung himself up and onto his feet.

His hands. No weapon. Where was it?

And he walked past Gett and out past the donkey.

Gett took one more step, out of the gap, another step, away from it, another, clear now, the carts receding behind him.

The hit had not come. Kob Meke's men had not moved.

The flour-covered road stretched another twenty paces ahead of him. Behind, his path was lined with his precise, black footsteps in the whiteness. His escort emerged, leaving his own footsteps.

As they always did after moments of danger, His fingers and toes ached. Gett wondered why that was. He supposed it was important, indicative of some fundamental aspect of being human, but it wasn't something amenable to investigation.

Without looking back, he strode out of the steaming district.

Why? Why had there been no hit? Were the hitters not here? Had they spotted Kob Meke's takedown team? Had they abandoned the hit from the first when Gett had returned to the Palace? Had he been wrong, misread all the signals? Gett's mind ranged across the possibilities. Would the Imperial Mother think he had deceived her? What would she do?

No, there was a hit. But they were careful, focusing on

survival. And very few officials would have been able to walk through that steam and crowd without flinching if they knew a hit was coming. If Gett had been running this assassination, he would be reasonably sure now that his target was not escorted.

The transition out of the steaming district was always abrupt. And always came, if not as a surprise, at least as an event. The street led up to an intersection with a large, tree-lined avenue which, because it ran north-south, always had a strong wind scraping through it. And so from the warm steam of the boilers, one always emerged quite suddenly into cold. And the light returned and the dusty dark stone of the street was again in sharp relief. It was as if he were leaving a winter of beauty and returning to one of hardness.

No hit would come here at least. And it was even more deserted than usual because people knew it was the main avenue for cavalry deployments. They'd come galloping through here yesterday and nobody wanted to be in front of that, or even worse, suspected of watching for it. He hurried across the street. Just ahead was the carved gate that led into the brothel district, the final section of the city he usually passed though to get to his villa.

The wrought wood gate marked the transition line between that region of the city administered by municipal officials and that directly run by the Palace.

As he stepped through the brothel district gate, he considered what to do. The buildings on either side were mostly three stories tall, and accreted more than built as business had accelerated in the peace of the last reign period, the single-storied buildings growing upper floors that, plant-like, hung over the dark and dirty street.

Foot traffic was heavy here, the kind of place marked in red on the planning charts that Gett used to pore over. Ahead, the

THE EUNUCH

street branched into three possible routes. Straight ahead, and the widest route, was the Jurchen district. To the right and through an alley was the Muslim Huihui section. And from a short curving street a little farther down you could get into the Chinese district.

He had presented his assassins with a killing opportunity. They had not taken it, probably wary Gett had surveillance. It was possible that they would spot his escort, but a fully deployed Imperial Surveillance Squad, at peak strength was running a substitution through the street of at least a hundred followers and this was more than enough to follow Gett with no repeats for at least three times the distance to his villa.

Gett decided the worst choice was probably the Jurchen district. It was under-populated — the Jurchen women who worked there were low quality. A Jurchen woman had to fall far before she would end up here. So in the whole district, at any one time, there were probably no more than a hundred Jurchen prostitutes. Because most of them were dregs, there weren't many customers either. Farther, it was heavily regulated. As the ruling people, the Jurchen authorities paid special attention to the district and it was run by a magistrate. The prostitutes stayed off the narrow, dirty streets and the pimps and enforcers stayed in their doorways — the streets were almost always empty. Bad for a hit. Safe, but not the place to bait a trap.

Similarly the Muslim Huihui section. Strict prohibitions on premarital intercourse made this a heavily-trafficked street, and both male and female prostitutes were available. But again, it was over-policed and run not by the central municipal government but instead by a Huihui council tasked with keeping order.

The best and most obvious choice for laying a trap was the Chinese district.

Gett had noticed something about wars and famines — gaunt, desperate starving people haunted the streets, but the brothel districts were filled with beautiful women. Women who in normal times could have done other things, gotten married, been expensive mistresses, worked as maids, had fallen below a cutoff and had, through the complexities of a thousand decisions, wandered through their lives to this point, selling pussy in a shitty brothel. It was when times were *good* that the girls were ugly; the beautiful ones had opportunities to do other things.

It was the same with the Chinese. As an officially inferior people, they were denied access to the best jobs in the Palace and in city administration, and so a Chinese girl was much closer to that line, and much more likely to fall below it.

So the Chinese brothels were popular—you could get better service, quality girls, two or three of them, for the same price it cost to screw one ugly Jurchen.

Not only that, but the whole district had very little oversight from the municipal government. Pimps fought in the street. The girls hooked out in the crowds. Brokers bustled around with the customers waving discounts and pen and ink drawings of their girls. Big Character drawings all over the walls: Save Us Southern General, Southern General Yue Fei.

Which made it more fun but also made it perfect to bait a trap.

Gett turned right and, robe kicking along in the cold, shuffled into the bustle of the Chinese prostitution district. Immediately Chinese architecture reached out above him—the red columns, cloud painted roof supports and cat-shaped eaves, the complex and detailed filigreeing of the world that spreads across those places into which Chinese settle themselves.

The street itself was essentially just a long winding alley. The same tall, leaning buildings, motionless, decaying things. Hanging at such an angle that the eaves of the opposite roofs almost touched in places. And the street itself, at pavement level, wasn't much wider, three arm spans at most.

THE EUNUCH

Packed into that was the crowd, seething like a dirty river, it was a physical thing crowded in on itself and flowing down the narrow street. Not usually this crowded in the early morning but the Examination was just two days away. Gett, immediately crushed into it, was carried along with the current.

He was taller than almost all Chinese and most Jurchens so he could see over their heads to watch the route ahead. The crowd stretched with no breaks all the way to where the alleyway curved off to the left and could no longer be seen.

Most houses had open doors. Attached girls came out into the crowd and also sat within the brightly lit entry halls. Girls, too, sat in the upper floors and windows.

It was always a shock to come out of the steam, which blocked sight and muffled sound down to soft taps and hisses and to emerge here — the pimps yelled, the girls laughed to each other. Hundreds of attempted conversations like a wrestling match, full of hostility and energy, as they all clambered over each other.

Gett liked it; it was why he chose it as his route every night. He liked the raucousness, walking quietly through it soaking it into his skin after the claustrophobia of the Palace.

And obviously it was perfect for a hit. Perfect not just because of the crush of people but because the interaction of the crowd with the girls set things up perfectly.

It was the way the hooking was organized.

The interaction was very structured. The goal was to get the guys into the house. To do that, each house usually had a stable of about twenty women, but also had three good girls, really high quality from big families in the south who had come to work in the Palace but hadn't made the cut. Each house needed one for the street, one for the lobby and one for the upstairs.

The first thing the client saw on the street was the house's number three girl — usually wide and soft but experienced. This got a customer's attention. The next thing he did was look into the bright doors of the house. Inside sat about five girls, but only one or two opposite the door, and here would sit the number two girl, also quality — better than the first, thinner, less like a whore. And the other ones, you could only see their legs or arms as they gestured in conversation with each other, everything else blocked by the doors.

Then, the customer looked up. And there, in the window, he saw the number one girl.

Always young, a girl who looked like she'd just come off her father's farm, had been taking care of her baby brothers, sewing with mommy, and was now sitting in this window, defenseless, alone and, for a price, you could walk upstairs and defile her.

And for an operation, especially an assassination, it was important because it shaped the movement of the crowd. The guys moved in nervous brittle groups, embarrassed but excited, and the number three girls, like weeds on the bank of a river, managed to snag the customers while the number two and top girls kept them waving there in the fast flowing current.

So the crowd was moving, dense and with discrete knots that formed at random. Diversions always worked in these spaces; each individual felt personally threatened. So for the few seconds the assassin needed, the crowd's attention would be focused exclusively away from him.

Gett scanned the crowd. They had to be here; had to have decided to take this opportunity. It was their last chance before he got to his villa and their best shot. But, where were they? Who were they?

Gett looked to his left. Customers walked next to him, ignoring him, he was obviously a eunuch. They were organized in their tight, nervously laughing groups. There was a group of Chinese salt sellers just behind him, and another group of Jurchen

THE EUNUCH

kids, probably sons of officials in the Ministry of Rites based on the way they were dressed. The salt sellers were hanging back, waiting for them to move on in that Chinese, head-bobbing, smiling way.

To his right was a group of six soldiers, from the size of their arms Gett figured they were from a crossbow battalion; peasant kids from way out nowhere, in the big city, getting ready to fuck their first beautiful girl.

Up ahead was a tight little group that was a possibility. Two guys, one Chinese and one Jurchen. Their angular hats with horse hair fringed tasseling marked them as Palace meat procurers — on the road for half the year inspecting pig farms — a bad job but one that gave them experience with prostitutes. That there were two of them was suspicious. They made their inspection rounds individually — them, a slave and usually two sub-ministry inspectors. When they were in groups, they were in the Palace attending planning sessions for special events. So you rarely saw two together. Rarely, that was the problem with ops like this, because *sometimes* you did. And even if Gett had not cared about establishing really whether or not these were his guys, tapping them out would, and the assassins would disappear.

He watched Kob Meke's surveillance squad move into position around the two meat inspectors — watched in so far as there was a subtle shift in the crowd. Gett didn't know who were his escorts and who weren't, and they were good so they were hard to spot but as he watched (and it was almost like the way snowflakes delicately cease to fall as they come in contact with the hair on your arm) bits of the crowd began to attach themselves to the meat inspectors.

The meat inspectors began to argue — not obviously flamboyant yet — but Gett knew it was coming. He figured about one minute to go before the fight, and then immediately the hit would come. Kob Meke's team clearly saw it too. From behind Gett, a tight knot of short little men appeared — they were dressed as Palace entertainment costumers — a few men in flamboyant reds and blues, clearly in the brothel district looking for boys. Gett knew one of them, not well, but had worked with him on a mission once. He was a takedown specialist, an expert in clawing down strong, competent, armed fighters quickly and safely. He giggled and laughed with his friends and kept pace with Gett.

The Jurchen meat inspector yelled, "Your mother's cunt! I'll stomp you down!" and swung a fat roundhouse at his friend. The Chinese inspector screamed back and grabbed his arm. They went down.

Just heartbeats now. Gett tensed himself. He forced himself to watch the scrum up ahead. He had felt this before — the tensing flaring explosion in his skin when he knew a blow was coming, could almost physically feel it, wouldn't even be able to distinguish between the real one and the one in his mind when it came. Everything in him scratched, wrenched at his mind to turn around, but he gripped down hard and forced himself to stare at the fight. If he turned, looked for the hitter, they would know he was surveilled, and would disappear.

Kob Meke's takedown team of squealing makeup guys giggled and clapped their hands, and ran a little bit forward but managed to keep by Gett's side.

Here it came.

There were two of them. Both of them were within two arm spans of him when they moved.

One of the girls broke off her hooking clade and swung towards Gett. Not one of the quality girls but a slag, old and clapped-out, no more than a year before she died or started selling under one of the river bridges for food. Gett's (and he knew his escorts') mind was cycling through the calculations.

THE EUNUCH

Was she the hitter? Not likely. Hookers made bad agents — it wasn't worth it to infiltrate a girl in for a long haul and if she had just come today, the pimps wouldn't have let her stay — they regulated the streets, were territorial. But the timing, she was coming right for him.

At the same time, one of the ministry kids peeled away and went right at Gett. Had he attached himself? He was in the back of the group. Had he just tagged on to them and they hadn't even known?

Probably just a second now before one of them pulled a knife.

So here it was finally. Time slowed down. The slag, took another step forward. Gett could see her shoes, see the tiny splash they made in the cold dark water dribbling beneath her feet.

He could see the kid, see his hand reaching behind his back, slowly.

He could see his escort, the make-up giggler, watch his eyes, not moving, straight ahead, wouldn't make his move until the last minute.

The slag's foot came up out of the puddle, tiny swirling droplets clinging to it, her other foot fell; she was less than an arm span from Gett now.

The kid too, had closed the distance; his arm was coming out from behind his back.

Gett's breathe now was coming out as if the air in his lungs itself had frozen, crystallized and was ice locked on to the slow moving universe itself.

It was coming now, less than a heartbeat. He saw the giggler tense for the jump, two more men plus a hooker began to turn for the takedown, the kid's hand came fully out from behind his back.

The slag; time slowed down in Gett's perception so much that she was frozen in mid-step, one glistening drop hanging in midair coming off her shoe. And ever so slowly, almost so imperceptibly slow that Gett couldn't perceive the shift, she began to smile.

And then it all sped up again, the kid stepped forward, showed the slag the money and she took his arm. Gett's foot hit the ground and just like that, he was past. Again he had been wrong. Again it hadn't come.

His escorts had held back and he moved, footfall following footfall, forward with the bustle of the crowd, the strange triangulation of bodies lost now behind him in the incessant shuffle, lost forever, disintegrated into the nothingness that it had been.

Fewer than a hundred steps later he was through. His house lay just down a side alley, he turned and made his way, still wary but surprised, down its narrow confines.

The hit, when it finally came, came almost as an afterthought.

十三

IT WAS PROOF they were professionals. Gett moved slowly down the alley, just steps from home, past a low weathered door and over frozen entrails left by a meat seller. Suddenly a small man next to him and another to his front tripped just enough to block his way. The knife came out, just as Gett had thought it would, and he reeled backwards.

It was a close thing. The hitter was fast. The knife flicked up to slide in under his ribs. But Kob Meke's men were just enough faster. The hitter went down. His partner went down simultaneously. Kob Meke's men pinned their arms and crowbarred open their mouths in case they had poison. In three heartbeats, the operation was over.

Gett watched them, and as he always did, tried to feel compassion for his assassins. He after all, had been there, seen what they saw, thought their thoughts, and knew the thousand complex reasons they could be here.

They sat silently on the ice-cracked freezing ground. Two Chinese, small compact men with small blank faces, the third, Jurchen, large, thicker with a stoop, the one who had been tasked with shifting his attention.

Around them, the dark frozen street was illuminated with sharp morning sun. Because the takedown had just occurred, there was not much of a crowd yet: a few ragged day workers gathered off to the north side of the street peering through wind slitted eyes, teeth jutting out like horses as they smiled and bobbed their heads, as if amplifying the vibrations of the rumors rippling through the city.

The three hitters, suddenly no longer a threat, were almost ignored. The attention of Kob's men had subtly shifted to the aftermath: how to keep the crowd back, was the correct length of binding cord available, how to, and with whom to decide, the best route to transport them back.

So the three men were very alone.

Gett tried to feel compassion because he knew what was waiting for them — an interrogation, but after that punishment. There were terrible penalties for the attempted murder of an Imperial Servant. Not death. Mutilation. First their tongues cut out, then ears punctured and eyes burned away. Then arms and finally legs removed. They would be carefully nursed back to health by Imperial physicians. Healthy, they would be turned over to a charitable organization of the Capital, there to live out whatever time remained to them in the quiet echoing chamber of their own minds.

So there was room for compassion.

But he never felt it. What he felt, as much as he tried to control it, was hate. As he stood there on the frozen street, breath still heavy and jetting out of his mouth in fast, crystallizing shafts of fog, the idea that they would snuff out his life; that they would leave, collect their pay, and continue living; that even more, after his annihilation, the world would continue on unaffected, burned inside him.

He walked over, threading his way past Kob's men and carefully, with as much control as he had, beat the first man. Fists pulled back and a fast succession of spear-like strikes to his face,

THE EUNUCH

bringing him down on his back with blood smashing out of his nose. He did the same thing to the second one, and also to the larger Jurchen.

And they took it. They knew that they had worse waiting for them. Kob Meke and a skeleton team stood back near the alleyway gutters, watching.

He stood back up, wiped the blood on the inside of his robe, and walked back down the alley to Kob Meke. Kob's men yanked up the assassins and hooded them. Imperial guards, in hard leather armor and short swords were pushing through the gathering crowds farther up the alley.

Gett pulled Kob aside and they stepped into a side alley. A trickle of dirty water meandered across the thin ice into the middle of the street.

Gett said, "I have to go rest."

"Now?"

"I need to sleep. I can't trust my judgment."

"Alright, well th-th-that's some luxury eh."

Gett stood there deciding how to answer. He recognized that he faced three problems.

The first was that he needed to get back to the Palace to interrogate these men and quietly pull Curdeger aside and tell him that the Imperial Mother knew.

The second was he had to sleep. He knew himself, knew his limits and knew he was at them. It was not that he couldn't stay awake, but that his thinking was impaired, that he would make a mistake — this time possibly a fatal one.

So the third and final problem was Kob Meke. Not stupid, he knew that these men were valuable. That whoever held them held a weapon. But Kob Meke, to formulate it bluntly, was not big enough to use it. Like a child holding fire, it was a weapon too powerful. And Kob knew it. So he was looking for a way out — or, more specifically, he was looking for a direction in which to jump.

"You want some advice?" said Gett.

"Sure, G-Gett, yes, I'd love some."

"Bring them back and transfer custody to the Imperial Mother."

"I don't know Gett, eh? A b-b-bit out of the nor-nor-normal channels, you know?"

"True, but she'll want to talk to them before anybody else."

"True. I suppose Chief Han will as well, eh? And Enforcer Sulo?"

"They will."

"Ha ha, well I wouldn't want to offend them you know. Tough problem."

It was the essential problem.

Gett said, "Send your guys back and request a bodyguard escort from the Imperial Mother. You can transfer custody on the way. So before you arrive in the Palace they're no longer your prisoners."

"Hey, that's an idea. Although they'll know what happened, you know?"

"True." Gett was silent for a moment, watching the water trickle through the ice. "When you carry a bag, one shoulder or the other has to feel the weight."

"Ha, I su-su-suppose that's true, eh. Do you think you could write that up as a request, you know, Chief Investigator requests Imperial custody, that sort of thing?"

"I could."

"Th-th-that would make everything so smooth, you know?"

"Do you have the proper colored rescript?"

"I do, actually."

Kob Meke gestured to one of his men who reached into

a pouch, shuffled through it, and pulled out a yellow and red square piece of paper, already chopped by the Surveillance Sub-Department. He handed it to Gett.

Gett said, "I'll request Imperial custody, but you have to get it chopped by the Imperial Mother's secretary."

"Hmmm, do you suppose it could be just a straight requisition?"

Gett kicked a pebble near his shoe. In situations like these, pared away, as they were, to the bone, the only thing left was the truth.

"I can't do it that way. It's too dangerous for me. I need you to be involved too."

Gett watched Kob think about this, watched him look at the prisoners, the crowd and consider his options.

There were three facts that Kob was considering: First, the Imperial Mother was the safe choice. Second, Gett, by signing the rescript, had involved himself in the paper trail. Third, it involved Kob himself just enough so when the time came to jump, he would only have one choice.

Gett looked at Kob to make sure that he was all right with that. Finally Kob lifted his head. Looked at Gett. Nodded. Gett signed the Imperial Request and handed it to him.

Kob moved off to his soldiers.

Gett entered his villa.

He stepped through the door set in the wall that surrounded his garden and a guard closed and locked it from the outside. Gett leaned back (but not, out of long habit, against the door, instead, next to it) and closed his eyes.

He was scraped out. As tired as it was possibly to be and still function. And inside that scraped-out emptiness reverberated two small hard things. The first was the operation. He had been the target of a killing. It had happened before and would happen again but he would never grow used to it. The relief that came after it was like an explosion, like he remembered an orgasm to be, roaring through his body like fire until it closed in on itself and became that small thing rattling through his insides. The second thing he felt was the relief of his refuge. In the Palace he was on display. His every action (as he watched the every move of others) was observed. He had done everything over the years to modify his presumptions and, on some level, the basic ways he thought, so that the control he had to have in the Palace came naturally, as an outgrowth of his motives and position instead of as a rigorously maintained suit of conscious armor. But he couldn't get rid of it completely, and it was a heavy, constricting, chest-tightening thing.

But when he entered his own villa, when the door shut, all his guards outside the walls, the soft inner parts of him suddenly could sag as that armor dropped away and his body and his mind unclenched together.

In his bedroom, he kicked off his soft cloth shoes and for one painful moment he contacted the delicate cold of the wooden floor. Then, shifting from one foot to another, he pulled back the bed coverlet stuffed with un-spun silk and slipped beneath it. He pulled his outer robe off and pushed it out onto the floor then pulled the cold cover over his head and descended into the dark crevice of its ceiling.

And almost in the same way that the panicked emergency response to the concubine's murder had spread from the single small point on the floor of the antechamber, here too, Gett's consciousness began to spread out. From deep beneath the coverlet, he sensed the walls of his bedroom, shaded by the heavy paper on its high windows. Beyond that he could sense the garden with its twisting maze of shrubbery, almost seemingly organized to confuse and mislead the dirty fingers of influence from over the walls. And as his mind spread farther, he could feel those high walls surrounding his home. He could feel the nervous shuttle and whisper of the city, and he could feel the heavy, distant frightened movements of the Palace. And one by one each of these successive layers went dark for Gett. The Palace faded into a void, the city went quiet and dark, the walls of his home closed in, his garden disappeared and the world shrank to this very small cave in which his heartbeat began to slow.

...awoke. Looked at the angle of the light. About two hours. The Hour of the Dragon. Not enough time to feel good but enough to think clearly. He had the cover pulled up around him. He blew into the shaft of light. His breath crystallized in the brightness. He pulled his robe from the floor and slipped into it still under the covers. He grabbed a fresh bag of betel nuts.

Quickly he was on the street walking toward the Palace, head clearing in the sharp, face-slapping cold of the morning.

The main gate of the Palace was impressive. Built to be so, it towered over the square onto which it opened. Wood as thick as a horse's body, dark forbidding red, and twice the height of even a man as tall as Gett, it projected Jurchen power down onto the heads of the Chinese who scuttled past it. And now, as Gett arrived at the guard house beneath, feet stamping in the cold, he confirmed what he had seen at a distance as he approached.

The guard had been doubled. And they were rigid, frozen to their spots with fear. Even more impressive, they stopped Gett's palanquin and asked for papers. Gett handed them to the head guard. He turned to the guard nearest him, staring, like a statue of ice, out at the square.

"What's going on?" Gett asked.

The kid blinked but said nothing. Gett waited for a minute. The kid shivered from the cold but kept silent. Gett turned to the head guard who was, with extreme meticulousness, going through his papers. "Why the doubled guard?"

The head guard didn't look up. "There is no doubled guard."

Get thought about how to re-phrase his question to make it easier for the frightened guard to give him a real answer. "Why has the strength of the guard been increased?"

"The Palace Guard is always at its maximum strength."

The head guard, blinking and tense, handed Gett back his papers. "You are cleared to enter."

The gate guard opened the small door cut into the main gate and Gett hesitated for a moment, watching the frightened guards, then he stepped into the Palace. A stillness fell over him. Something had happened. Changed. He looked ahead of him, down the long stone corridor. A few eunuchs hurried down it towards the outer gate. He carefully watched their expressions as they passed him. Panic. Something big. Gett made a left and shuffled along the wide corridor of Evanescent Light and into the Courtyard of Benevolent Rejoicing. This wide courtyard marked the transition into the western quadrant of the Palace and across it was Curdeger's analysis section. It was empty. But halfway across, there was movement in the distance. Gett saw on the other side of the wide courtyard, six guards dragging a struggling figure in white robes, the uniform of a harem administration eunuch. Gett didn't stop, but he watched the guards drag the eunuch all the way along the edge of the courtyard then disappear around a corner.

THE EUNUCH

Continuing through the courtyard, Gett considered this. It was not, in and of itself, strange. Unlucky or stupid people made mistakes in the Palace. Or, Gett thought about how to frame it more accurately: people made mistakes and those mistakes were used by others. So to see someone, especially someone from a bureau as fraught with competition as the Harem Administration, struggling with the consequences of a mistake was unremarkable. But six guards? For a eunuch? For, as far as Gett could see from his distance across the courtyard, a kid.

Gett stepped off the courtyard and into the corridor that led to Curdeger's analysis room, in which Diao Ju most likely still lay, now reduced to shreds.

The door to the room, when he arrived at it, was closed and locked. He knocked. No answer. He knocked again. He heard shuffling inside.

"Analyst Curdeger?"

No answer, and the shuffling stopped.

"Analyst Curdeger, it is Chief Investigator Gett. I would like to talk to you."

Again, no answer.

"Curdeger, it's me Gett."

"Analyst Curdeger is not here," said a frightened voice.

"Where is he?"

"I don't know."

"Why?" This stumped the voice for a beat.

"He didn't tell me."

"Who are you?" asked Gett.

"I'm nobody," the frightened voice said through the door.

"Well, not nobody. What do you do?"

"I'm just a morgue assistant."

"Why are you so nervous?"
"Everything has been moved forward."
"What? What do you mean?"
"The book."
"What?"
"The book."
"What book?"
"The one that the Emperor found."
"What book did the Emperor find?"
"It, there is no book, the, what is in it is false."
"What is the book? What happened this morning?"
Shuffling inside the door then silence.
"It's okay, I am a Chief Investigator, I am just looking for Analyst Curdeger to discuss a case."
Silence.
Gett felt foolish standing outside a door, negotiating with a stuttering twenty-year-old. He waited for another minute. Banged on the door again but got only more silence.

Gett tapped on the door of the Hall of Imperial Records. The door was not tall but it was very wide. Gett had always felt that this was as it should be, symbolically proper for the Imperial Library. But he felt exposed now in the empty room that led into it. In the distance he heard the clipped, ringing sound of what he knew to be a bladed weapon impacting metal—not armor, though, something else he couldn't identify.

He waited. He tapped on the door again.
"Who is it," came Lao Kou's pipe-shredded voice.
"It's me, Gett."
The huge door shuddered open a crack and Gett slipped in.
Lao Kou stood behind it, pipe in his mouth. In the daylight

THE EUNUCH

he always looked terrible and sick, skin like a corpse, eyes like blood jade. He locked the door with his long bony hands and turned to Gett.

"Where the fuck have you been?"

THE BOOK, Gett finally determined, had been found under a chest in the original antechamber. And this, from the moment he was told, struck Gett as odd, because the room had been checked thoroughly by an enormous number of people incentivized to find whatever was there. Yet, there it had been found, pushed deep back into the shadows.

What happened after the discovery though genuinely surprised him. Not that such a thing could occur; but that with all that was going on, someone could be so stupid.

The book had been discovered during a post analysis cleaning by a janitor seconded to the Bureau of Sanitation, and the possibility that it was overlooked evidence had (unfortunately) occurred to the cleaning crew. They, having no experience with this sort of thing, did not know which of the many bureaus within the Palace to bring it to. So they brought it back to their offices in the southern quadrant of the Palace and the bureau chief made the—in hindsight catastrophically poor—decision that as it was a document, it should go to the Central Secretariat.

This it did.

When later, the events that led to its dissemination were reconstructed, it became clear that the following had occurred: The Chief Secretary had been frantically awake the entire night managing the flow of documents that Diao Ju's death, the alert, the investigation, and the Examination had created. At dawn, that torrent had slowed to a trickle and he had decided that it was an opportunity to sleep. He had been so for about an hour when the book arrived.

The eunuch in charge made the decision not to wake him. In any case, it is debatable whether the Chief Secretary would have done anything markedly different.

The second decision the eunuch in charge made, and the one that would have so much of an effect on the rest of the investigation, was not, from the perspective of his mandate, bad or even one that was out of the ordinary: he ordered copies made, upon completion to be forwarded to all authorized ministries — no small job for the scribes — but they managed it.

This meant that, a few hours later, all fifty-two pages of the murdered Concubine Diao Ju's diary went out to the following offices: The Ministry of Espionage, The Bureau of Enforcement, the Ministry of Records, the Harem, and the Sub-Secretariat administering the Bureau of Palace Investigations, the Office of Concubine Fecundity, and finally the Ministry of Sanitation, as it had been they who had originally brought in the document and through a clerical error, had been added to the list.

Arriving at each of these offices, the diary was read first by secretaries tasked with managing correspondence, and then (in the offices with smarter secretaries) quickly shuttled to the Ministers or Bureau Chiefs: Urgent. Read immediately.

Which most of them did, and at that level, almost all of them realized that a disaster had occurred and began the process of damage control: documenting how the diary had come into their ministry, meticulously numbering who had read it, establishing a chain of possession from the moment it had come into their offices. And then sending out runners to ask for audiences with the Emperors' executive officers to explain that they had contained a damaging and malicious document, carrying hastily constructed but extremely voluminous documentation to back it up.

The diary itself was long, covered front and back with a small controlled script written with a stiff brush. But the relevant passages were short, no more than five or six pages out of the entire diary.

The Emperor's reaction when he first learned that such a document had been disseminated was muted. He ordered an investigation into how it had happened and retired back to his chambers. But over the next hour, a steady stream of directives had flowed from his quarters: arrest this minister, investigate that bureau, place the Palace in a state of alert. And it was in these incremental but inexorable steps that the Palace had descended into chaos.

"You have a copy," said Gett.

Lao Kou, sitting on his stool, smiled, showing his yellow teeth.

"We have the original."

"Really?"

"Of all the places such a thing is likely to be sent, here is the least contentious destination."

"And?"

"We will be all right. I have met with the Mother."

They were quiet for a moment, Gett prising himself into the gritty folds of Lao Kou's needs, and Lao Kou silently smoking, accepting the necessity that he do it.

Lao Kou would not willingly allow himself to be drawn into the fraught and undulating web that was spreading across the Palace, especially now that it was heaving with the panicked struggle of so many of those caught up in its sticky

THE EUNUCH

fibers. But while nihilism and evil Lao Kou could deal with (in fact felt comfortable swimming in these murky waters), chaos was distasteful; it was, by its nature, unmanageable and so represented for Lao Kou the very apex of danger.

"I need to see the whole thing, the original," Gett said.

"Of course."

"How long will it take?"

"About an hour. There will be a great deal of paperwork."

Two officials from the Central Secretariat were called to witness the process through which Gett was required to go in order to have legitimate access to the book. The first step mandated that he request it, in writing, and delineate what data he required and what portion of it he wished to read. This request, and each point listed within, was transferred to the Head Librarian (in this case across the room, but under the watchful eye of the witnesses) who was required to respond, again in writing. This Lao Kou did, in the affirmative, again under the quiet frightened eyes of the Secretariat witnesses. A time and date — half an hour from the time of request — was set, and a secure reading chamber was arranged in which Gett would read and the Secretariat witnesses could watch and in which Lao Kou could physically handle the book.

And so, just under an hour later, seated in a cramped documents room, the Secretariat witnesses standing so close that their robes rustled against his and their frozen breath fogged the air in front of him, Gett began to read.

Lao Kou slowly and carefully (with a delicacy that came of long practice with both very old and very valuable documents), while his pipe smoldered in a small scaffold well away from the diary, turned the pages.

When Gett finally finished, and it had taken a good hour, Lao Kou was clearly feeling the bite of withdrawal. So when Gett finally sat back, pensively, Lao Kou slipped off his stool, creaked over to the side table on which his pipe sat, now unlit. He pulled it up, lit it with a bit of paper fired from the heating charcoal, sucked off a long deep drag and sat back while it spread itself into his mind and defanged the slithering tiny beasts of his addiction.

Gett was silent for a long moment as he considered the import of what he had just read.

The diary's essence could be excerpted to three entries. They were: the beginning of Diao Ju's relationship with the Emperor, its middle, and its end.

The entries started early, from the time she officially entered the Palace and began her interaction with the Emperor. But these early interactions were rituals, formalized to achieve a religious goal. The earliest crucial entry recounted her first scheduled sexual liaison with the Emperor. It was the first time she interacted with him in an environment that was not formally structured. The entry was dated, Gett had noted, almost exactly two years earlier:

> *It is possible that I have a problem. I need to write this down so I can think about it.. Today was my first day with the Emperor. The eunuchs have been calculating for three days, and last night they informed me that the result had come. The preparation, because it was my first day, took a long time, almost four hours. Most of it was to make it more likely I would get pregnant with a son but some was to make me more beautiful. I was nervous because it's important, I have to get pregnant, but also for my status with the other concubines. They're watching, and how the Emperor treats me afterwards will determine what they*

THE EUNUCH

think they can do to me. But I've learned I can't control being nervous. So I accept it and try to do what I need to do through the nervousness. After all the preparation, a full formal group of Eunuchs took me to the Emperor's bedroom where I waited before the Emperor came in. There was a ritual for our first time. It was short, though, with only five eunuchs who burned "two papers". The Emperor told me to go to the bed and get undressed. I did. Then he did too. But then I don't know what happened. He couldn't become hard. The experiencesI had before I came here didn't prepare me for it and because I hadn't prepared, I failed. I could have done something different but I didn't know what. In all the times I've had sex in the past it was simple so. I couldn't think of a solution fast enough. The Emperor tried for a while but because he was soft he couldn't get in and he failed. When he rolled off of me I knew that I only had one final opportunity but the best I could do was to roll over and whisper in his ear, "We'll have another chance in a month." A little later he just got up and put on a robe and walked out. The eunuchs rushed in, put me in the "pregnancy position" and performed another ritual. Why did they put me in the pregnancy position? They can't have not known. I think they did know but to not do it would be to admit that they knew. After the ritual they took me back to my room.

Following this was a series of similar entries. But as her second year began, the tone changed:

I need to find a solution. Today was the ninth time that I have visited the Emperor and he was again unable. He again became angry and beat me. I have not discussed this with the others here, only my cousin on my trips home. But third wife Sugai and seventh concubine Liu Suhua, with whom I play the Poetic Game visit the Emperor at least twice a month and I am sure that they have the same experience – I have seen bruises – but I am too afraid to discuss with them because they could use this as a way to denounce me to the head eunuch. And in fact discussing it with them would do me no good. At best it would confirm that they are in the same situation. I would gain no useful information – and no information that I don't already have. So I must think: I cannot secure my position or rise through a pregnancy. But no one else can either, because the Emperor is unable to have sex with his wives and concubines. Can he have sex with other people? Men? Animals? Children? I must watch for this. I am in no more danger than anyone else. I have to figure out a way to be in less. Also, Argul's dismissal has not been discussed but I believe it is related to this. But how can I ask? If I am too curious they will wonder why. If I am not, then I can't protect myself.

And finally, her last entry, dated five months later, the night before her death:

I believe I may have put myself in danger by making a terrible mistake. Four days ago, when my scheduled day arrived, I was transported to the Emperor's bedroom after the proper ritual. Nothing has changed. But this time when the Emperor was beating me, I made a mistake. I laughed. Immediately he stopped and stared at me. And then he walked out of the room. I was collected an hour later at the appointed time. I believe that the Emperor thinks I was laughing at him and at his deficiency. I wasn't. I was laughing at, I'm not even sure what, the ridiculousness of

THE EUNUCH

my situation and my inability, after almost a year and a half, to find a solution to it. But the Emperor beats me for his inability. I believe he will find a way to revenge this slip I made. And when he does, every ally I've made will desert me.

And then what appeared to be an entry made on the same day but later:

I have been scheduled out of sequence for sex with the Emperor. If I run I'll be caught. If I go I'll be killed.

Gett knew that now, as he sat here, there were probably in the Palace three hundred people who knew what was written in this diary, at least a third of those had read it directly. Some portion of those people had already leaked its contents, in whispers, in don't-tell-anyone-else confidences to friends, family and others outside the Palace. And so the diary, the words of Diao Ju damning the Emperor, had already slipped the ropes of the Palace and were galloping through the city.

So the question was: what state of mind had the discovery of this diary and especially its wide distribution, induced in the Emperor; what had it caused the Emperor to want? The present Emperor had held his position for only three years. The accession had been uncontested (or more accurately: weakly contested, no accession could be un-contested). He was young, insecure. Unsure how to be an Emperor, unsure how people saw him, and straining to be the person that he thought, in his sketched and fragmented understanding of what it meant, an Emperor should be.

This diary threatened that identity. It portrayed him not as an awesome, terrible man, but instead: a frightened kid who can't fuck a girl. A lot of people would have to die to prove the diary was a fake.

And the thing was: *it was a fake*. Clearly, it couldn't be anything but a forgery. No Palace concubine would write one. Their rooms were regularly searched and any other girl who saw it would denounce her immediately or read it and save the knowledge of both the crime and the contents for when it was needed.

And Diao Ju would know that, had clearly demonstrated that she wasn't stupid.

But as Gett read the diary, he was struck by how much it sounded like how he imagined her to be. It contained, of course, long passages in which she laid out tracts of loneliness or anger, but embedded within that soft flesh was a hard calcified matrix of thought about the problems she faced and a probing, searching attempt to work out the solutions available to her.

And from the analysis of her by the vetting team, from Gett's own re-creation of her path back to the inner quarters and from Gett's long experience with people *like her*, he came again and again, as he read this diary, to the same conclusion: This is as if it were written by her. But it was not. So whoever wrote it had known her intimately and for a long time.

Gett turned to Lao Kou, still sitting quietly behind him. "What's the security setup?"

"Ordos units moving through the Palace with arrest orders on Ministers and Bureau Chiefs who touched the thing."

"And those guys are under interrogation. Screaming names."

Lao Kou nodded.

"What's the cull?"

"Now, I'd figure about a hundred. Should peak some time tonight."

"Chinese mostly?"

"Of course. But not all."

"You have the list?"

THE EUNUCH

Lao Kou shuffled off his stool and over to a new pile of documents. He pulled out a rolled Imperial arrest order. Handed it to Gett and hopped back up on his stool. Gett scanned the order.

> *For disseminating vicious lies about the Emperor and slandering his family and illustrious ancestors, the arrest of the following traitors must be made:*

Gett's name was not on the list. Gett's bureau was not even on the list. Did it mean anything? Gett, the person legally empowered to investigate this murder, should have gotten a copy, in fact should have gotten the original. But he hadn't. Gett skimmed the names, he knew most of them. Gett calculated, in the absence of any protection, he had about two days before somebody named him as a co-conspirator. Torture was hard. And Gett, in the two times he had been tortured, had screamed everything he could think of to make it stop.

And Gett, as Chief Investigator on a case in which a piece of evidence like this had been missed, was a person those being tortured would think of.

A day at best.

The Throne Room was dark. The Imperial Mother invisible. Gett on his knees.

"I need your protection," he said.
"Why?"
"I am going to be named during the interrogations."
"Why?"
"Because I'm a believable target."
"Maybe you made a mistake."

"I have made many, but this book is a plant."

"Why?"

"It is the same with the knife. Someone is framing the Emperor."

"Why?"

This was the essential question. Why? Why frame the Emperor—a man above punishment? It was a question that Gett, since he had come to the idea that this was the goal, had been pondering.

"I think someone is attempting to make him look..." Gett paused to set himself, because here he was stepping out onto ground that was brittle and thin, "ridiculous."

"It is impossible to make the Emperor look ridiculous."

"Of course, and so I must speak in ways that clearly do not represent truth but instead represent what..." again Gett paused, attempting to place the footsteps of his words with precision, "what it is possible some people could wrongly believe."

"You may speak."

"If a person were to look at this case based on the evidence of this book, the location of her body and the provenance of the knife, he could reconstruct the following sequence of events: Imperial Concubine Third Class Diao Ju is sexually unsatisfied. The Emperor is unable to engage in sexual intercourse with her and anyone in his harem, so unable to give them the one thing that ensures their status: a pregnancy. Concubine Diao Ju records this frustration in her diary. Then when she is called for an unscheduled sexual event with the Emperor, she brings her diary. They attempt sexual intercourse. The Emperor fails. Concubine Diao Ju, after dressing to be carried out, does something, says something which enrages the Emperor. He stabs her with a knife from his bedroom. She runs and dies in the antechamber just beyond the inner quarters. Her diary falls out of her hands and

THE EUNUCH

slides under a dresser in the room. The Emperor, embarrassed by his anger and its cause, hides the knife where he thinks no one will find it. Here in this room."

Gett, having finished, waited. If she wished, it would be irrelevant that he had bracketed his statement with a declaration that it was false. That he asserted a person could believe it was an executable offense.

"Why would someone attempt to make the Emperor look ridiculous?"

"I don't know yet."

She didn't speak for a moment. Gett could hear her breathing.

"What do you want?"

"I request that the Imperial Mother grant me a pass, chopped in the Imperial Mother's name, that all inquiries into my investigative activities be passed to The Imperial Mother's Secretariat. And I wish the Imperial Mother to put out a notice that any investigations into my involvement be terminated."

There was another long pause. Gett did not move. His head to the cold floor, he could feel the enormous columns rising on either side of him, the dragons curling around them, hovering over him, powerful and watching.

"There are bureaucratic issues," said the Imperial Mother.

Gett waited silently.

"From a bureaucratic standpoint, this is a difficult thing for the Imperial Mother to do."

"I see."

"There are no bureaus that are under the direct control of the Imperial Mother," she said.

"That is true."

"So it is difficult for the Imperial Mother to control them."

Gett simply waited.

"But in times like this, righteous officials often must find solutions to issues such as these," she suggested.

"I understand, Imperial Mother."

With a slight swaying of the beads, she was gone. Gett raised his head up from the floor and stood up on his creaking knees. On his long spindly legs, he made his way out of the audience chamber, torches casting his shadow in a flickering shuddering chase.

Gett ran his hand along the seam of the small drawer that was set in the lacquered box on his desk. The dust was undisturbed. He squatted down, his knees creaking, and looked at it from a lower angle, a trick he had learned many years ago — if dust had been sifted there to cover an intrusion, the way the light hit it was distinctive — real dust fell and accreted slowly but directionally — dust that had been placed was usually (but not always if the intruder was experienced) sifted horizontally onto the surface, shifting the angle from which you viewed the surface you could usually see that.

But, nothing, or at least an experienced break in.

As he continued his inspection of his small private office, he began to consider. He was discomfited by the fact that he genuinely didn't know what to do next. The investigation was sculpting in his mind a structure that made sense to him, insofar as the goals of those involved were were sculpting it. And there were a number of possible points on that structure that he could now examine in more detail. Too many in fact, and thus his indecision.

He considered his assassins: Almost certainly he would get no useful information from an interrogation. At best who hired them. Probably just a middleman. But there was a time issue. They were in the Imperial Mother's custody, but that custody was being subjected to pressure; it couldn't last forever and at

THE EUNUCH

some point others would gain access to them and he most likely would lose it.

Gett crawled over the floor looking for displacement of the markers he had set. Even looking very carefully, he saw no movement. He had to contact Kob Meke's harem informant. He needed to understand the structure within which all the behavior that he had pieced together had occurred, and probably contributed to what had happened. It was the most valuable information but the least pressing in terms of his immediate danger.

He climbed up on his chair and looked at the sill of the high window. It was slatted against the cold and and let in sharp shiny strips of afternoon light. He examined the cracked paint of the window sill. Such things were extremely useful because if anyone had forced the window, small chips of paint would flake off and there was no way an intruder could avoid it.

Again, nothing.

The Imperial Mother had (carefully) offered him a straight deal: transfer control of his investigating bureau to her, get protection. To create an official remonstrance to the Emperor was a major undertaking, a day's work at least to absolutely make sure that it was without errors of writing or protocol—all of which carried severe punishments. That he had to do it was unquestionable. It wasn't a matter of if, only when and how. And when had to be soon—he figured he had a day at most until she withdrew her protection.

A few more minutes of careful checking confirmed what he had predicted. No one was breaking in yet. It would happen but maybe not for another day or two. Not that he would ever store anything valuable here. It was essentially just a room, tucked away in an unused corridor in the Ministry of Tax Assesment. The cold part of the Palace, far from Enforcement. And a far walk through many winding courtyards to even the nearest Palace guards. In part, it was a convenient place to come when he had to deal with the ebb and flow of paper that rose and fell like a tide during an investigation.

But more importantly the office served as a net. Anyone who was interested in him would target this place first—because it seemed like a safe start. They would find nothing. Gett, however, would know that someone was reaching out of the darkness for him, desperately seeking a way to survive and seeing in his fall, a counterweight to their survival.

By the time he had carefully put everything back in its place, he had made a decision. He sat down, out of breath, and called out to a courier. He pulled over a small strip of paper and a brush. What to write? In truth, it would be safer, from an evidentiary standpoint, to deliver the message in person and verbally. But to emerge, without reason, out into the Palace halls during a cull like this was unwise. He would be watched, and the event—a Chief Investigator visiting another Bureau Chief at this time—would be reported. But the constant flow of messages that whispered through the halls was a background noise. Unnoticed.

Gett, after a moment's pause, wrote:

> *Kob, Meke, Chief of Counter-Intelligence, 2nd Class, Bureau of Counter-Espionage, Capital Region*
>
> *As regards the investigation into the death of Concubine Third Class Diao Ju, The Office of Investigation of the Eighth Secretariat requests an interview with evidentiary research witness. Please determine availability and interview location.*
>
> *Signed: Chopped*
> *Enchenkei Gett, Chief Investigator,*
> *Bureau of Palace Investigations*

THE EUNUCH

He handed it to the courier who whisked it away.

Gett looked at the angle of the sun coming in his window; about an hour and a half at least before he would get a response.

Scheduling an interview with an informant was a tricky business. It couldn't be too clandestine—if somebody noticed, they would also note that the meeting was clearly meant to be secret. Questions would be asked. And the whole thing would collapse and come out in excruciating and often fatal detail. But they couldn't be ostentatious either. Kob Meke clearly had someone inside the Harem on his payroll. Such things were dangerous up to a point, but for the most part tolerated because almost everyone had informants. But the harem, because of what it was, held an incrementally larger step of danger for all of them, for Kob, for Gett and for the informant, whoever he (or probably she) was.

Gett popped in a fresh nut and as the high hit him sharp and hard, so too did a thought that had been lurking about, itching at his mind: Over the last two hours, Gett had noticed a change coming over himself—a strange but calming one. He had felt it when he had arrived at the Palace gates, it had crept over him as he learned about the book, and now, sitting here in his office with the maelstrom swirling around him, he had sensed why: He was no longer alone. Whereas the previous day he had been a tiny threatened speck, a smudge in the Palace easily erased with the flick of a thumb. Now that same hand had loomed up, curled itself into a fist and was thundering down, randomly and furiously, and *everyone* was threatened. He was no longer the focus of hundreds of eyes because those eyes had now turned, terrified and malevolent, to look at each other. And he could therefore now do what he did better than others: fade into the background, move through the interstices of their fears and in the small pockets of truth he found, creep slowly to the solution to the problem that had been presented to him.

Right now, outside of his small office, the Emperor's personal agents were arresting a first tier of officials. Most of them were the less clever or unlucky; the ones who either had not had enough time to react when they received the diary or who had reacted badly, either ignoring it or not immediately seeking out the Emperor.

The hand of the Emperor would begin to penetrate deeper into his bureaucracy, a second, less involved tier would feel his hand brush past them, and the arrests would begin again.

He heard more shouts far away from his office, distant but panicked. Kob Meke's response, if it came, wouldn't come for at least another hour. Gett decided that the best thing to do was to wait. So he sat back in his chair and did just that.

十五

THE SECRETARY handed Gett a small folded prescript. Gett opened it. Like-ink spilled across the thin, brittle paper favored by Counter-Espionage was Kob Meke's un-careful brushwork.

> *Counter-Espionage has arranged that interview with the witness pertaining to the murder of Class Three Concubine Diao Ju will take place at the Hour of the Monkey. Interview location will be the Offices of Counter-Espionage, Surveillance Sub-Directorate*

Gett rolled up the note. He thought about destroying it. Clearly it was an interview with a Haremite—Gett had all but explicitly asked for one. Thus, dangerous. But it was a paper trail. It established protocol.

He put the prescript in his waist pouch.

※

There was a fastidious meticulousness to Counter-Espionage—rooting out spies and traitors in the Palace—that Gett appreciated. It was difficult work. Not so much like most work was difficult in that it was strenuous or dull. Instead it was difficult on the mind.

It did not attract people who relied on a common sense of truth. Instead, those who flourished in the rich nightsoil of other people's secrets were the ones who dug with feverish precision, following all suspicions through to the fullest branching termini of their roots. They sifted through an enormous, bewildering complexity of detail. They remembered it at all times. Then they carefully drew thin, reedy lines of supposition between the isolated smudges of fact that allowed faint, dirty pictures of a possible reality to emerge.

They were people who functioned poorly in the real world. They lost themselves in the navel-gazing shadows of their suspicions. But in Counter-Espionage they had dropped down through the earth into a strange world that suited them.

Because the most successful were not the ones who were rigorous. The most successful were the ones who, even if their obsessive digging scratched out a thousand lives, *never missed the real thing*.

Always, when Gett walked through the dark, dirty corridors of the offices of Counter-Espionage, he saw the character of its occupants reflected in the exuded sense of the place—dark, small, complicated rooms, a pale occupant, under a tiny candle light, surrounded by documents. Like thin moles digging in dark soil.

The only exception to this was Kob Meke's office, he ran operations, his family wouldn't let him get trapped in the dullness of analysis. He gathered the dirt the pale creatures in their horrible offices grubbed about in. His office was full of sun muted through paper-covered slits high in the wall. Fat bottles of sorghum wine lined the bright red tables under the window. His desk was clean. Somebody (probably him) had put a bunch of yellow and fuchsia flowers in a vase.

Kob sat smiling, waiting for Gett.

"Have a d-d-drink."

Gett sat in one of Kob's chairs. Not Imperial issue. Delicate ivory inlay scrolled around the careful woodwork. Family

THE EUNUCH

furniture.

"Alright," Gett said.

Kob poured some white sorghum wine.

"D-d-dry glass."

"Dry glass."

They knocked it back. Kob smiled.

"I can give you t-t-two hours."

"Should be enough."

What d-d-do you think you'll ask her?"

"You know, procedures and scheduling in the harem."

"It's a friendly session. We've got it record-d-ded as a confidential witness interview so it's on record as having happened but her id-d-entity won't be in the report."

"How'd she get in?" Gett asked.

"In a way that nob-b-body saw. Same way she'll go out. St-tart?"

"Sure, but alone."

"I could listen and you'd never know. It's my int-t-terrogation room."

"Of course. But it's more important that you not be in the room for her to talk openly to me."

"Right."

"And how much of this do you really want to hear?"

※

As they walked down the corridor to the interview room Gett assessed his exposure. All events in the Palace could be construed as having relevance to Counter-Espionage — so an interview was standard. It was why, probably, Kob Meke had set it up this way. But his arrival would be logged. And the reason for his interview recorded.

Gett signed in and entered the chamber. Sitting in the dimly lit (but comfortable as it was for friendly sessions) room was the informant. Gett immediately understood Kob's caution—this was an Imperial concubine.

She was looking out the high window set next to the ceiling, squinting. If you looked closely (and Gett was) the tiny but deepening dragon claws around her eyes stood out. Same with the mouth, a tiny craquelure of lines articulating down off of the corners. So, early thirties. The colors on her tassels indicated she hadn't had a son. So, about to be retired.

She sat quietly, not acknowledging them. A little short, a little dark, from a Western Desert tribe. Thin. Huihui, probably.

Kob slipped out. Gett sat in the chair across from her. He gave her a moment and then began.

"Why are you here?" Gett asked.

"It's all in the records."

"No, why are you here talking to me?"

"That's a stupid question."

"Why?"

"I could lie."

"True."

"So why ask?"

"Your answer tells me about you."

"Not much."

"Not nothing either."

She allowed herself a brief, very small upturn of one corner of her mouth for that.

"Why does it matter?" she asked.

"Because why you're here determines a lot about what you'll tell me."

"What do you want to know?"

"First, why you're here."

She looked at him. There was a sophisticated meanness in

her eyes. The kind that didn't necessarily suggest she was a bad person, just a careful one, used to complexity.

"Money."

"How much?"

"Enough."

"Why do you need money?"

She gestured at her robe. "I'm a Concubine Fourth Class; from a second-tier tribe."

"What do you do for it?"

She fixed him again with the stare. Then smoothed her robe. "What do you want to know?"

"Who's giving it to you?"

"The money?"

"Of course."

"You really expect me to tell you?"

"It would help."

"Help who?"

"Help me."

"How?"

"It would help me because if I know who was giving you money I might get some insight into why they want you to talk to me."

"Why do you think?"

"Well, somebody wants me to solve this murder. Or they don't," said Gett.

"Which do you think it is?"

"I was hoping you knew."

She said nothing. Gett sat, thinking about what to ask next.

"Did you talk to her often?" he asked.

"Who?"

"Diao Ju."

She laughed at this. "I'm a Class Four Concubine. Third-level concubines don't talk to us. They have their own living quarters. They talk to and hate each other, not us. We see them occasionally walking past us in the halls. We are required to respect them by staring at the floor." She smiled. "They slip past us like a fragrant wind."

"How do the schedules get made?" Gett asked.

"The Chief Harem Daoist makes them."

"The Head of Harem?"

"That's right."

"The sick one, always drinking the medicine?"

"Yes."

"How specifically? What goes into his calculation?"

"The girl's birthday, the season, the Emperor's birthday, the balance of earth and fire in the Palace, proven fecundity, intelligence, race, and special requests."

"What are special requests?"

"Sometimes the Emperor prefers one girl over others."

"How much does that factor in the calculation?"

"It depends."

"On what?"

"On how much the Emperor prefers a specific girl."

"So he can request one but she doesn't necessarily get given to him?"

"It depends on how he requests her and how much control he has versus his mother over the process."

"This Emperor?"

"This Emperor what?"

"Does he often make specific requests?"

"Not very often."

"But it happens?"

"Of course it happens."

"Who does he request?"

THE EUNUCH

"No one girl all the time."

"Recently?"

"The past three months?"

"Sure."

"He requested out of turn Xu Xianlan, Arghut Hakim, Tololo Hugulu."

"How many times?"

"One extra time for each."

"Why?"

"They're prettier than the other girls and two of them are not Chinese or Jurchen. Arghut is from the Western Desert, Tololo the western high plateau."

"Has he ever specially requested you?"

"No."

"Why?"

"You would have to ask him."

"What specifically is the calculation? I mean not what goes into it but how does he add up the girl's birthday, the season etc?"

"It's secret."

"Secret meaning you don't know? Or you can't tell me?"

"Meaning I don't know."

"Who knows?"

"Only the Harem Daoist."

"How does he know?"

"The information is the property of the Emperor. It is given to him when he becomes the Harem Doaist."

"Is the fertility of the Imperial wives monitored?"

"It is."

"How?"

"Temperature and inspection."

"Inspection of what?"

"Of their vaginas."

"Does the Harem Daoist have access to this information?"

"Of course."

"Does he use it in his calculations?"

"Imperial Wives whose numbers are appropriate are scheduled for sexual intercourse with the Emperor during their fertile periods."

"Fertile wives take precedence over fertile concubines?"

"Yes."

"And First Class over Second Class, etcetera?"

"Yes."

"Jurchens over Chinese and other tribes?"

Just a stare.

"So it would be possible for a Third Class concubine to have no sexual access to the Emperor during the time in which she could become pregnant?" Gett asked.

"Yes."

"Or a Fourth Class one."

She looked at him for a bit before answering. "Yes, that happens."

"How many times had Diao Ju been scheduled out of her fertility window?"

"I don't know."

"You mean you don't know at all or specifically?"

"Specifically."

"Roughly?"

"Most of her scheduling was outside the window."

"Why?"

"I don't know."

"Did she try to change that?"

"Yes. For the past four months her schedule was re-arranged."

"In what way?"

THE EUNUCH

"She was scheduled for intercourse with the Emperor during her fertile period."

"Why?"

"Why what?"

"Alright. How?"

"I don't know."

"But what would you guess?"

"That she had done something to make the Emperor like her."

"And if she hadn't?"

"Then she had made the Chief Harem Daoist like her."

"That goes in to his calculation?"

"What do you think?"

"So she comes into the Palace as a Class Three Concubine, she has never had sex with the Emperor during the time window in which she can get pregnant. Then suddenly, four months ago her schedule is re-arranged and she has sex with him during each of the four succeeding windows?"

"That's right."

"Who did she replace?"

"No one."

"I mean on those four days, did she replace any other girl's fertile window?"

"Two girls got pushed forward a day. One was retired. The fourth was pushed back a day."

"What were their responses?"

"Nothing."

"Why nothing?"

"A day makes no difference."

"Yeah, but two days might, then three, then a week. It's water down a hill."

"It can be."

"So these girls must have been angry."

"Yes."

"So what did they do about it?"

"What can they do?"

"You tell me."

"Of course they are angry. That is known. Every time a girl is moved off the pregnancy rotation she is put in seclusion to minimize conflict."

"And so they were put in seclusion."

"No."

"Why not?"

"They weren't moved off the pregnancy rotation."

"But they were shifted along it."

"They were."

"And so they were angry."

The concubine sat silently for a minute. She looked at her hands, squinted out the window.

"I think you misunderstand the way their minds work. They were angry but they were frightened. They are still meeting with the Emperor during their pregnancy period and so all of their attention is focused on that—it determines the course of the rest of their lives. If a girl wants revenge, and they do all the time, she'll try to get it later."

"Who were they?"

"The girls that got shifted?"

"Of course."

"All that is recorded, you don't need to get it from me."

"It would be easier."

"Lots of things could be easier."

"And the retired wife?"

"Concubine."

"And the retired concubine?"

"She was scheduled to be retired anyway."

THE EUNUCH

"What was the reason given for her rescheduling?"
"No reason is ever given."
"But what did people assume?"
"How can I speak for other people?"
"What did you assume?"
"I assumed that she was old."
"Did you like her?"
"The retired concubine?"
"No, Diao Ju."
"No."
"Why?"
"I don't like any of the girls."
"So it wasn't that you disliked her specifically."
The Concubine Fourth Class thought about this for a moment. "She was devious."
"Unlike the rest of the concubines?"
"She was different."
"How?"
"Hard to talk to, hard to get along with. Smarter than the other girls. Angry."
"So they disliked her as well."
"Yes."
"Always?"
"Yes."
"What about recently?"
She thought about this. Gett watched her. She was thinking not about what she had seen but instead what to tell him.
"Recently she was different."
"How?"
"Nicer."
"Nicer how?"
"In a way almost like she had watched how a normal

concubine acts and had figured it out and had copied it—but copied it well so that it seemed genuine."

"Who were her friends?"

"She had no friends."

"None at all?"

"None."

"Why?"

"None of the girls have friends."

"I don't believe that."

"Then why ask me questions?"

"What would four months of rescheduling cost?"

"In what?"

"In gold."

"Rescheduling for four times access to the Emperor during a concubine's pregnancy window?"

"Yes."

"About twelve jin of gold."

"Twelve?"

"About."

Gett was astonished. That was about enough to pay for the rice for an entire village, fifty to a hundred people, for their entire lives.

"Does that price change?"

"Of course."

"Based on what?"

"Whether the Emperor already has a son. Whether he has daughters. Whether the months are going to be ones that favor getting pregnant with a son. Whether they calculate the energy flow to be strong or weak. Whether the Emperor is old. Whether a concubine is new or about to be retired. That sort of thing."

"Is it normal for concubines to have no pregnancy access to the Emperor?"

"It's common."

"Common but not normal?"

"It happens."

"But usually to girls who have made a mistake or are undesirable?"

"Yes."

"Or are about to be retired?"

She looked at her hands, and back up at the bright, high window. She sat that way for a moment.

"You know you have what you need. I'm finished."

"I have a few more questions."

"No."

Gett waited for a moment then nodded, stood up.

"Should I wait for you to leave?"

"No."

"Why?"

"Kob Meke has arranged for me to be taken back to the Harem."

"Thank you."

She said nothing, but nodded. It was as if she was trying to figure out, from his questions, what had happened and how it would impact her.

Gett stood. He watched her for a very short moment as she sat, motionless, waiting. She was in a tough position. Clearly aging. Clearly smart. This had clearly been arranged to give her exactly the access that Diao Ju had gotten before she died. It was unlikely to be anything else. And not probably arranged by the harem administrator—instead probably for a cash payment that could then be made to him for a re-interpretation of the scheduling portents to give her a few months of pregnancy window scheduling. So she, like the other girls, was hard. And also clearly smart enough to realize from his questions that she had put herself in personal danger by agreeing to the interview. Gett guessed she was meticulously assessing their discussion in her mind, trying to figure out from what he had asked and what she knew and had kept from him, the parameters of what had really happened and in how much danger it put her.

Gett turned and walked out of the interview room. He wondered what Kob Meke, who undoubtedly had listened to the whole interview, thought about it.

Diao Ju's schedule had changed recently. She was not an Imperial favorite. Like this concubine, she was also not Jurchen. She had cut some deal. With whom? If she had cut it with the Harem Daoist than it would have been for pregnancy access. If with an outsider then probably for money to buy that. But what did she have to offer? Who would pay such a high price for it?

Gett made his way out, passing, quietly like a rustling shadow, the candles of the analysts. He stepped out of Counter-Espionage into the courtyard that connected it with the Ministry of War, pulled up his robes and hurried across the cold stones, squinting into the wind.

GETT HURRIED. There it was, the tiniest thread that had, with the shifting of the fabric, softly eased itself out of the weave and was now dangling tentatively in front of him. He headed for the library. Lao Kou was still there, reading, like a dark statue. He heard Gett and turned around. His back now to the candle, his face in shadow.

"More reading?" asked Lao Kou.

"Yes."

"Of course."

"I need the Harem records," said Gett.

"Those are quite restricted."

"Yes."

"Case going well?"

"Hard to say," said Gett.

"Mmm?"

"Many brush strokes. Few pictures."

"As it is always. Which specific harem records do you need?"

"Schedules and special passes."

"Just that?"

"Probably."

"I have heard a few things," said Lao Kou.

"There is a lot to hear lately."

"Yes."

"No solution yet then?"

"No. But possibly one in sight."

"Yes? When?"

"Impossible to say."

"Mentioned your library record requests in your reports?"

"Only the paperwork. Nothing else."

Gett watched Lao Kou think about this. The largest risk for him was simply time — how long before he and his library became a target? How long before the case came to a close? Implication was inevitable if it took too long. He took one last puff of his pipe, extinguished it (carefully and fully) in a small black pot of water and laid it on his knotted desk.

"Wait here."

And with that, he shuffled away into the darkness of his library, a mole, burrowing through dark and secret truths. He returned with an armload of brittle scrolls, the white of the paper visible first emerging from the gloom. He laid them on the reading table in front of Gett.

"These are the schedules running back for three years. Schedule Changes are marked in a separate addendum but with references and a marking number in the master document. All entry, exit and special passes are noted in the Harem Security Report. Need anything else?"

Gett looked at the scrolls. Unrolled he estimated them to be about twenty arms' length worth. A concentrated afternoon.

"I will start with this."

Lao Kou nodded and disappeared back into the darkness.

The documents themselves were opaque and dense. Not meant for reading but for checking. Gett first settled himself into the schedules; it would be these that incentivized the girls, structuring their lives. It took Gett a solid hour to get through them and another one to correlate them with the changes since added and itemized by the Harem bureaucracy.

THE EUNUCH

After two hours of careful reading, Gett had established the following:

Over the past three years (and not before the present Emperor's ascension going back as far as seven) there had been nine schedule changes. Each change had been made to the schedule of a second or third-rank concubine. The routine, from the first concubine leading through three years to Diao Ju, had not deviated—a girl was, from the moment she entered the harem, assigned a *bad schedule*—one that ensured the impossibility of a pregnancy. After a few months, the girl's schedule suddenly changed to one that perfectly matched her fertility cycle.

Following this schedule change for each girl, another important change was made. It had taken Gett a while to dig it up because references to it were oblique in the main text, simply numbers specifying an addendum. But after about an hour of cross-referencing, Gett pieced it together. Each girl, after being granted a schedule change, was assigned a no-escort pass—allowing her to move around both the inner and outer Palace unescorted. The sign-outs and sign-ins for these passes were difficult to find but they were there, deliberately classified as training transfers and so (cleverly) filed separately from the harem records under a different bureau heading.

Each pass was granted, signed out and signed back in within five hours of a sexual scheduling with the Emperor—every single one, running back three years, with the exception of the first, which was probably some sort of dry run.

Gett thought about this—there was a puzzle here. First, the security around a concubine is precisely highest just before and just after sex so as to ensure that the impregnation process is inviolable. An outside pregnancy that begins at that same time is the most difficult to detect.

Second, the schedule changes were backwards. In every

instance Gett had ever heard of, a concubine had bribed her way out of the harem for a sexual liaison—in other words, she was doing something, paying somebody and getting out of the harem was her goal. It was extremely difficult, was punished usually with death and so was extremely rare. But here, the only conclusion that Gett could make was that *the liaison itself was the payment* for the schedule change. The Emperor's concubines were...and Gett considered long and hard about how to phrase this in a better way in the report he would finally have to make... the concubines were being *pimped*.

"It's trouble," said Sulo.
"That's what it looks like."
"What happened?"
Gett walked him through it as they sat in Sulo's dark workroom.
"Who did it?" Sulo asked.
"I don't know."
"Who you think?"
"I don't have a theory yet."
"Big problem. Lots bad results."
"Yes."
"Wait. Hey!" Sulo yelled at one of the servants standing at the door, "Go and get a scribe." Very quickly one came, sat down and flattened his scroll, waiting.
"Alright. What do you want, Gett?"
"I need the surveillance records on Head of Harem, Gogoro Shen."
The scribe wrote quickly, recording their conversation.
"No. He's not involved in this."
"How do you know?" asked Gett.

THE EUNUCH

"Gogoro is good. Can't do this."

"I agree."

"If he's not involved, why you need?"

"He's Head of Harem. The girls were being pimped. It's somebody in the harem."

"Not him."

"Correct."

"So why you need the records?"

"It's the place to start."

"Even if he's not involved?"

"Yes."

"He is not involved."

"Yes, of course."

"Anybody else who can change the schedule?" asked Sulo.

"A few."

"Who?"

"Three harem priests, the harem security, the Imperial Mother. Maybe a few others.

"See! Go torture the priests."

"Then?"

"Maybe they confess."

"Maybe. But there are lots of reasons to change a schedule — sickness, seasons, whim."

"Ask the girls."

"What do think they're going to say?"

"They are honorable Wives of Emperor. They will tell truth."

"Yes."

"See, alright. Gett, I got to tell you something."

"What?"

"It's my experience, it's like a thing I learned."

"Please."

"It explains why it's not him."

"Yes?"

"People like him are baited."

"Baited?"

"On the way up. The Emperor is always testing loyalty. Over maybe twenty years, he has passed many tests."

"So?"

"So me too."

"You what?"

"I passed the baits. The tests."

"So?"

"So I know what it is like."

"What's it like?"

"All the time you are aware. Something happens, you think — is this real or a test? Never relax. He would think maybe this is bait too. He got where he is, he's very careful."

"Of course."

"So he wasn't involved. He wouldn't risk it."

"Of course."

"Yes."

"But I still need the records."

Sulo sat back, running through this conversation.

"Alright, because it's a formal request, investigator to ministry, I am *forced*."

"Yes."

"Alright. Hey!" Sulo yelled at the servant again. "Go get the surveillance report."

The boy ran off to get it. They sat in silence, Sulo staring at his hands. The boy came back with a scroll.

"I give to you only because you are forcing."

Gett took the scrolls to his office and unrolled them. One was

THE EUNUCH

a record of the previous three days of Gogoro's life. But also, surprisingly, the scroll contained a further five separate days before the murder, not contiguous, but five days at intervals of about three months. The last three days were headed: *Surveillance at behest of Bureau of Palace Investigations.* The second episodic record was titled: *Security of high officials.*

That was interesting — interesting that it happened, of course — but also that Enforcement was tasked with it. Gett wondered if they actually had been. For a brief moment he wondered if it was a mistake.

The documents were very concise:

For the two days after the murder, Gogoro had worked and slept, nothing more. Every day a sparse report of a trip between sleeping quarters and the harem. Since Gogoro lived in the Palace, there was a notation of a short walk then meticulously, each hour, "nothing to report".

Except for one deviation the day of the murder. Gogoro left the Palace to go to the other side of the city and visit an orphanage. Even more interesting was that it had been established as an orphanage *three years ago*. When Gett looked at the longer set of records, this side trip also appeared as the only anomaly in an unbroken record of trips between quarters and harem over many months.

▦

Gett had decided to wear an investigator's tassel on his hat. It swung back and forth when his palanquin rocked as his bearers skirted the side of the narrow alley. Four Palace eunuchs accompanied him, each also fully dressed-out. Some of the gutters were slick with ice, but the center of the street was a churned-up sludge. The tassel annoyed him, getting in his eyes as they moved back and forth across the slush, but in situations like this it was better to have it.

Gogoro would find out about this visit. With that knowledge would come the understanding that Gett had ordered him followed. Not unusual. Not a reach beyond Gett's mandate. But Gogoro would note it and he would store it away. The tassel, and the accompanying eunuchs, provided Gett with just enough bureaucratic cover to make it hard for Gogoro to take revenge. In any ensuing investigation, Gett's presence at the orphanage would be entered in the record because he had dressed officially for it and was accompanied officially for it.

It was still dangerous, though. And Gett was unhappy about that as he turned the corner, stepped out of the lowered palanquin, over the center of the street and to the doors of the orphanage courtyard — old, peeling paint and unlocked.

Gett always walked into spaces carefully, especially unfamiliar ones. He pushed open the doors and looked in. Empty cracked stones. Chinese style — a simple open square ringed by raised rooms and a long landing. No obvious dangers. He walked in, checking behind him, leaving his eunuchs outside the door. Stopped in the middle. In the room ahead, through the door, he saw children. Without preamble, he walked up the short stairs and entered quickly, checking behind him at the door frame as he did — no one there.

Inside maybe twelve kids. Two old women. All filthy. They stared.

Gett stepped back out to the veranda, looking up at second floor windows for people looking back at him. Left-hand side, into the sun, movement, but the glare made him unsure.

On the right, a workroom? A scratching noise. Gett walked over and stepped in. The room faced north, dark and cold. A young Chinese man at a desk. He looked up. Literate probably, assuming he could read the scrolls he was holding. Shaven-

THE EUNUCH

headed, common for scholars to prevent cheating. Thin but not naturally so. Brought on by hunger. Small, slitted hard-to-read southern eyes. Chinese.

Gett waited. The scholar stood, then down and kowtowed — twice for rank, once for Gett's Jurchen racial superiority.

"Honored Imperial Eunuch, what may I do for you?"

"Please stand up and get me a chair."

The scholar did so quickly, then, frightened and tense, returned to the floor, kneeling.

"I am involved in the investigation of the murder of an Imperial concubine," said Gett.

A bit of surprise passing over the scholar's face.

"You expected something different?'

"We had heard something different," the scholar said carefully.

"Which was?"

"It is not important. The city is full of rumors now."

"In this city full of rumors, which particular rumor did you hear?"

The scholar considered how to safely answer. "We heard that three concubines had been executed."

"For?"

"It was not clear."

"We are establishing the movements of all the principal people of the harem on the days leading up to the murder of a concubine."

"Yes, of course."

"That includes, even though he is not a focus of our investigation, the Head of Harem, Eunuch of Standing, Gogoro Shen."

"A great man."

"Yes," said Gett.

"He comes here often."

"Yes, our records show that. So I am here."

"How may I help you?"

"Of the many reasons to hold the opinion that he is a great man, what is yours?"

"I'm sure you know."

"Why would I know?"

"I mean you are here, so you know."

"He is a great man, but I don't know him well. Why would he come here, to this orphanage?"

"He is... he is a friend of our home."

"Your personal home or this home for unwanted children?"

"Here, of course."

"What specifically does being a friend mean?"

"Head of Harem Gogoro Shen is not... he is not suspected of having committed a murder?"

"He is not."

"Or of being involved in any way?"

"There is no reason to suspect him. This is a normal part of every investigation in the Palace."

"Of course, but you understand my worry, I'm... I'm sure."

"Maybe, what is your worry specifically?"

"Of causing difficulty."

"Of causing him difficulty?"

"Yes."

"What could you say that could cause him difficulty?"

The scholar paused for a moment, finally. "I don't know."

"You are afraid of him?"

"No... of course... he is from the Palace. But... it... he is a friend of the orphanage."

"What does 'a friend of the orphanage' mean?"

"The money we have to save these children comes from him."

"All of it?"

THE EUNUCH

"He arranges it."

"All of the money to run this orphanage comes from him?"

"Yes."

"How much money is that?"

"I'm not sure of the exact number."

"But you must know in a general way."

"The sum?"

"Yes, for a year to run the orphanage."

"It varies greatly and you are a representative of the Palace. You deserve an accurate answer."

"But roughly?"

"I would feel more comfortable if I could check our records. Since it relates to the Eunuch Gogoro Shen, I wish to be accurate so as to not cause trouble."

"For him or for you?"

"For everyone."

"This year."

The thin Chinese scholar thought nervously. "This year we have spent twelve cash."

"For the whole year?"

"For most of it. But the year is ending. This will be close to what we spend for the year."

"And this is a normal year?"

"Relatively normal."

Twelve cash. It was an astonishingly small number. Almost pocket change for a bureaucrat from the Palace.

"And only your orphanage received money from Gogoro Shen?"

"We didn't receive it from him directly. He organized the funding."

"How many orphanages did he organize funding for?"

"Ten that I know of."

Gett considered this, still a tiny sum.

"And this is why he is a great man?"

"It is part of it. He was kind."

"Kind?"

"To the children."

"In what way?"

"When he was here."

"When he was here, he was kind to the children?"

"Yes."

"Is that rare?"

"Yes, it is very rare."

"How often was he here?"

"Once every few days."

"And what did he do?"

"He played with the children."

"And then?"

"And then left."

"How did he play with them?"

"How?"

"What specifically did he do?"

"The things you do when you play with children. Share their toys, make faces, that sort of thing."

"And nothing else?"

"For the most part."

"And the other part?"

"He would discuss funding sometimes."

"And?"

"And we might talk."

"About?"

"Nothing specific, general talk. The weather, that sort of thing."

Gett felt like he was getting nowhere. When one powerful

person was asking questions about another powerful person there was always fear. Because it was easy to be caught in the middle. But here, with this small man, while of course there was a sense of anxiety, there was no panic, the sort of horrible existential terror when a person feels descending upon him the choice of who to betray.

"Have any other people come here to ask about him?"

"No."

"In the past five days, how many times has he been here?"

"One time."

"For?"

"Financial arrangements for the next month."

"Nothing else?"

"No."

"For how long?"

"I don't remember. A few hours."

Gett looked back across the courtyard at the children in the dirty room.

"When do they leave?"

"They don't leave. They live here."

"No, I mean at what age do they have to move out?"

"We have the funds to keep them until they are ten years' old."

"Then what?"

"Before they reach that age, we arrange for labor in the city for the talented ones. The others we arrange to leave the city for farming."

"Any other occupations?"

"There are."

"Which?"

The scholar hesitated. "I'm sure you know."

"Why are you sure I know?"

"I just... it is... you are an investigator."

"How common is it?"

"Many of the children don't wish to leave the city. It is difficult to force them. And the pay is higher, especially when they are very young."

"Why?"

"It is attractive."

"So how often?"

"Maybe half."

"Half the children?"

"Yes."

"Boys and girls?

"Slightly fewer boys."

"How much do they cost?"

"One and a half cash."

"That is enough to run the orphanage."

"It is paid to those who arrange it and is split with the child. We don't see any of it."

"Why so much?"

"They are attractive but also the energy flow through them is very strong because of their youth."

"It is legal in the sense that it has been regulated bureaucratically by the city management?"

"Yes, that's how it has been regulated."

"And in this completely legal framework was the Eunuch Gogoro Shen part of the managing apparatus?"

"No."

"No?"

"No."

"Was he in any way connected to it as a... person who had a stake in its success?"

"No, of course not."

THE EUNUCH

"Did he use the service?"
"No no no!"
"No no no?"
"I'm sorry, I thought you knew."
"Knew what."
"His difficulty."
"He is a eunuch, I know."
"No, his other difficulty. Here."
"What was his difficulty here?"
"He was trying to close this unfortunate path."
"In what way?"
"From the Palace."
"And?"
"And it's still going on."
"The moving of these children?"
"His efforts to shut it down. He is a friend of the orphanage."

There was a noise outside. The children were moving out of the room.

"It is time for the children to eat. I must arrange it. Do you have more questions?"

"Not for now."

"I am here every day if you do. Ready to help in anyway."

"Thank you."

The scholar hesitated, torn strongly somehow. Finally, "May I ask you a question?"

"Yes."

"You are a Eunuch of Standing?"

"I am."

"And you feel I have answered your questions honestly?"

"It's hard to say."

"Of course, but in the future it may be confirmed that I did. Is this true?"

"That is true."

"And thus I would have done you a service. Assisted in this matter."

"Yes."

"And that is the sort of thing deserving of sponsorship."

"Sponsorship?"

"For the Examination."

"The Imperial Examination?"

"Yes."

"It is in two days."

"I mean the one in two years."

"That is a long way off."

"It is important to be sponsored, and to prepare."

"Gogoro Shen has not sponsored you?"

"He has."

"So?"

"We need three sponsors to be allowed to take the Examination."

"Three?"

"Yes."

"Why?"

"To show our character. And since I have been shown to be of good character by my management of this orphanage and my truthful answers to your questions…?"

"You manage records?"

"Yes."

"In your records, would there be memoranda of his visits?"

"There would be."

"Show them to me."

They were elegantly written and clear. It was good to have

educated labor. On the scrolls, Gogoro Shen's visits were clearly marked; green ink to contrast with black for non-Palace visitors. A short look over the scrolls showed Gogoro over a span of five years had been here roughly fifty-four times (there were a few notations from the same days so it was unclear whether he'd come twice or stayed but engaged in two separate activities.) In the commentary on the schedule, for each entry, it was written: funds brought, and a notation of the amount. Always different but always small.

"I will take this."

"Of course, Investigator."

"Thank you."

"May I help you in any other way?"

"No, this is enough."

"I am honored to have been of help. You will consider my request?"

"Yes."

Gett thought about himself, thought about these people. Village girls were denied a Palace posting and ended up as prostitutes. Eunuchs were castrated, didn't secure a Palace position, ended as beggars. Scholars took the Examination, failed and ended like this. Small men, growing older, in poverty, all the money of their villages exhausted. Working for a bed and a desk to study on.

They all disappeared into the city like grain casings scattered by wind. The discarded husks of the very few who slipped through the cracks and into power.

Gett stepped out of the scholar's cold room. Walked across the courtyard, carefully now because it was full of children. He stopped in the middle, considering. The wind was blowing at his ankles and under his collar onto his neck in a way that he hated. He felt he had missed something crucial. It was picking at his arm. When he walked to where he could see his eunuch escort outside staring back at him, clearly frightened, he knew what *it* was. He turned toward the central room with the children, and walked up the few steps to the landing

Gett stepped into the room. It was the same—the filthy children, the filthy walls, the filthy women. But there was one thing that hadn't been there earlier. One thing that was not filthy. A man sat with his back to the door in conversation with one of the women. He was wearing a clean robe from the Palace. A frightening one that indicated he was a Eunuch of Standing.

Before Gogoro Shen turned around—and he would in just a few short heartbeats—Gett had to decide what to do. He could back out quietly, maybe even before Gogoro turned around, even though the old crone's head was already rising and seeing Gett.

He could stand and wait. It was coming. The crone was looking at him now and it was just one flick, two flicks of the eye before Gogoro would notice it.

Or, a third choice. The only one, really. Because Gogoro already knew he was here, had come precisely and only because Gett was here.

"Head of Harem Gogoro Shen," said Gett.

Gogoro turned around. Saw Gett. No reaction. Just silence for a moment. Thinking. Looked at Gett. Looked behind him. Looked at the children. Finally:

"Investigator Gett."

"It is an honor to meet you here."

"You are here to visit the children?" Gogoro asked.

"No."

"Of course. Please sit down, Investigator Gett."

"Thank you."

THE EUNUCH

Gett sat on a small cushion. The children played just a few arm-spans from them, jumping and squealing. Gogoro watched them for a while.

"How is the investigation going?"

"It is confusing."

"I expect that is normal."

"It is up to a point. This is more so than usual."

"And it has brought you here."

"Yes. We had you followed, of course."

"Of course."

"This is not a formality. Everyone is a suspect."

"As it should be."

"This was the only odd thing about your schedule."

"Is it odd?"

Gett thought about this. "Yes, it is."

"Why?"

"Most everything else you do is either related to your home, to the Palace or to the harem. This is the only exception."

"So you are here to see what this is all about?"

"Yes."

"That makes sense."

"So what is it?"

"First, before we talk, look around you, what do you see? Don't tell me, but instead sense it."

Gett looked out at the room to see what Gogoro saw. He saw the filthiness. He saw the old broken women and the children, mostly boys. As he was looking, one of them ran to a corner, pulled out his penis and pissed. One of the old crones yelled something in an ugly dialect. The boy finished, urine rivuletting into the center of the room. He ran away laughing with the great cataclysmic triumph of a four-year-old. Two other boys stomped in it, splashing urine sideways. Gett looked back at Gogoro.

Gogoro stared at the boys. Finally he turned back to Gett.

"Investigator Gett, let me ask you a question. May I?"

"Of course."

"Do you eat when you are sick?"

"Yes."

"Do you enjoy it?"

"No."

"Why?"

"It is hard to taste and smell food when I am sick."

"So you enjoy it less. Correct?"

"Correct."

"Yet you still eat."

"Of course."

"Why?"

"Hunger."

"You are hungry. A compulsion to eat. What is hunger, can you describe it for me?"

Get thought about this. Difficult to describe except as a tautology. "You are right, it is a compulsion."

"So you eat."

"I do."

"But you taste nothing."

"I taste less."

"Yes, less. Exactly, the ability to sense to food, the ability to enjoy it and receive pleasure from it has been taken from you and yet, and yet, you still eat. You are compelled to by your body."

Gett waited. Gogoro was silent for a moment. The long folds of skin hanging off his face. He lifted his cup of medicine. Drank again. Winced. One of the young boys blundered through between them.

"Another question, Investigator Gett."

"Of course."

THE EUNUCH

"There are many scholars in the Palace who come from very small places."

"That is true."

"From far south, even."

"True."

"Do you know that in some places they even eat brown rice?"

"I do."

"Do you eat it?"

"I do not."

"Why?"

"I don't like it."

"Yes, you don't like it but the thing is, people develop a taste for it. These southerners have grown up eating it. So when they come to the Palace, they still want to eat it. Have you seen this?"

"I have."

"Often they eat it in private. It is a habit they are embarrassed by."

"I have noticed that."

"What did you do?"

"In what sense?"

"When you saw someone eating brown rice, or you knew that someone was, did you make a report about it, that sort of thing?"

"Of course not."

"Did you go to stop him?"

"I did not."

"Why?"

"It has nothing to do with me. There is no law forbidding it. And even if there were, it would not be my mandate to investigate that specific crime."

"Exactly! It is not the kind of thing that concerns the official business of the Palace."

"That is true."

"In fact you probably said to yourself, that is his habit, not mine and who cares. Possibly you didn't even think about it because it was such a small thing. So and so eats brown rice because he is from the south. Someone else drinks fermented milk. Different tastes."

"Yes."

"And what do you think would have happened if you had made a report or talked to him and said stop eating unhusked rice?"

"Nothing."

"Nothing officially or nothing in his heart?"

"Nothing officially."

"But in his heart?"

"He would be resentful."

"The empress or other Palace officials?"

"They would most likely not care."

"Exactly! A pointless exercise. You would have antagonized him and achieved nothing!"

Gett left soon after, and now sat in his workroom. He was genuinely at a loss. Gogoro was the most likely person to have managed the selling of these concubines because he had the most access to the means to do it — he controlled their schedules, could change them at will and so could incentivize the girls to accept it. Gett could, if he wished, take this information to the Imperial Mother. She might authorize torture for Gogoro, she might not. If Gett was sure Gogoro had done it (and sure the Imperial Mother herself wasn't involved) then it was an easy thing.

But Gett wasn't sure. Gogoro could re-order the schedules of concubines if he wished — in fact had probably done so many times. But most of them (maybe all of them) would have been

THE EUNUCH

for legitimate (or at least bureaucratically justifiable) reasons. Nothing about the discreet changes in the records would stand out. The same was true of no-escort passes, even around the time of sex with the Emperor. They were a fact of life, and were documented carefully. There was no way—from the documentation—to prove which ones were dirty.

The bigger problem, the problem that stopped him not only from acting on his hunch, but even more made him *unsure* about Gogoro's involvement was—as Sulo said and Gett knew—*motive*. Candidates for positions like the one Gogoro held were vetted for a long time before they were elevated. They were tested. Baited. Their family histories were investigated. It was a long process. It took years. And so the people who made it into those positions were not so much careful as they were *naturally unmoved* by enticements.

A normal man—if you offer him the right thing—will eventually risk it and take the thing. So over the long grinding years it took to rise in the bureaucracy to these positions, normal men were weeded out. And left, at the end, were those like Gogoro, who *seemed to have no desires*.

And this was the whole problem. Why would a man with no desires risk so much?

Thus the orphanage had stuck out to Gett, an anomaly. Something that might yield a dark, secret, and expensive desire. Instead, a dead end. This kind of sex was less common among eunuchs than people thought, but common enough. Its failure as a motive: *sex with children was cheap*, not something that required the enormous funding provided by pimping Imperial concubines. A dead end.

Gett arrived at the courtyard of Fervent Matriarchy and paused, thinking, as he stood in the twisted shade of the iron trees. Curdeger had promised him an analysis of the poisons, and he might have it by now. But also, Gett had to warn him. Curdeger's mistake in his inspection of the corpse had reached the ears of the Imperial Mother. Reached her *through* Gett. She wasn't incentivized to tell anyone, or, even more importantly, to use it against him. But Curdeger needed to know she knew. And it had to be Gett to tell him.

But Curdeger was gone. Not in his office, not in his morgue. He was somewhere safe. Somewhere he could ride out the next two days. But not somewhere that would, just because he was there, cause suspicion. Curdeger was a careful professional. He would have made the right choice. Gett stood motionless in the cold.

Gett announced himself to the Chinese door boy, hidden behind the dark red door of Curdeger's villa. He heard the boy's padded footsteps move away into the house. After a long moment, the footsteps returned.

"Wait," the boy said in accented Jurchen.

Gett did. Quietly standing in the long alleyway upon which Curdeger's gate opened. The house had been an Imperial gift, and somehow, Curdeger had not lost it when he lost his court position. Inside, Gett knew, he was being watched. It was important for them to determine whether Gett was signaling anyone. They would monitor him for a bit to ascertain if he had an escort (or even more dangerous, if he had been followed).

It took them a while to do that, and also just to see what he would do — people often betray themselves if just given enough time to do so.

Finally, if not satisfied, at least assured that there was no immediate danger, the door creaked open and the tiny Chinese boy beckoned him in, saying, "Come."

Curdeger sat, unsurprisingly, alone in his barren outer room. Curdeger's house was large so, especially as his present position didn't merit it, a danger. Curdeger, always careful, had clearly moved everything of beauty away from his outer hall. He had prepared it to accord with his status: fallen official, on hard times, still living in the big house, but inside everything of value has been sold.

There he sat in a hard ash chair with a clay teapot at his side, sipping from a rough cup, waiting for Gett.

Gett, as he walked toward Curdeger, almost before he had taken two steps, felt something. There was a sense, clinging to Curdeger's body, crackling from his hands to his eyes to his legs, like distant lightening between clouds. Gett glanced at the room again. It was empty except for the two of them.

Curdeger smiled.

"You came home," said Gett.

"Yes."

"Your home is very beautiful."

"It is not what it once was."

"But possibly in the future?"

"Who knows what the future holds. I can only concern myself with the duties of the present."

Gett sat. He sipped the tea Curdeger poured for him, thinking about how to begin. The steam curled around his face in the cold room.

"The present is difficult," Gett finally decided to say.

"Yes."

"With the murder of the girl."

"It is unfortunate."

"And also the many things that have been brought out into the light through this investigation."

Again, there it was, like the miniscule crackling of very dry flint sparking off Curdeger.

Gett, gently, began to edge himself toward the point. "The Imperial Mother, as always, is interested in all of the details that make up events in the Palace," he said.

"It is her intelligence and ability that make her so," said Curdeger.

"Yes. I have reported everything regarding my findings to her."

"I see."

"Because she is naturally interested to know not only the details but also how they were discovered."

"Yes, I see."

"As you say, her intelligence and curiosity lead her to ask many questions about the events surrounding her. We, as her servants, realize that her genius will often suggest solutions that we had not contemplated. Thus when she asks questions of us it is important to give her all of the information we have."

"Of course. Please wait a moment."

Curdeger stood and walked slowly over to a low and scratched drawer in a corner. He pulled out a small piece of paper and a brush and ink. He came back to the table.

Curdeger said, "My department has been working very diligently on this problem."

"Of course."

"I have findings."

"I had hoped you would."

"I apologize that you were not able to find me in the Palace."

"It is immaterial. I have found you now. What has your

THE EUNUCH

department uncovered?"

Curdeger poured out a bit of ink in a scoured stone. There was no water to cut the ink so he poured a spot of tea into it. He brushed out a set of characters on the paper. Then pushed it over to Gett.

Oddly, he had written it out in Jurchen; the phonetic equivalent of the Chinese herbs.

Curdeger said, "This is the poison that was used to kill the girl. We were lucky. It was the third we tested for. It is also luckily rare and only sold in three shops in the Capital."

On a second piece of paper he brushed three names.

Again, he wrote in the awkward, official Jurchen. Which was odd, because the shop names were certainly written in Chinese, a language Curdeger could of course write.

"These are the shops that sell it. They are in the Chinese quarter."

"Thank you, Analyst Curdeger. This is invaluable."

"It is my job."

"I will immediately contact these shops."

"Yes."

Gett sipped his tea and considered now how to edge his way into the warning he had come to deliver. But he hesitated: Curdeger was afraid and he had done this odd thing, writing Chinese terms in Jurchen.

And then, like a soft lapping ripple on the side of a boat, Gett understood what had happened.

Gett sipped his tea again to give himself a moment. "I apologize for interrupting your important work in your home," he said. "I must allow you to return to it."

"No, please stay."

"Unfortunately I cannot."

"I will see you to the door."

Gett stood. Curdeger pulled his own heavy body up out of the creaking, small chair and they walked to the door of Curdeger's anteroom, across the bare, dark carpet-less stone floor.

"I will visit with the results of our investigation into these shops."

"I am at the service of the Chief Investigator."

Gett stepped into Curdeger's untended garden. He was let out the door by the Chinese boy and was again on the street.

Gett, as his palanquin moved gently through the bustle of the city, considered what had just occurred.

Someone was there. Someone had come to see Curdeger. Someone who had been hidden. Who? From the Imperial Mother? Regardless, the question would now arise: Why had Gett been there? Why had he not waited for Curdeger's return to the Palace? What relationship, beyond that of a Chief Investigator and a Crime Scene Investigator, did they have?

If it were an agent of the Imperial Mother, even the taste of a lie was enough to bring death, enough that Gett would be subtly pulled under when the opportunity presented itself. If he told her the truth, she would ask, Why? Why was Gett crawling quietly about and out of her gaze, to warn another that her eyes were on him?

Curdeger had warned him someone was there, in a code, the odd writing.

It was now late morning. The sun had cleared the high eaves of the houses that led up to the large square that fronted the Palace and so while the ground was cold and gray, the bit of sun that flickered across Gett's face as he walked was welcome, and a bit warmer than the surrounding air. A small pleasure as he considered his problem. He paused a moment in a bright patch

THE EUNUCH

and surveyed the Palace from just off the main square.

The guard had been quadrupled. Hard, short men in full armor, spears bristling, like malevolent red porcupines, squatting at the main entrance. A cavalry patrol of three rode past the gate every two minutes. Gett calculated, if the entire perimeter was patrolled at this level, that an entire battalion had been deployed. It was a real defense patrol; short swords only. No banners. Not for ceremony or intimidation; for killing.

Most of the vendors who normally operated at the edge of the square had closed up. There were few customers and to stay meant to be suspected. The city could sense the movements in the Palace, knew bad things were coming. So walking up to this point had been odd—the complexity of the city had sheared itself away, like dirt shaken from roots until all that was left at their tips was the barren, rough skin of the Palace.

Gett pulled up his robes and pushed out into the wind of the square, his mind still occupied with the question of how to warn Curdeger. A large red ant moving across wide, gray precisely laid-out stones.

Halfway to the gate, Gett's mind twittered, like a lone cicada. He continued forward but, like the scattered responses that follow that first buzz, danger began to tick quietly in his mind.

Seconds later, the gate guard began to deploy, moving out silently to quick, sharp single commands, uncoiling into a fully deployed battle array, spears outwards, first rank down on one knee second braced, standing.

Gett's eyes followed the gaze of the spearmen out to the main avenue that led to the Palace.

A procession of Imperial Examination palanquins, bobbing and weaving, was slowly moving its way up the cleared avenue toward the square. The scholars' palanquins were white, each carried by four Chinese; short but muscled. They had a heavy escort of swordsmen to hold back the usual, but on this day non-existent, crowd.

Gett looked up at the Palace wall. Along this stretch, and visible from the square, were twelve guards. That meant probably another twenty out of sight and professional spotters every few horse lengths. So probably about thirty people who could see him.

His existence here was not unsanctioned. But two things made it dangerous. The first was simply the fact itself. Exposed, he would have to stand there for a least a half an hour before the formalities of the entrance of the Examination testees were concluded. Because he was the only one there, other than the guards and the procession of scholars, his presence would be noted in precise detail—to omit anything would be to risk a fuller report by other watchers.

He would not be allowed admittance before the palanquins. But if he were to attempt it, that would be noted as a breach of protocol. He couldn't back out of the square because that too would be noted and the question would arise, why had he left? An inquiry would be made.

Such things, once begun, were unstoppable.

And so these small events were dangerous, especially now.

Gett had no choice but to stand, unmoving and exposed, like a cold-stunned insect, in the middle of the square. Even that would generate a report. Questions would be asked about his intentions, why he had chosen to observe the entrance of the scholars at such close proximity. The best, and it was far from good, that he could do was to meticulously follow protocol. That at least would merit a non-mention in the record.

The head palanquin held the top scorer from the *Provincial* Examination. He led the procession into the Palace for the *Imperial* Examinations. Red tasseling meant he was Chinese.

THE EUNUCH

The fringe meant that he came from a peasant family, so two marks against—inferior origin and inferior race. But this was the Provincial *Jinshi* so almost a full kowtow, only holding back in reference to the occupant's racial inferiority.

The last thing Gett saw though as his head descended toward the stone was the lead scholar turning his head, his robe slipping off his neck just a fraction, revealing the odd dark birthmark on his neck. The same birthmark Gett had watched shifting in the firelight of the Throne Room as this scholar stood alone in the carnage. As his head reached the stones, Gett wondered if there was a lesson here. The scholar had risked, he had survived. Had the Emperor forgotten him? Forgotten the humiliation? Gett tucked it away in his mind, a question not about life but about the young boy who sat on the throne. At least it answered one question though. Gett now knew where the arrogance came from. The Provincial Jinshi was always in at least the top five scorers on the Imperial Examination. Destined for power. And they always knew it. Gett averted his eyes. His head a finger's breadth from the cold stone, he watched the shadow of the palanquin pass over him. The second approached. Number two from the Provincial Examinations. Tasseling marked this one as Jurchen, from a bannered tribe. So even though this was the second-place holder, protocol required a full kowtow. Gett pulled himself back up and then prostrated himself, knocking his forehead against the stone of the ground.

The first palanquin slowly moved forward. The skin on Gett's forehead began to freeze. The dark shadow of the second passed over him. He carefully lifted his eyes to assess the remaining eight.

They would be much simpler, a mix of Chinese and Jurchen but their status as scholar testees, taking the test tomorrow, meant racial origin took precedence; a half kowtow for the Jurchens and a simple kneel for the Chinese.

This Gett, his knees now very cold, did.

The procession passed, finally, into the gates. Gett waited the mandated duration then carefully stood up, joints cracking, knees stiff and frozen.

He walked slowly to the gate and signed in.

As Gett walked through the long entry passage, red painted walls echoing his footsteps, he thought about the procession. All scholars; testees of the Imperial Examination. When his race had first occupied this region, close to a hundred thousand Chinese sat for the examination every three years. In the chaos of the subjugation, the tests had been suspended, but recently, because they were useful, the practice had been resumed. Now, less than a decade later, the numbers were pushing above the fifty thousand mark again.

So these young men were the distillation of that. Six months of testing, three enormous culls, had brought them to this point, one out of every ten thousand who had taken the test. It was an extraordinary achievement. And having worked alongside many of those who had taken the tests and gotten here, into the Palace, Gett knew that, whatever flaws they had, they were all deeply and frighteningly intelligent.

And what Gett was thinking about as he walked down that long passageway was why this fact nagged at him, like a tiny, quiet insect scratching at the nub of his mind.

十七

GETT, NOT WANTING to bring attention to his presence in the Palace, was trying to dress in the dark. He could tell by feel that he had chosen the proper robe — the ceremonial scarlet phoenix — and he had managed to get one thin arm into a sleeve. But now he was hunting about for the other, which thus far, he had not found.

Finally he had to open his door. A thin, bright line of cold afternoon sun cut in. The sleeve was exactly where it should have been, and perplexingly, exactly where he had been hunting for it.

He slipped on the robe, stepped out into the corridor and locked the door to his workroom.

There was a limit now to how inconspicuous he could be. The robes made him taller, more powerful, more radiant, stronger — symbolically, the perfect embodiment of the perfect servant of a perfect Emperor. They were not comfortable. But they were frightening.

The shop was dark, a cluttered rectangle about the size of a man lying down. A gray counter divided it in half. Behind it, standing in the shadows, was the thin, pale herbalist. His hands, stained as were most of those who prepared medicines for a living, rested on the counter. He didn't move when Gett stepped into the shadowy interior. He persevered in his immobility as Gett approached the counter.

"Good afternoon," said Gett.

"Good afternoon, Honorable Eunuch."

"You are the owner of the shop?"

"Yes. I am the full owner." His voice was professionally quiet, years of particulate fumes having scraped away its original timber, reducing it to the herbalist's rustling whisper.

"I am Enchenkei Gett. Eunuch of Standing. Chief Investigator for the Palace."

"It is always an honor to serve a member of the Inner Court."

"It is an honor to serve there. I would like to ask you a few questions."

"I hope I will be able to answer them."

Gett pulled out the piece of paper on which Curdeger had written the name of the poison. He watched the shop owner's expression as he handed it to him. It did not change. But Gett had discovered that many of the men who ran these shops were palsied from the repeated handling of their medicines over long periods of time, and so often what seemed to be calm was, for them, only an inability of their faces to react. The thin, dry owner studied the name of the chemical.

"Do you know it?" asked Gett.

"I do."

"What is it?"

"It is a poison."

"Why?"

"Why what?" asked the shop owner.

"Why is it poisonous?"

The dry old shop owner nodded. He paused to think about Gett's question, clearly one of those careful men for whom exactitude was a virtue and slow deliberateness it's natural expression.

"It is poisonous because once it has been ingested, it settles in

THE EUNUCH

the stomach. Slowly the heat of the stomach changes it from its phoenix essence to its dragon essence. If this dragon essence is in the presence of the earth and water elements it then becomes a poison."

"How long does it take?"

"How long does specifically what take?"

"Death."

"It is very slow acting and variable."

"Give me an estimate."

"A long hour."

"And how long before the person who ingested it will begin to feel its effects?"

"Every person is different."

"Roughly."

"Three quarters of that."

"Why do you know this?"

"It is what I do."

"You mean you sell this poison?"

"I do not."

"But you know about it. How it works."

"In my training we learned how to prepare it."

Gett and the dry old man stood together at the counter and didn't speak. Finally Gett said, "Often, when a representative of the Palace arrives in a place to ask questions there is a sense that one is standing next to a sleeping dragon, one that could inadvertently roll over, in its sleep as it were, and crush a person."

The old man nodded.

Gett continued, "That dragon, today, is not asleep. So such an inadvertency would not occur. But the inner court wishes to find a person who purchased this medicine. Meaning that dragon is interested, has noticed you and will remember your answers. I, as its representative, could wish it were some other way. But it is not."

The dry old man pondered this for a moment.

"I did not sell it. But I suspect I know who did. I am sure there is a shop named 'The Gold and the Fire Expert Medicinal Preparations' on your list, yes?"

Gett did not answer.

The old man continued, "Undoubtedly the medicine was purchased there."

"Why?" asked Gett.

"Because that is a rare poison and it is always purchased there."

"How do you know?"

"It is a small community that buys and sells these things."

"Yes, but in such a small community how do you hear these things—'Oh, so and so has begun to sell a deadly poison.' that sort of thing?"

"No, it is not like that."

"Then what is it like?"

"The preparation of a poison like that is complex. It has fifty-eight discreet ingredients and another twenty that are required as reacting companions in its making. When I go to purchase stock, I see what is low and high and what is not available. I know who has been there before me. Over time it becomes clear who is buying what and so making what."

He looked at the paper again.

"Yes, definitely, it is the woman who runs that shop who sold this."

The woman, proprietress of the shop, sat in the back. The shop, and more so she herself, were brightly lit.

"Could I ask you a few questions?" asked Gett.

THE EUNUCH

"About the past you mean?"
Gett thought about this. "Yes, about the past."
"I thought so. People always recognize me."
Gett paused again.
"Recognize you as what?"
"What?"
"What do people recognize you as?"
"Me."
"Recognize you as you?"
"Yes, of course."
Gett paused for a moment to think about that.
"Who are you?"
"Ha ha ha. It's all right. I'm Lan Xiaoping." She waited for his reaction. Gett had found though that, during an interrogation, when one reached a point like this, of confusion, it was best to say nothing. The fact of the interrogation itself and the fear generated by his uniform, usually prompted the speaker to explain.
"*The* Lan Xiaoping. The dancer from the Palace."
"Now?"
"No, in the past."
"I see."
"Of course, I'm sure you've seen me. That's why you recognized me."
Gett looked more carefully at her. She was at least thirty-five years old, so while not actually old, certainly the last time she danced at the Palace was at least fifteen years ago.
"That's very interesting. I'm sure I have never heard of you, but as I am a Eunuch, I am often not invited to the dancing events of the Palace."
"Oh, of course! I'm so sorry!"
"There is no way you could have known." Except, of course, for his Eunuch's robe, which for any one who had spent any time

in the Palace, marked him, unquestionably as one. "I would like to ask you a few questions."

"Of course! All of my relations with the Palace are excellent!"

"Wonderful," said Gett. He pulled out the piece of paper. "Do you sell this?"

"What is it?"

"You don't recognize it?"

"Oh, there are so many chemicals. To know each one is not so important. It's more important to cultivate business relationships like I do. I have excellent relationships with all of the Palace suppliers. We're discussing a relationship in which I would supply all of the Palace's chemical needs."

"That sounds very lucrative. Do you think there is any way you could check if you sell this chemical, and if you sold any in the last few days?"

"Well, I just don't know. I don't recognize it."

"You could, for example, check your records."

"Oh! Of course! We dancers and actresses, we start out as geniuses, but we're surrounded by so many fools that we become foolish too, ha ha."

She pulled out a sheet on which was recorded recent sales. She squinted as she went through it, clearly blurry visioned of the near type.

"No, I didn't sell any of that."

"You are always at the counter?"

"Yes, I can't trust anyone else to do things right."

"Of course. But possibly when you are arranging your external business activities?"

"Then, yes, of course. But in the last few months I have taken a break from that."

"I see."

Gett paused, thinking about how to continue. He found this

women, and those like her, difficult to question. Most people have something to hide. Usually it is related to the case in question. Often it is unrelated but, still, it is one specific thing. But people like this, where to begin?

"This is a poison," said Gett.

Gett watched her. It was as if he could see her mind chew this piece of information, swallow and digest it, then watch the nutritious particles of her answer float up into her consciousness.

"Oh yes, of course. Now I remember! We who sell chemicals are a very tight-knit, mutually supporting network of friends in this city."

"Of course," said Gett.

"We have to be," she said.

"Yes."

"But I feel, because of my excellent relations and long history with the Palace, that I should mention something."

"Of course."

"And when they are as close as mine are, with such large business arrangements pending, I feel responsible."

Gett waited.

"Zhang Xuwen of the 'Gold and Water Balance Shop'. It is on your list?"

"I cannot say."

"I'm sure it is. He is such a successful, clever man. Very calm, never excited. And he speaks so politely, always quietly, almost whispering."

"And?"

"He is very close to me. I know he sells this. I tell you because I know he would not want to be party unwittingly to anything in the Palace. Possibly he does not understand as well as I do, because he does not have the kind of high-level contacts that I do."

"That is very moral of you."

"Yes! I know! That is really a defining characteristic of who I am. It is what keeps me humble, which is hard to be when you are one of the most famous dancers in the Palace!"

Gett thought for a moment about what to do next. Continuing to question her would probably be useless; he could bring them both in later if he really had to.

A quiet businessman who clearly had been doing this for a long time, and a newcomer, somebody's ex-mistress probably, this shop given to her in a fit of absentminded lust. Now she was hanging on desperately. Along came an opportunity. Gett had his money on the businessman.

Gett checked his list. One more shop.

He had an enormous forehead. And, unusual for a Chinese especially as he was not excessively old, possibly tipping into late middle age, he was losing his hair in the manner of the Huihui. To honor their god and his prophet he had a long, meticulously groomed beard. He watched as Gett entered his shop, the last on the list. He had a bright-eyed, smiling stare.

"Good afternoon," said Gett.

"Allah willing yes," said the bearded shop owner brightly.

"I have a few questions I'd like to ask you."

"Alright," said the shop owner, eyes still fixed on Gett.

"This mixture, do you know it?" Gett said as he slipped Curdeger's paper on to the counter.

The shop owner looked at it, put it down.

"I sell that."

"Really?"

"It's a poison, you know."

"Yes. I know that," said Gett.

"People who eat it die in agony and it takes a long time."
"Have you sold any recently?"
"Yep."
"When?"
"A few days ago."
"Do you remember to whom?"
"I do."
"To whom then?"

The bright-eyed shop owner smiled. He said, "You know that just down the street is the brothel quarter. The girls who work there, most of them don't like it. But you know, they made the choice. They are girls who can *accept fucking for money*. Somebody comes to them and says, 'Hey, I want to fuck you!' and they say 'Alright! That'll be five coins!' And then they get the money and go fuck. Somebody else comes comes by later. And the hooker, her pussy is still sore and this new guy he says, 'I want to fuck you in your butt and cum in your ass and watch it leak out.' and the hooker, if she's a professional, says, 'Alright! But that'll cost extra! And I want to be paid first. And see, everybody *expects to pay*. Nobody goes to a hooker and says, 'Hey, let me fuck you up the ass for free'."

"How much do you want?"
"Fifty coins."
"That's a lot."
"Your boss can afford it."
"You accept an Imperial guarantee?"
"Of course."
"Why? You trust it? Trust that you won't be cheated?"
"I make poisons."

Gett nodded.

"Write it out and chop it," said the bearded owner.

Gett did.

The shop owner, as soon as this was completed, yelled out to the back of his store, "Xiao Liu! Bring me the records from four days ago."

A minute later, a rumpled but pretty thirteen-year-old girl brought out a messy ledger. The owner looked through it, eyes twinkling.

"Here it is. He bought it on the tenth day of the month. Then he went to the guesthouse around the corner."

"How do you know that?"

"It's in the ledger."

"That he went to a guest house?"

"No, just what he bought."

"Then how do you know where he went?"

"I followed him."

"Why?"

"He wasn't from the Palace."

"So?"

"It meant that somebody from the Palace would come looking for him eventually. I'm careful with the Palace."

"Which guesthouse?"

"Eternal Spring Xu."

"Next to the South City Gate?"

"Yeah!"

Gett thought about this.

"Describe him."

The owner smiled. He ruffled through the ledger for a moment then found a piece of paper and pulled it out.

"I wrote it down so I wouldn't forget anything." He studied what he'd written for a minute. "He was short and black. Chinese. He was dressed in bad taste and his clothes were cheap. He was obviously not cultured like you and me. He stuttered and he had a Western Desert accent. He was nervous and he counted out the money to buy the poison really carefully. He is not the guy you are looking for."

"You wrote that down?"

"Yes."

"I mean the last bit, about him not being the guy you are looking for?"

"Yes."

"Why?"

"Because he isn't."

"No, I mean how did you know?"

"That he wasn't the guy who you would be looking for?"

"Yes."

"He's just some loser."

"Why?"

"He's just some guy. Hired by the guy who really used the poison."

Gett thought about that for a moment.

"You can tell that?"

"Yep."

"How?"

"Real clients come in, they know what they want, don't want to be seen, come at night. These other guys come during the day. They don't know what the fuck they're doing. They're obviously spending somebody else's money because it's always in a little separate bundle somewhere. Your guy is probably dead already."

Gett considered this.

"I'll be back with more questions."

"Of course. But it won't be free."

"Of course."

Gett pulled up his robe to walk out and noticed the pretty thirteen year old gathering up the records to take back into the rear of the shop.

"Your daughter?" Gett asked

The shop owner stroked his long beard and, showing all his teeth, smiled brightly.

"Nope."

As Gett stepped out of the shop, stepped into his palanquin and he and his guards turned left, towards the guesthouse. It had begun to snow—not hard—but the gentle sleepy kind that deadens all sound and converts everything upon which it falls into smooth white shapelessness. Thus, it was as if the complexity of the world had begun to disappear around Gett.

Gett thought of himself for a moment, as if he could see from far above, looking down through the silent, gently falling snow, a tiny red point, like a drop of blood, rolling slowly across a wide expanse of nothingness.

As if the complexity beneath it did not exist.

THE GUESTHOUSE would be unfruitful. There were maids, food carriers, other travelers, tiny retiring, wall-clingers who paid attention to earn a living. And so, whoever this person was, he wouldn't have accepted his poison in such a place, so full of eyes. Anything of interest—recruitment of this man, where, when, money, purchasing arrangements, handoff of the poison—all happened elsewhere. Where though?

The guesthouse was next to the City Gate, the entrance letting out right into the main thoroughfare. This purchaser of the poison must have entered through it. Probably there, in fact, as he emerged from it like a wind-blown seed from a flower, had been spotted and assessed. Exactly right to serve as a sacrificial cut out. So, a drifter, not too rundown, unattached, in need of money. He had been followed. Approached. Where? Not here. Somewhere quiet. Not, probably, knowable. He had purchased the poison. Handed it over, again, somewhere not probably re-constructable. Then, flush, having had an unexpectedly fruitful encounter in the city, he had left, probably as part of the agreement he had entered into. Then, somewhere outside the city, killed.

The gate.

Gett's bearers skirted the slush in the deep depression at its center of the street and turned onto the Avenue of Glimmering Brilliance that led to the Main Gate of the city.

And suddenly he sensed someone. He turned his head.

There, coming up on his right, blue eyes locked on his palanquin, strange angular features twisted into a smile, was Chief of Enforcement Sulo.

"Gett."

"Enforcer Sulo."

Out of respect, Gett stepped down from his palanquin.

"Lets walk," said Sulo.

"Alright."

"Yeah. Where you going?"

Sulo's guards hung behind, as did Gett's minders. The two of them walked through the crowd surrounded by an odd bubble as people noticed and avoided them nervously.

"The Gate," answered Gett.

"Which gate?"

"Of the city."

"Main Gate?"

"Yes."

"Why?"

"Someone checked into an inn near it. What he did in the inn is less important than what he did before and after."

"What do you think he did after?"

"Ran."

"So you think he is dead?"

"Yes. But I want to make sure."

Sulo, in his aggressive way, thought about what to ask next. Gett preempted him. "May I ask you a question?"

"Ha. What question?"

"Why are you here?"

"Here in the city?" asked Sulo.

"No, here with me right now."

"I'm Chief of Enforcement Bureau. I need to know where your investigation is. I need to know when to do the arrest."

THE EUNUCH

"Not for a while."

"Yes," said Sulo. "Maybe."

Gett said, "You know otherwise?"

"No. You tell me now what you know."

"Here?"

"Here not so many stupid cunts."

Gett considered as they walked slowly through the snow. Sulo had had him tailed. Then had shown up himself. Anything he could want to know he would know soon. It meant he wanted to know now.

Gett asked, "What specifically do you want to know?"

"Who kill the girl?"

"I don't know."

"Why she killed?"

"I don't know."

"But you're a smart guy, always have a theory."

"Yes," said Gett.

"Say it."

"I think someone who knew the girl well, before she became a concubine, killed her in a way to humiliate the Emperor."

"Can't humiliate the Emperor."

"Right."

"He is unhumiliatable."

"True."

"So?"

"If it was an affair, and it probably was, there'll be a record of it, and him, or her."

"Her?"

"It happens."

"Ha. Yeah."

Sulo, uncharacteristically, became silent. And oddly they walked together like that for a few moments. The two strangely tall men, gently skirting thin lakes of slush and sparkling mud. Alone together and oddly comradely because of their shared height in a rarefied solidarity above the heads of others, as if, on the busy street, they had their heads just above very cold turbid water. Finally Sulo spoke.

"Yes, I see. You go back to your investigation. I wait for your arrest order."

"Of course. Thank you for your interest, Chief of Enforcement Sulo."

"No thanks. My job."

And with that, Sulo peeled away and his escort, which had been hanging back, immediately surrounded him, only his black head visible, floating away in the disturbed waters of the crowd.

Gett was alone again in the snow. He knew now. Sulo's visit a confirmation. His arrest had been ordered. Sulo was holding it, delaying the moment as long as possible. If he derived some benefit, he might stretch it. But there was a limit. A day. Hours maybe.

Gett approached the Gate, always impressive, designed to be so. It was about the height of three men. The wall in which it was set, about double that. Close to fifteen hundred people flowed through each day, mostly day workers and vendors.

What struck Gett each time he had business here was not that the gate was large, instead that it was small. The dark red wall of the city divided the Capital from the world; a thick demarcation of the fetid, roiling center and the vastness outside. This minuscule pinprick was the only connection between the two. And the embroidery around that pinprick was a manifestation of this importance. The guards, the secrecy, the magnificence, the upkeep. A hole, Gett thought, but like many in this case, very restricted.

THE EUNUCH

The Gate Guard had been strengthened to almost triple its normal complement. And they were examining people with much more care than usual. An unlucky Chinese merchant was pulled aside as Gett approached. As they beat the merchant, Gett was admitted, obviously a Palace official, and he was escorted to the office of the Keeper of the Gate, deep within the wall itself. Within minutes, Gett was in front of a small man, standing behind a small desk. The disparity in their heights was so great that Gett actually had to bend down slightly to hear him as he talked softly.

The Keeper of the Gate said, "We are always honored to have a servant of the Emperor here in our district."

"We are all servants of the Emperor."

"True, but the light shines more brightly on some of us because of our proximity to the fire."

"It is my honor to be here in the office that manages the flow of the Emperor's many loving subjects into this city," said Gett.

"It is nothing, a small post."

"I am engaged in an investigation."

"I have heard that an investigation is in progress."

"Yes, and it has led me here."

"Here?"

"Yes."

"How has it led you here?"

"I wish that I could tell you more but I cannot."

"Of course."

"I need to know if any bodies have been found in the last five days."

"You are from the Palace? I mean, that is where your offices are located, correct?"

"Yes."

"Possibly you could inspect our gate and report back to the Palace on our management?"

"Now?"

"You are here, it is convenient."

"It is possible but it is not convenient," said Gett.

"It would be a useful thing to do. Each of us has a duty."

"I would like to look through your records and discuss your recollections of the last few days."

"Of course, possibly a walk, then we talk?"

This was impressively, unbelievably stubborn. Gett was an investigator from the Palace. A thing to be feared. Yet, this challenge.

"If that is what you need to push these memories to the front of your mind, then I am not against that," said Gett.

The gatekeeper came out from behind the desk. Very short in that placid, compact way that many short but competent men are. The gatekeeper guided Gett out of his office set in the honeycombed city wall and down a long, dark cold corridor to a door that let out, to Gett's momentary surprise, right into the bustle of the gate's wide tunnel passageway itself.

The width of the passageway was about that of two men lying across it head to feet. It was crowded. People trudging past Gett and the Gatekeeper as they stood there for a moment watching this human river flow through this bottleneck. Gett counted. There were people flowing *in* through the gate, But a much greater number *out*. Out in a way that said—to someone who knew how to spot it—that they expected to be away for a while. No bags, but many clothes, bulging pockets—a shuffling unobtrusive exit. Not an exodus. But not a trickle either. They had that tension about them that Gett had seen in many people before—one foot in front of the other, muscles clenched until they stepped over each threshold they had constructed in their minds. Here the gate. Then an outpost. Running.

"We screen them," said the Gatekeeper, "take for example

this man."

"The one leaving?"

"No, the one coming in."

Gett pulled his attention away from this silent frightened flight. The Gatekeeper indicated a short dark man shuffling along in the large crowd.

"He is a beggar's pimp. He runs a ring of about two hundred and fifty beggars in the Capital. He takes half their earnings and arranges for his beggars to be situated in the most valuable begging spots in the city and to not be molested by the magistrates. We would like to restrict his entry into the city."

He paused for a minute.

"And there is a recruiter."

Gett looked and saw a thin, tall Jurchen pulling Chinese peasant girls aside. The man, who was handsome, walked up to a young girl amidst the flow. He was, Gett could tell even from this far away, polite and respectful, with the grace that comes from a household with money and the culture it buys. The Chinese girl was at first nervous, but she finally nodded and smiled after he had whispered in her ear.

"He is a recruiter for our brothel," said the gatekeeper.

"Your brothel?"

"Yes, we have a brothel on site. We have the best girls because as keepers of the gate we have access to them before anyone else. They are housed in dormitories here and much prized by clients."

"Why?"

"As I said, because they are the most beautiful. We have first access and so of course choose the highest quality girls."

"I see."

"But more importantly, the energy flow of the gate has been calculated and their dormitory has been situated at a nodal point of the in-flow. You do know this gate is in a direct line with the

Emperor's mate-producing room? For our Chinese customers, that energy concentration in the girls is even more important than their beauty."

Gett listened surprised. All of this was not illegal, that was the wrong word. But it was activity that fell outside the rights and responsibilities of the gatekeeper of the main gate of the city. It was odd in the extreme that he would tell Gett all this.

Gett asked, "And you organize this?"

"I do not. It is not part of my job."

"But you allow it to occur."

"Yes. I allow it to occur."

"Why?"

The gatekeeper paused, "Why does anyone let anything occur?"

So, a righteous survivor. Offended but powerless. Gett arrived, an opportunity arrived. So, at least Gett now knew the trade.

Gett said, "This is all very interesting."

"Yes."

"And impressive."

"Yes."

"There will be people in the Palace interested in it."

"Really?"

"Yes."

"As I had hoped."

They watched the ebb and flow of travelers though the gate for a bit.

Gett finally said, "So, the records."

"I now remember that four bodies were found over the last three days. They have been buried but can be easily exhumed if you need to identify them."

THE EUNUCH

Gett travelled through the freezing streets, heading back to the poisoner's shop. He considered whether the poisoner would ask for money to identify the body. Probably. Gett thought about why this didn't bother him. He decided it was the fundamental honesty of it—unfairness grated on people, but meticulous evenhandedness albeit infused with evil and greed, was less distasteful. A lesson, Gett decided.

The street was cold. The wind, a hand drawing a chilled finger across his face, then picking up, digging down and scraping along his bones.

He stepped from the hard brittle glare of the snow-swept street into the darkness of the poisoner's shop. The poisoner, bald, bright eyes watching Gett, was still there, in exactly the same position in which Gett had left him and was still smiling.

"Hello," said Gett.

"Welcome back!"

"Yes, thank you."

"What can I do for you?"

"I need you to identify a body."

"Of course!"

"I need you to do it now."

"No problem. It won't be free though."

"I could make you do it."

"That's true, you could!"

He knew Gett, in the end, in the interests of convenience, under time pressure, would not.

"Where did you find him?" asked the poisoner.

"Near the Gate."

"Not at the inn?"

"No."

"Did you go there?"

"No."

"Why?"

"I didn't think I would learn anything."

"I guess that's why you're the detective. Pretty clever. I wouldn't have thought of that!"

"I have arranged for you to be met at the Gate. They will take you to look at the bodies. Come to my office when you have finished."

It began to snow again as Gett returned to the Palace. Not hard, but enough so that it caught on his eyelashes and lips in the way a new snow does, gently grabbing you.

The whole thing was confusing.

In that softly falling cocoon Gett thought about what he knew. The girls were being pimped. What was the payment? Unknown. But something significant. The harem managers, logistically, had to be involved. Gogoro was the obvious person but you didn't reach a position like that without having been tested. The risk was huge. Financially it would be a way to get very rich, but what could you spend the money on and not be noticed? Nothing really. Especially for people who were watched like Palace officials were. Gogoro visited his orphanage. He gave them money but it wasn't the sort of money that you would get from pimping Imperial Concubines, just petty stuff and it didn't seem to be a front for anything. Other than probably sex. Maybe Gogoro just liked kids.

And then it hit him.

十九

THE SUN WAS setting. It's heat dissipating quickly. Gett could feel the cold unfurling itself around him, freeing itself as its jailer slipped below the horizon.

Gett's palanquin twitched back down the narrow streets. The night would be complex. He had only a short time. He arrived at the poisoner's shop just as the sun finally set. Its light lifted off the ground, the long hard shadows of just seconds previous, evaporated into the muted grayness of dirty ice.

He stepped inside. The bearded and bald poisoner with the bright eyes sat smiling.

"Who sold the Harem Eunuch Gogoro Shen his medicine?" asked Gett.

"What did he do?"

"Who sold him his medicine?"

"Again, you will pay me?"

"Of course."

"In writing please."

Gett put it in writing.

"I sold him one of the ingredients."

"One of the ingredients?"

"It is a complex medicine. And very expensive."

"What does it do?"

"We have these medicines, they are based on ancient recipes and the old recipes say they do a thing."

"What does this one do?"

"You're here on official Imperial business. You're not a customer. So I can't say it does a thing. That's ancient people saying it. You see?"

"Show me the recipe."

"Of course."

He disappeared and a few minutes later came back with an old scroll. He unrolled it for Gett. A long list of ingredients. Text about dosage. And finally, the usage for which the medicine existed, short and concise.

"To eunuchs," asked Gett.

"Yep."

"And old men and people with injuries, that kind of thing?"

"The people who designed the medicine thought so!"

"Just function or also re-growing structures?"

"The recipe isn't clear about that. I don't know."

"Does it work?"

"I can't say it does or it doesn't. People smarter than me thought it did. If they thought it did, then it probably does."

"But in the selling of it, what have been the results?"

"He was the first person to buy it. The recipe was hard to find, he gave it to me, from really old documents! And the ingredients are expensive!"

"How much?"

"For the whole medicine, including preparation fees?"

"Yes."

"Fifty thousand cash."

Gett was surprised. Enough to feed four villages for a year.

"That's for how much medicine?"

"One dose."

"And one dose should be taken how often?"

"Once every three days."

THE EUNUCH

"Fifty thousand cash every three days?"
"Yes."

Gett stood there for a long moment staring at the small piece of paper. On it was written:

Restores the generative capacity in those who have lost it.

Gogoro wanted to have a fucking kid.

Gett considered what he could achieve with an interrogation of Head of Harem Eunuch Gogoro Shen. By the nature of the job (and so probably by Gogoro's because he had been attracted to and thrived in it) it was a job that gave a discreet man great power. The harem eunuch had at his disposal 1) women whose fate he controlled when they were low-level concubines and his decisions set their futures. 2) From them, he had access to the pillow talk of the Emperor; collected rigorously and carefully sifted, it provided the thin gold flakes of advance warning. 3) In the same way, by proxy, he had the Emperor's ear.

So, powerful. For Gett to slide in with a second interrogation was dangerous. If Gogoro were involved somehow in Diao Ju's death, then Gett's visit, and especially the questions he was asking, would alarm him. His attention would shift. Gett would be a target. If he was unassociated with the murder he would see it (rightly because that is how it would be seen by others) as an affront during a moment of temporary weakness. A reprisal would be necessary. So, same result.

Gett sat in his office for a bit trying to come up with a solution to this problem. Eventually he decided he had one.

Gett felt his knees freezing into the black stone floor. The twin dragon columns spiraled up into the darkness above him. The Imperial Mother sat unmoving behind her silk curtain. She let him wait for a long time.

"Speak," she said.

"I believe you should question him."

"Why?"

"I cannot."

"Why?"

"It is too dangerous."

"For you?"

"For both of us."

"Everything I do myself is more dangerous for me. This is why you exist."

"Not this."

She paused for a long time thinking about this. Not about her rights, but about the dangers.

"Explain," said the Imperial Mother.

"Gogoro has great resources. He is Head of the Imperial Harem. An interrogation I perform is a warning. One that you perform is a signal."

Gett waited, his head to the floor.

With the young girls in the harem, there was a layer of softness under their skin, a tender layer of fat that Gett remembered fantasizing about and touching. But by thirty-five years of age — and even earlier with worriers — that softness had burned away and was imprinted on a woman's skin, and with much greater clarity, her skull. Thus it was with the Imperial Mother as she watched out of the bead curtain, carefulness in her forty-year-old eyes.

THE EUNUCH

Gett raised his head to listen to to what was happening in the wider room. He could not see the officials but he knew that they were down from the dais assembling in the hall. He strained to hear, or more precisely to differentiate through hearing, which footsteps belonged to whom. Sulo's hard shoes were easy, they came cracking in aggressively, stopped and turned when he realized what this was. Han Zongcheng's were more difficult but Gett thought that he could pick them out. Not hesitant but careful as he shuffled in, saw what this meeting was to be, stopped, reordered his thoughts then took his place. Curdeger's too, were easy; there was a tiny creak from his shoes because of his weight. Chief of Surveillance Squads 2nd Class, Kob Meke, unsurprisingly, lost in the shuffle of feet. An interesting fact though, worth a mention to him as a matter of professional interest.

And finally, a silence, a lack of any footsteps from Head of Harem Gogoro Shen because he knelt in the middle of the hall, unmoving, head to the floor in the full kowtow of the accused.

And thus did Gett, from his position, for the first time in his life, in the quiet nook behind the Imperial Mother's screen, listen to and watch her perform a questioning; one that over the past hour he had discussed with her in meticulous detail, but one that she would now perform on her own.

She began.

"Why did you organize the pimping of the Emperor's concubines?" she asked.

"I did not organize such a set of activities." Gogoro Shen's voice was gravelled with lack of sleep.

"We know that you did."

"This terrifies me because it is in conflict with reality. Could I ask you to please show me what causes you to believe this slander against your honest and faithful servant."

"You may not. Who was it who purchased these services, both over the last three years and specifically on the night that the concubine Diao Ju was murdered?"

"I cannot answer that question because it assumes that both such a thing existed and that I organized it. Both suppositions are false."

"Who would have?"

"Who would have purchased sexual liaisons with the Emperor's concubines? Nobody."

"How was the ex-filtration of the concubines managed."

"I do not know because such a thing did not and could not occur."

"Why?"

"Because I organize the security. No security setup is flawless. Especially one that is built to be discreet. And most especially when it is under constant slow assault by people seeking to influence the Emperor like this one was. But we have a lot of experience and we have learned from every mistake that we have made with our concubine security and I would not say that a security breach would be impossible. Nothing is impossible. But a sustained breach over three years with not a single clue coming to light, not a single murmur, is as close to impossible as a thing can be."

"What security mistakes have you made?"

"The honorable Imperial Mother is asking in general?"

"No, give us a specific example of a security mistake you made, what breach it led to, why it was a mistake and what steps you took to rectify it."

Silence for a moment. Gett saw that Gogoro's hand had begun to twitch.

"Four years ago it was discovered that one of the corridors through which Class Four Concubines were escorted could be

THE EUNUCH

entered at one unsupervised intersection. A special pass allowed access to the Imperial Bakery which connected there. It was not discovered at first because between the time the bakery pass came into existence and the passageway being vetted for concubine transfer, work was done to fix rain leakage. The two paths did not cross originally but post-repairs, they did. It was exploited by an official to gain access to the concubines and befriend them. When we discovered it, we switched to an alternate route. It took about a month to get the Baking route switched, after which we brought our concubines back to the original corridor."

"Did it cause any problems?"

"It is just an example of a security flaw we found and fixed. One of many in a constantly on-going process, Imperial Mother."

"Why was the concubine unescorted?"

"It is common for concubines and wives to pray at the shrine of fecundity after a meeting with the Emperor. They must be unescorted."

"How many times has this happened?"

"It is recorded every time. I do not know. But it is not new and not secret."

"How much did the clients pay for this service?"

"For what service?"

"For the service of providing them sexual access to the Emperor's concubines."

"There was no service so that question...is unanswerable."

"Then humor me. How much would a person pay for such a service if it did exist?"

"How is that possible to know?"

"You mean to tell me that in thirty years of service you have never had an offer to arrange a liaison with a concubine?"

Silence. Gett, from behind the curtain began to squint. He could just make out, other than the twitching, Gogoro's forehead had begun to bead with sweat. And with this Gett began to think. The shaking hand. The sweat. They were *odd*. They should be telling the Imperial Mother he was frightened. But Gett had watched too many interrogations and he knew Gogoro wasn't afraid. Something began to scratch at Gett's mind.

"Of course there have been offers, but there has been no average number."

"Calculate it or make a guess."

"I would say that a liaison with a concubine would be worth… may I have a brush and paper?"

"Why?"

"I will write the number, I do not want anyone to know it."

Quickly he was given this, and in very tiny script he brushed something. He folded the paper and it was brought forward to the Imperial Mother.

"That much?"

"I have had offers for more, but if it were to be run as a business, then that would be a price that was sustainable."

"Why didn't you report those offers?"

"I did. They are all in the harem records."

"Why did you want that money?"

"I did not want it."

"Why could you have wanted that money?"

"I am a servant of the Imperial Bureaucracy. I have a generous salary and no debts. My expenditures, to quiet just this kind of speculation, are submitted every week to the Secretariat Audit. The Secretariat Audit is charged with financial audits of all bureaus above grade seven. If my expenditures have been misrepresented and not discovered or if such a crime was committed in collusion with the Secretariat Audit then a much deeper and wider problem than this murder exists."

"Let us do this. Imagine yourself an investigator. Carefully look

THE EUNUCH

at your life. What have you spent money on? List it up for us."

"It has been done in much more detail than I can do here."

"Then do it in whatever detail you are able, now."

"I have one property in the Capital. It is my residence. In that residence, I have four servants—all wholly-owned not salaried, and my ownership of both the property and the servants is free of debt obligations. I have an honorarium. A quarter of it goes to covering my expenses. Another quarter I hold. And roughly half of it is dispersed to my extended family. That's it."

"Who arranged these liaisons?"

"There were no liaisons, only the occasional conversation and as I explained we always quickly rectified that."

"Who had the access and know-how to arrange these liaisons?"

"The only person who understood the schedules enough and had enough control over the security and transfer procedures to arrange for something of this nature is me. And this is how I know that no such arrangements occurred because I did not make them."

"How was the money transferred to you?"

"There was no money."

"How could it have been transferred."

"I have never engaged in such activity so I have no idea how illegal money could be transferred."

"Why would someone pay to engage in sexual intercourse with a concubine?"

"I have no reasonable answer."

"I don't believe you."

"That I don't have an answer?"

"Correct."

"As it has never happened, how could I?"

"Posit theoretical reasons."

Gogoro again was silent for a moment. His breathing had developed a rasp. Others in the hall had begun to notice. Faint rustling whispers began, just at the edge of hearing.

"Love for a concubine. The only way that he can have her is to pay for her. The second might be the thrill of it—the most dangerous sex, with the ultimate forbidden woman. The third…I can think of no more. No one does it. It is too dangerous. The reward is too small. There is nothing that could motivate a person to organize it or engage in it."

Gogoro was pulled out of the hall by four guards, down a long hallway and through a small door into a side room in semi-darkness. Gett, following behind, could see he was having trouble keeping his feet now. The sagging skin of his face shadowed deeply in the weak light. Gogoro finally stumbled. Gett motioned for the guards to allow him to stay down.

He walked to him. "We know that you have people working right now to get you out of here."

"I have honest people who know I committed no crime and who fear for their own lives if capriciousness is allowed to determine the fate of an honest servant of the state working for my release."

"No, we know what you did. Here is the reality. Having arrested you, the Imperial Mother's hands are now tied. She can't allow people to arrange for you to be released. And she knows that it will happen. You are owed too many favors by people who have the Emperor's ear. Especially obviously his wives. So you are going to be tortured, they will get the identity of the buyers from you, and you will be executed by evening."

Gogoro took this in. Gett knew he had considered it.

"It is how it must be," said Gett.

THE EUNUCH

"Torture."

"Yes."

"Is there anything that can be done?"

"Nothing. Your arrest decided this."

"Yes, of course."

"So, reality. You have a mother, father, cousins. You know that they can all be executed, down to the fifth level of relatedness. And you know that the Imperial Mother will do it."

Gogoro's breath was rattling badly now. Gett's mind was buzzing.

"Now saying this as a threat. It is abhorrent to me. I have stood where you now stand. But I am a messenger. Both from her to you but also in the other direction. We need to know who bought Diao Ju on the night."

"Can you untie me?"

"I cannot. You are not under my jurisdiction."

"I want my last discussion to be one that has dignity."

Gett considered this. He looked at the guards.

"No I'm sorry."

"Why?"

"You know why."

Gogoro accepted this. He took a moment then spoke, his voice quiet.

"What is the purpose we have in life? It is, we are born, we grow. And slowly we learn how to be attractive, how to seduce women. It is odd. I believe that even the pleasure of sex must have a purpose, you know? Why? Why should sex be such an important part of our lives? It creates children. But why so wonderful? It seems that it could just as well be... something else, boring, unhappy. I have thought about this, considered this question. In part because of the condition we both share. We are removed from the considerations of this question from two directions — on the one hand, we do not have these desires nor do we have the physical ability to satisfy them if we did. Second, others recognize this incompleteness in us, and so we are removed from the aspects of life that are predicated on a possession of them. And the surprising thing to me in my life has been how much of life this closes off to us. Almost as if the entire reason we exist is to pair off men and women, to assign them to each other and then to force them into sexual intercourse. To cause them, by every means that exist, to do this. I do not have to explain this to you. I know who you are and I know that you have considered these questions, have asked them to yourself at night and alone. So now you come to me you say, 'Gogoro, you face annihilation, you will die today.' I will die today! Erased! And the world will continue. The only difference? I will be gone and generation and generation and generation will follow, absolutely unchanged, not even knowing that I was cut out of that stream right here. I am the terminus of my line. Think about that. My line has existed since we humans have existed! All of those generations. All of those struggles. Thousands of generations of seductions. Thousands of rapes. Thousands of young happy people in love. One after another in a perfect unbroken string. Think of the difficulty. Think of how unlikely that was! How difficult! And over the course of my life I came to realize that it all ended with me. I was the terminus of those thousands upon thousands of triumphs. I was the final failure. So be it. You wish me to admit I arranged the concubines. You say 'who else could have done it?' You tell me I will die today. That is a tiny chip of a part of what is ending today. Later or earlier I am a eunuch. So you will kill me. The Imperial Mother will kill me. You will torture me. I must tell you how I did it. And with who! Fuck you all. I choose annihilation. I choose it for my family. Kill them all."

Gogoro vomited blood and bile all over the tile floor.

THE EUNUCH

Gett's mind ground through this methodically and fast. In two heartbeats he understood. But as he reached forward, Gogoro's head dropped down. His death was not instantaneous. It never was when you ingested poison. Bloody foam from his throat. Convulsions on the floor. And through it, with wild dying eyes, he looked at each one of them in turn, the three guards and finally Gett, carefully, with hate.

The guards, terrified but competent—they all were at this level—went about the hard panicked business of prying his mouth open and forcing him to vomit. They knew it was futile. But the best they could hope for was banishement, and the worst, unthinkable if their prisoner died. As Gogoro lay twitching on the floor Gett knew this sealed it for him. He was here. This was all that mattered. He had been too slow to see it. The shaking, the sweating, the shortness of breath. Gogoro must have taken it before he was brought in to the Imperial Mother's Hall. Must have known there could only be one outcome.

Then one of the guards, through hard clenched teeth said something to the other as he grunted with the exertion of squeezing Gogoro's stomach. He said, "It's bad energy for us."

And with that, Gett finally but tenuously grasped the thread which had been dangling in front of him the whole time.

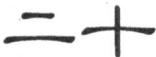

Curdeger watched Gett, waited for him to speak. Not out of protocol, (Gett, with higher rank, had precedence) but instead out of surprise. Gett was back, and Curdeger had clearly decided to simply wait. They sat in the sparse receiving room. Curdeger on a wooden stool, Gett, as required, across the room in Curdeger's raised receiving chair.

"I have a matter to discuss with you," said Gett.

"Please."

"It is related to this case but not to your investigation and analysis of the crime scene."

"Then it would be outside the scope of my mandated rights as they relate to the murder."

"It would."

"I will of course answer any question that I can and that I have the right to answer."

"You built the wing of the Palace in which the Imperial Child Producing room is located."

"Designed and oversaw the construction. That is a recorded fact."

"And so you also designed and built that room."

"Correct."

"According to what guidelines?"

"According to harem fecundity guidelines."

"Could you list and explain them to me, specifically, what

THE EUNUCH

they are and how they shaped the final architecture of the room?"

"That is a very broad question and so it is difficult to answer precisely."

"What are the goals that inform the design?"

"Again, there are many."

"What are the most important?"

Pondered this for a moment.

"Most important to whom?"

"To the bureaucracy that manages the life of the Imperial family."

"Security, fecundity and the production of a male heir."

"Those are stated or unspoken goals of the design?"

"Stated."

"And how do they influence the design?"

"They also influence the construction."

"How do they influence the design and the construction?"

Curdeger, already careful, slowed down.

"There are restrictions on the dissemination of that information."

"What are the restrictions?"

"There are only a very few people who are allowed to know it."

"Who are they?"

"I can't say."

"But it is who I would think it would be."

"I cannot say."

"Am I on that list?"

"You are not."

"Yet, I need that information."

Curdeger nodded. Thought for a moment.

"Such things, such choices, are difficult to make in the absence of an official statement from a person superior to me."

Gett pulled from his robe the scroll chopped by the Imperial Mother, passed it to Curdeger who looked at it carefully. He would, Gett knew, read the content of the scroll and understand its meaning—Gett had wide powers but their edges were underdefined. This request fell on those outside edges and so was problematic—to not grant the request was unsafe because Gett was a direct servant of the Imperial Mother (or more precisely her son, but in most cases this was the same). But he was also on firm, guidelined ground in refusing it—sanctity of the harem, lack of definitional clarity in the rules. Reduced to their essences, both bad choices. He could be found to be in bureaucratic fault for either, it was a matter only of outcome. A dilemma.

"Could I be briefed on the progress of your investigation and why its continuance requires this information?"

"Of course."

Gett told him the steps he had taken, and how it had led here.

"And you feel that the victim took advantage of, or was part of, something that took advantage of some systemic aspect of the harem wife allotment system?"

"Correct."

"So?"

"So it seems they have arranged it in a *Chinese* way."

"Jurchen ways are superior," said Curdeger.

"Of course, but as in all things the Chinese have *some* wisdom." Curdeger was silent for a moment. Gett had noticed that in both discussions with and interrogations of the young, they are often afraid of a pause, as if the answer to every question should sit at the edge of their minds, ready to leap down and stride cogently out of their mouths. In the very old, or experienced, there was a reversal. They, when confronted with a choice, or the realization they had been led onto unfamiliar ground, would stop to think for a moment, allow the conversation to hold. Curdeger did this—was silent for a long time, unmoving, without expression as he thought through the possible outcomes for him. Finally he looked back up at Gett.

"I cannot list for you the things we take into account, but I can answer questions."

"I ask, you answer?"

"Yes."

"What factors are taken into account when building the Emperor's son producing room."

"Many. Again, that is possibly too broad a question."

"What factors are taken into account to influence the union to produce a healthy son?"

"Security, Energy Flow, comfort, in that order."

"How is security built in?"

"Could you ask a more specific question?"

"How are the entrances secured?"

"Each corridor is a tenth of a *li* long and three doors are built into stone walls, they lock from the inside so only the inside eunuchs can open them."

"Are there entrances other than the doors?"

"All entrances are doors."

"Are there entrances other than the four doors that I know about?"

"There is one passageway in the floor that leads to the Emperor's personal area of the Palace. It is locked from the outside because of its specific use."

"What is its use?"

"It exists to allow the Emperor free use of his will."

"Does he often use it?"

"I can answer only questions about the construction."

"Are there other entrances?"

"No."

"Are there other exits?"

"No."

"Are the doors part of the mechanism that regulates energy flow?"

"Of course."

"What are the others?"

"The position of the bed relative to the room and the position of the room relative to the gates of the city and so by extension, the full and the new moon."

"What relationship specifically?"

"The four doors are aligned so that the energy flow from the gates is uninterrupted if it is a male month but blocked if it is female."

"How?"

"In the female months, the moon does not accurately align with the gates and thus does not align with the doors leading into the room."

"Meaning the moon aligns how?"

"Meaning that you have a line of sight from the Palace gate to the city gate to the setting moon."

"In the male months."

"Correct."

"And the Emperor's passageway?"

"It was designed in such a way that it does not impede this flow."

"Does it enhance it?"

"It does not."

"What else?"

"Those are the structural issues."

"Are there other issues that you know of?"

"I know that there are issues of time and issues of sexual intercourse. But they are outside the scope of my knowledge and mandate."

"Do you feel qualified to speculate on them?"

"I do not."

Gett stepped into the Questioner Arigh's offices. Again, the irritating young Jurchen kid from the Harug Clan sat in attendance.

"Still here," said Gett.

"Of course," said the boy.

"I have come to see Questioner Arigh."

"Please state your business."

"It is as it was before. I wish to speak about matters relating to an investigation."

"The same?"

"The same."

"Not solved yet?"

"No."

"Why?"

Gett considered how to answer (considered also whether he had to, as he had decided that the boy would not survive the purge, not from a top family).

"I am not smart enough," said Gett.

The boy thought how to respond.

"Please go and tell Questioner Arigh that Chief Investigator Enchenkei Gett is here to see him."

The boy did, and Gett was left alone—in silence; the walls were thick, the interrogations went unheard here. Quickly, the boy was back, and Gett was led (through the quieter hallways this time) to Arigh's office. He stepped in. Arigh was waiting for him.

"Gett!"

"Arigh."

"What the fuck is going on?"

"Do you mean with this investigation or in general?"

"Both."

"We have made much progress in the investigation. In general, you might know better than me."

"What do you know?" asked Arigh.

At heart, an interrogator.

"You first," said Gett.

Arigh thought for a minute.

"I have all the people who saw the book down here."

"And?"

"Completely fucking awful deal for them, you know. Completely useless. But it has to be done."

"And?"

"Well it's dangerous for me, isn't it? They're all fucking bureau heads. So it's an hour of torture, enough to say we did it. Then in I rush, Oh I'm so sorry, this was a misunderstanding, orders from over my head, let me put you in this holding cell while I get it sorted out. Fucking mess. I'm dead if this keeps on. Hurry the fuck up."

"I have a few questions."

"What kind?"

"Questions I have to ask in my capacity as a servant of the Emperor in the course of the investigation."

So there then, pleasantries over. Everything official until Gett left the office. Arigh pulled back in on himself.

"As a fellow servant of the Emperor, I will answer all questions with my full knowledge and expedite the investigation to the best of my abilities!"

"You are a credit to your position in the investigatory apparatus."

THE EUNUCH

"It is an honor to be told this by a Palace Investigator!"

"My question, then is, do you know how the Emperor's male energy flow is monitored and managed during his sexual encounters?"

"What do you mean specifically by know?"

"It is a systemic process. Do you know the rules of the system upon which the management of the Emperor's sexual energy flow is based?"

"I am not part of that bureau."

"Yet you have interrogated many of the people who are."

Out now. A choice. Set carefully and properly in front of Arigh.

"It's hard to confirm that, Gett. The records are secret."

"You have to choose now."

Arigh was silent. For Arigh, only danger. Interrogations he had had to do would come back to him — You tortured me! It was ordered; I kept it to a minimum. But people remembered torture, it wasn't a thing like a fight in anger or even the killing of a loved one — those could be excused. Torture, and Gett had seen it again and again, was never forgiven. Arigh had holding cells full of officials. Had they done anything? Yes. But nothing Arigh cared about, in truth nothing important. Yet, he was tasked to interrogate them. He would put it off for a while, there were tricks to shift responsibility. But still, he ran the bureau, it would come back to him.

Finally, it was as Gett had expected.

"The interrogations are secret, Gett. I'd be lying if I said things like that didn't happen, but we don't record the information. We'd be breaking protocol if we did."

"So there is no transcript of such an interrogation?"

"Right."

"But there is a record of who performed the interrogations in which the information was conveyed."

"No."

"Why."

"We don't keep records of the information so we wouldn't have noted in which interrogations it occurred."

"But if you remembered."

"Gett, you know how it is. Nobody talks about who does the questioning, especially not here. Half the guys come out and go back to their positions."

Gett waited.

"I can go through it with you but I need you to have the right authorization."

"What is the right authorization?"

"A memorandum from the Emperor or the harem."

"The Imperial Mother has issued one."

"Show me."

Gett did.

"I want a copy."

"I can't give you one, but we can have a witness to attest that I have it and have shown it to you."

Arigh's Chinese boy was bought in.

"A Chinese witnessing isn't going to stand up in a hearing. He doesn't have status," said Gett.

Some arguing with his staff. Finally the stupid Harug Clan kid was brought in. Document witnessed.

"We don't have anything from the harem," said Gett. "You'll have to do without."

Arigh nodded.

"You know how it works," said Gett.

"Fucking unreliable Chinese."

"No, I mean the harem. Specifically the sex. You know how it works."

THE EUNUCH

"Yes, sort of."

"Why?"

"It's in the nature of the thing, you know. We bump up against it."

"And what do you do?" said Gett.

Arigh looked at Gett, considering. "Well," he finally said, "there's nothing that isn't useful."

"How do they organize it?"

"I don't know all the details."

"Tell me what you know."

"Interesting stuff, not supposed to know it."

"Of course."

"Can't be avoided really though."

"No."

"You are questioning somebody, they stole some money, it's part of what they tell you in the natural course of things, its part of, say, how they stole the money. They took advantage of some part of it, you know how those things go."

"I know how they go."

Arigh was nervous—interesting in and of itself—so Gett considered how to proceed. In general, these sorts of conversations need a transition, something physical so that the interviewee felt the shift from engagement to interrogation. It moved them into the mindset that they sat in front of someone to answer questions. It was both more difficult—he was used to being on the other side—with Arigh, but also more straightforward because he understood the process.

Gett shifted his robes. Looked down, looked back up. Put the documents he was holding aside and looked at Arigh.

"How many haremites have you interrogated."

"Including what?"

"Everyone, concubines, wives, eunuchs."

"What about the secretaries and that sort of thing?"
"Anybody connected to the harem."
"Going how far back?"
"Since you were on the interrogation detail."
"Let me look at our records."

A long moment of shuffling in another room.

"About thirty-five. Some of them don't really work at the harem. Like for example some clerk tasked to liaise with them for a month. Usually, it's those people who have more problems."

"About thirty-five?"
"Give or take."
"How many eunuchs?

Checking again.

"Ten."
"Concubines?"
"Five."
"Wives?"
"None."
"Because?"
"Not allowed."
"The concubines for…?"
"You know, usual stuff. Stealing, disrespect."
"How many were punishment interrogations?"
"About half."
"The others for information?"
"Yes."
"And the eunuchs?"
"The same."
"Secretaries?"
"Mostly records errors."
"What about the Harem Calculation Bureau?"
"Yes."

THE EUNUCH

"How many?"
"One."
"Punishment?"
"No, information."
"What is the goal of the energy management for the Emperor's sex?"
"Manage the sex so it produces a healthy son."
"The sex itself or just the location, timing and such things?"
"All of it."
"Specifically the sex, how do they organize it?"
"They organize it on the son days."
"How do they organize it on the son days?"
"There is a run-up of about five days. The Emperor has sex on each day with a lower level concubine."
"About or exactly five?"
"It varies from three to six depending on the month."
"How low."
"Three."
"No, how low are the concubines, what level?"
"Under Second Class."
"One a day or…?"
"One a day."
"For what purpose."
"To build up his energy."
"What specifically is building up his energy?"
"He has sex with the concubine, under supervision. He doesn't ejaculate."
"To save up his ejaculation?"
"To conserve his male energy and suck the female energy out of the concubine."
"The not ejaculating achieves that?"
Arigh shrugged.

"They think it does."

"He holds himself and the energy flows out of her into him."

"Right."

"Then?"

"Then on the fifth day whichever wife has the right calendar numbers is brought in at the right time and in the right way and the Emperor has sex with her and ejaculates."

"The ejaculation plus all the male energy flows into her."

"Right."

"Must be difficult, the run-up."

"Yes."

"That's where the information comes from?"

"Yeah, mostly concubines who made the Emperor ejaculate."

"What's the punishment."

"Pretty serious. A day of torture."

"Maiming?"

"No, no maiming, but they don't forget it, don't do it a second time."

"But that's why you know."

"It's one of the main reasons I know. They tell me while we do the torturing. They're not supposed to and we can't even ask, but they'll say anything to make us stop."

"How long have they been doing it this way?"

"The sex you mean, or the torture?"

"The sex. It sounds like a Chinese thing."

"Since Emperor Zhanzong. After he married the Chinese, so about ten years. They keep it very secret."

"So, for a few hours after the Emperor ejaculates into her, she is filled with the most powerful energy in the world. Built up over days, amplified in the Emperor's body. Nothing more powerful in the universe. Anybody who had it inside her could do anything, overcome any burden, achieve any goal. And it can be transferred out of her through sex; the only way it can be transferred out of her is through sex. They believe that?"

"Yes."

"All of them?"

"It's a Chinese thing, but yes."

As the Torch and Lighting Management Bureau had been decimated in the last round of arrests, the shifting, orange-edged shadows that defined the Palace at night had been replaced by those which were moonlit, still and pale. Gett made his way through these clearly defined regions of light and darkness and thought: an improvement.

He could hear the faint scuffle of frightened people, around corners, hidden in doorways, just under the threshold of visibility, but watching him. He stepped away from the walls and crossed the muted courtyard. His feet were not loud; he had replaced his Shoes of Rank with the padded ones he wore in his office which, while not warm, were safer.

He reached a small door shadowed oddly by the moonlight falling through the empty curled branches of a persimmon tree — pale, diffuse, complex and disappearing into the darkness inside. He pulled up his robe, stepped over the lip of the doorway and into the complete darkness of the Palace interior.

Even though he couldn't see it, Gett knew that the corridor leading to the Library angled away to his left. He made his way by feel. Down the corridor of The Limpid Pool at the End of the River of All Springs with its inlaid woodwork, left into the staff corridor for deliveries with a rough unfinished floor, then out into the black emptiness of the Outer Hall of the Imperial Library. Carefully slid across the porcelain smooth floor, twenty steps, hands out in front. The library door, no give because it was so large and heavy. Hands spidered left and right to find the seam. The large handle. Found. Locked.

Gett knocked quietly. It echoed in the tiled darkness around him. Waited. Nothing. Knocked again. Waited. He whispered into the seam of the massive door. Again, louder. He put his ear against it, straining to hear breathing or careful footsteps. Nothing.

Lao Kou? It was possible he was on the other side of the door, breathing quietly. Smoking in the darkness, silent, careful. Or he had been arrested — sitting now (or standing) in a torture room or a freezing cell. Torture probably, if he had been arrested. Dead? Not likely. Lao Kou had survived this long, survived worse. So, hiding probably. Library locked from the inside. Probably. But… not knowable.

Another closed door.

He stood shivering in the cold darkness. Inside the Library were the records Gett needed — who knew her. Locked in the Library, but also locked in Lao Kou's mind.

Lao Kou knew that care and value were survival. There were on the order of ninety thousand scrolls below his feet. Lao Kou had filed every single one. The Library was a valuable resource of information and so power. There were periodic bureaucratic attacks — a new administration assigned by fiat, the system buckles, Lao Kou insinuates himself back to absolute control. Because he is useful. So not just the door. The door had a lock. Someone had the key but it represented the absence of Lao Kou. And without him, the information was inaccessible.

Or rather, Gett thought, as he stood in the total darkness of the library foyer pondering the problem, that wasn't strictly true. The reproductions of the documents were unavailable.

"How does it work?" Gett asked Sulo.

"You put it over words. Makes big. Old guys can read."

"May I try it?"

"Yeah, sure."

He handed the transparent ball to Gett. It was small, fit in the crook of the palm of his hand. Heavy, like the false jade made from melted sand, but transparent instead of dark and cloudy. Gett held it above one of the documents on the desk. The characters were much larger, similar to when falling raindrops bead on paper in moment before are. Gett no longer had to lean back to read them as he had become accustomed in the last few years.

Gett looked at the other strange things in Sulo's office. Mostly Chinese and Jurchen, but also many things from the tribe to which Sulo belonged. Some, like the tapered device, were odd versions of familiar things. It was almost identical to a water clock, but it was housed in the same transparent false jade as the ball, and used sand instead of water or liquid metal. Other things, like the circular brass tool with the etched markings, had the complexity of a geared water wheel, but it was much smaller, and was marked with sun and moon symbols. Gett put down the transparent ball.

"Lao Kou isn't in his Library," Gett said.

"Yeah?"

"I was wondering if you knew anything about that."

"What should I know?"

"Did you arrest him?"

"What you give me in return?"

"What do you want?"

Sulo grunted.

"I want you is solve the dog-cunt case."

THE EUNUCH

"Yes of course."

"No, I didn't arrest him."

"Did somebody else?"

"I think no."

"But you're not sure."

"Pretty sure."

That, for Sulo, was as good as saying, no, he absolutely was not arrested.

"Lao Kou is smart," Sulo added.

"Well, I need access to the documents in his library."

"Too bad for you, then."

"No, actually."

Sulo said nothing.

"The documents in the library are copies. The originals would work just as well."

"What documents?"

"The family registers and vetting reports for the test candidates."

"Where are the originals?"

"Prefectural Offices for their villages."

"How you know which Prefectural Offices if you got no records?"

"That information is stored separately with Security."

"That maybe takes a long time."

"It could be made to take a short time."

"Yes, maybe. So you got news?"

So, another deal then. Gett took out a fresh nut and started in on it—the thready hard sponge squeezing out the bitter juice.

"There's always news."

"How is the case today?"

"As you know, the Harem Eunuch, Eunuch of Standing, Gogoro Shen was arrested."

"I was there."

"And you know he killed himself after the interview."

"He confessed?"

"Sort of."

"He tell you who did it?"

"No."

"A waste."

"But I think I know how he was involved."

Sulo smiled, and sat back eyes half-closed watching Gett. Gett thought of the minds of people like this as if they were composed of intricate scaffolding, like the frame of a building that grew not larger, but denser and more opaque as the layers of bricks and mortar and glass of information were hung upon its complex skeleton.

"He was pimping the girls, but not for the sex," said Gett.

"For what?"

"For the energy."

Sulo considered this and then smiled. "He sells the energy transfer."

"That's what I think."

"I think only Chinese believe that," said Sulo.

"Times change."

"The Emperor's energy, in a girl. Like a bottle. You buy, you drink."

"Yes."

"Clever."

"Yes."

Sulo paused to think about what this meant for the case and so for him.

"Who he sell to?"

"I don't know."

"Why?"

THE EUNUCH

"He didn't keep a list."

"But you got a guess."

"I do."

Sulo waited.

"Over the last four days," Gett asked, "who would need it?"

Gett watched the answer come in to Sulo's mind and sprout up on to his face. It was mostly a good answer. Good because they were weak. Not (much of) a threat. But unknown so unpredictable.

"So," Sulo said, "you're clever. Go catch the bad guys now."

"I need your help."

"I'm not clever."

"I need an escort."

Sulo sat back and considered this carefully.

"Why do you need?"

"It is too dangerous for me to go alone."

"No, why you need the records?"

"I need to establish who knew her before she came to the Palace."

"The records won't show that."

"Not directly, but at least they will show which of the candidates is from the same place as she is."

"Maybe no."

"Maybe, but you know how these things are. There's always a shadow in the records."

Sulo had taken some care in selecting the weapons for the five guards that would accompany them to retrieve the records. A fight was unlikely but if it were to occur, then the short solid swords that the rear-rankers held were by far the most effective — stabbing weapons built for killing. But as the purpose of the escort was intimidation more than anything else, Sulo had considered the spears held by Palace guards and, in a more systematized and structured way, by Imperial shock troops. They were useless in a close fight but were recognizable symbols of Imperial strength. In the end, Sulo opted for both, instructing his men to throw the spears down if involved in a scrum. Thus, with spears up, red Imperial flags hanging from them, short swords tucked away in hidden scabbards, and crossbows hung on their backs, did Sulo, Gett and the escort party of five soldiers emerge on battle horses into the avenue that led to the outer gate of the Palace.

A thin, cold wind blew down the avenue, constrained by the walls that lined it. A single dead leaf tumbled along in front of them until it came to rest at the foot of one of the roughly thirty soldiers guarding the gate.

Even from this distance, Gett could tell they were not Palace guards. These were non-Capital troops called in for extra duty, at worst from the Ordos Sector and so with combat experience. A personal army of… someone.

Gett, Sulo and their escort approached slowly, the clip of their horses' hooves echoing in the cold hard air. When they were close enough, both Gett and Sulo dismounted. Sulo did not move out of the protective circle of his soldiers.

"Hello," said Sulo. "We are Enforcement Bureau escorting Chief Investigator Enchenkei Gett to outside Palace for a search. We need to go out the gate."

The Head Guard spat a fat red gob of betel nut saliva onto the dark paving stones. Gett watched him search his mind for an intimidating phrase, then, believing he had found it, smile.

"Dog fucker, I'm in charge here. Nobody comes in. Nobody goes out."

"Why?" asked Sulo.

"Orders."

"Yes, who ordered?"
"My orders."
"Who gave the orders?"
"Go fuck your bitch mother's cunt or I'll have my guards arrest you."

Sulo considered this for a moment.

"I am Enforcement. Good friend, bad enemy. You maybe haven't worked so long in the Palace, you know?"

The Head Guard shouted an order and his men de-shouldered their weapons and ranked up to fight. Sulo's escort drew their swords and spaced themselves at arms-width.

Sulo spoke slowly.

"I work here a long time. Everybody knows me. I don't know you. So you're new. You gotta learn the rules. You move or I kill you."

"With a five man escort?" asked the Head Guard smiling.

"Which bureau ordered the lockdown?" Sulo asked.

"None of your dog-fucking business."

"All is my business."

"Doubt it. Go fuck your mother, foreigner."

Sulo smiled.

"You look in my eyes careful now."

Sulo stepped forward, pulled out his sword.

It is a fact, and one Gett had observed it repeatedly, that there are men for whom violence is an extension of their everyday lives. Most men believe this is true of them. In general, it is not. So, when Sulo pulled out his sword, the Head Guard sneered, a posture to indicate his contempt of Sulo. Sulo swung back and cut off his head. Arterial blood sprayed up half again as high as the man's shoulder. The body still stood for a moment after the head hit the ground, then it too folded in on itself and collapsed, blood mixing with the red betel nut saliva on the dirty ground.

Nobody moved, shocked at the sudden, out-of-context moment.

"Nobody else has to die," Sulo said. "I outrank your commander. He is insubordinate. Open the your mother's rancid putrid cunt door or you are insubordinate too."

They did. Gett, Sulo and the five soldiers passed through. The Gate Guards stood back in silent fear and calculation, considering whether they would be punished or rewarded. Gett watched them each come to the same conclusion: it will be decided by caution, silence and luck.

The doors of the gate shut behind them and they were outside in the main square that fronted the Palace, half a *li* of emptiness lit only by the moon, buildings lost in the darkness at its edge, as if the flat paved plane extended out to infinity.

Ostentation was intimidation; Sulo's escort lit torches.

They moved off into the square. Halfway across, Sulo, without looking at Gett said, "Don't worry, people working for the Emperor lock doors from outside. They want to keep people out. Don't keep people in."

⁂

The Chief Guard of the Kob family home emerged from the house. He walked out through the ring of guards and up to Gett's horse. He indicated that Gett dismount. Gett did so and they walked a short distance into the shadows of the wall, away from the torches and the guards.

"You can come in alone."

"I need commander Sulo and two escorts."

"Commander Sulo, no escorts."

"Fair enough."

"No weapons."

"I don't carry one. Commander Sulo has a cavalry saber and a knife."

THE EUNUCH

"He can't bring them. He can leave them outside."
"He won't do that."
"He can bring the knife."
"Fine."

◆

Gett and Sulo sat in a room of the Kob family compound. It was luxurious—the equivalent of anything in the Palace. Shining floor, heavy Western Desert carpets, intricate scroll work on the screens dividing the wall. Candles made dark wavering shadows in the dim yellow light.

Gett knew that just outside, holding in their breath and placing their bare feet carefully, were probably twenty Kob family guards. Sulo knew it as well, Gett decided. So, an answer to one question anyway. Sulo was under heavy pressure or he wouldn't be here.

Kob Meke walked in. An old eunuch servant accompanied him halfway, bent over at the waist, bowing even farther to Kob Meke, Sulo and (slightly less) to Gett as he backed out of the room.

Kob Meke sat.

"Hey G-g-Gett, what is it you n-need from me?"

"You know we arrested Gogoro Shen, Harem Eunuch of Standing?"

"Yes, I'd heard th-th-that. Glad I wasn't at that audience. Nasty business."

"Yes. He was pimping the concubines."

"Nasty b-b-b-business."

"Yes, but lucrative."

"Selling the energy."

"Yes."

"I suppose it would be."

"Who do you think he was selling to?" said Gett.
"No id-d-dea."
"Come on."
Pause.
"Oh," said Kob.
"Yes, that's what I think."
"Hmmm."
"Your guys have been surveilling them?" Gett asked.
"Of c-course."
"Since?"
"Since they arrived inside the C-Capital prefecture. Give or take five days d-depending on when they arrived."
"Where are the records?"
"I'm afraid that's a security matter. C-c-c-can't actually tell you."
"You increase surveillance on the ones who passed?"
"Of course."
"So?"
"Well, I t-told you. I've notified the Palace that I have important family b-b-business and I can't give you access to the records."

Gett sat for a moment in silence. These meetings came always to this moment.

"Let's do this," Gett said. "I understand that it's a delicate time to be requisitioning records. But everything should be discussed. You have some new information that might be relevant to your surveillance activities. Maybe this is a family matter. We're here. We can wait for a bit for you to discuss how new information might affect your protocols."

"Well I g-g-guess that makes some sense, G-Gett. B-b-bit difficult to call a family meeting in the middle of the night, but I'll see what I can do."

THE EUNUCH

He smiled, got up and walked out.

Gett tried to decide if he had done the right thing. Kob Meke would be, probably already was, offended. And he would probably take some kind of revenge later. But it was likely to be small. More important was that Kob Meke was now in discussion with his father and brothers right now, in a separate room away from Gett and Sulo and the guards who surrounded their room silently.

Kob Meke returned.

"We talked about this, G-g-Gett and, well, we just think that, you know, your investigation is just pretty important, so w-w-we want to help."

"Wonderful."

"But those records are also p-p-pretty important. So we'll have to be notified of a movement in the case. First, you know? Before anyone else."

"The Imperial Mother is always first. I can notify you or your family immediately following."

Kob Meke looked out into the dark hall. Waited for a response. Got one. Turned back to Gett.

"Of course. That's what we meant. First Imp-p-perial Mother, then us. On all developments in the case."

"As it should be," said Gett.

Back in the dark streets, torches draping wavering light over empty streets, Gett considered the cost/benefit of forcing Kob Meke.

It was a risk, but a small one. Kob Meke had taken Gett's prisoners to the Imperial Mother yesterday. He'd chosen sides.

Difficult to step back from that. Tonight, two powerful bureaus show up at his family home. Kob Meke's father understood. Would have seen it coming. Kob Meke was young. A lesson for him, Gett thought. In any case, useful and successful; Gett had the scrolls.

※

Gett sat in his office. A fresh betel ground in his thin jaw. The hit was just coming over him and warming his face. The drug lump was building up in his throat. He slowly unrolled the first scroll. Within, it detailed the movements of the five hundred scholars who had arrived in the Palace six days ago to take the test that would determine the course and quality of the rest of their lives.

GETT BEGAN the reports.

The Kob Family had, as he expected, provided him with two crucial sets.

The first was a dense list indicating the origin of each scholar: village, prefecture, province. The second was a meticulous chronology of what they had done and where they had been after their arrival in the Palace.

Gett began with their origins.

It was not an easy task. The names of the thousands of small towns and villages from which the Examination Candidates had come—or lived in or moved to or passed through, it was all carefully recorded—were both difficult to remember, and also often repeated—many were near rivers, beside hills, in valleys, produced pigs, used red bricks—and the unimaginative names bestowed upon them reflected this fact. Helpfully, the Kob family had provided Gett with a map of these locations. But its utility was handicapped by the names. There were fifty-seven "Next to the Brown River Villages". Sixty-three candidates listed this village name as their place of origin. But there was no indication of which specific one—and they were scattered over an area covering tens of thousands of li. There was no indication of which of the thirty-five "Sheep Wool Towns" had produced a specific Examination Candidate. Or which of the twenty-nine "Narrow Valley Stream Villages" had produced another. On and on.

The whole thing would have been maddening. Except it wasn't. For Gett, it was simply deeply disappointing.

A careful hour of crosschecking showed that, regardless of the confusing nomenclature and useless map, none of the Examination Candidates had come from the place Gett had been looking for: Grain Sequester Prefecture. The nearby grain producing region the Palace had deemed important and thus sought to control through an Imperial Concubinage. The place where Diao Ju had grown up. And the place she had still lived when she was plucked out and into the Palace to be that Concubine. This stumped Gett, stumped him to the extent that he had to sit back and re-consider his theory: whoever killed her had known her, well and for a long time. But how? She hadn't been in the Palace long. Her interactions there were carefully managed and always monitored. If the Examination Candidate who killed her hadn't also grown up in her town, had no connection to it — and as confusing as these records might be, they were accurate, on pain of death — then...how did he know her? How did he know her so well?

How did he know she would make it back to the anteroom after he stabbed her? How? It wasn't a matter of passing through her town or a fleeting interaction in the Palace. It was deep, intimate, understanding.

A dead end.

He turned to the second set of records.

On the first day of the eleventh month, four hundred and eighty eight Imperial Test candidates assembled at the Palace Gate. That morning, six days before the murder, had been cold. The records showed that two candidates collapsed and were removed, their tests postponed for two years. For the rest, this was their last un-ritualized moment.

At the Hour of the Tiger, the doors opened and the candidates were escorted by Board of Personnel guards to the Courtyard of Evanescent Scholarship. Here they were grouped by province.

This was the first opportunity to breach security so it was watched closely. Separation achieved, the candidates were escorted to their dormitories.

Three guards on each room—to monitor their security but also to monitor each other for collusion with the candidates. The candidates were given an hour to rest. The remainder of the day was taken up by a series of security checks—examining their bodies for information cribs, interrogations, random offers of help to entrap them. All but three passed these tests. One of the candidates had written characters backwards on the inside of his leg that could be pressed on paper. Two more were weeded out by traps.

And finally a dense series of lectures on Palace etiquette and hierarchies—most of them would be in the Palace for only a short time (because most would fail the Examination) but it was important that while there, they followed protocol.

The report showed no unmonitored moment in that first day.

The next morning, early, at the Hour of the Ox, Examination Bureau eunuchs walked the row of dormitories waking the candidates.

Once empty, the rooms were searched. The report noted that two more candidates were eliminated for cheating infractions; they had hidden preparations for crib sheets, but the staff were expert at finding such things. They were escorted past the remaining assembled candidates, and out of the Palace. A small brand was burned onto their inner wrist. They were now marked and could never participate again. There was an appendix for an analysis of the cheating methods. Gett skipped it.

The remaining candidates, still close to five hundred, were marched in smaller groups to the Examination buildings. Their identities were matched against physical descriptions provided by provincial test officials.

This brought him from the time the scholars had been admitted into the Palace until this morning. Encompassing the time of Diao Ju's murder. The other pile of scrolls detailed the plans for tomorrow — the security and surveillance plans for the examination. Gett unrolled them and began to read.

Later in the morning they would be given paper and a brush from pre-sealed boxes then escorted to cubicles. The cubicles were an armspan wide. Square recessed boxes open to the room. A small lip jutted out as a bench. A board would be laid out in front as a writing table, locking them in.

The questions would be handed out. Then they would have until the next sunrise to answer them.

Security over the next seventeen hours would be both physical and analytical. The rooms were guarded by Bureau of Examinations enforcers, so no one could have access to them during this period. The Head Examiner was always in the hall but watched closely. The candidates even more so. So the kinds of opportunities that would allow a candidate to receive an answer from an examiner did not, for the most part, exist.

Again there was an addendum report. An analysis of prevention methods for the more serious and much more difficult problem of prearranged lenient grading. Gett searched through the papers until he found it.

It was long and number-heavy, but the essence of it: how to preserve the anonymity of the candidates? For example: if a candidate arranged for grading, he had to communicate to the grader — this is my test. Some embedded their names — first row of three characters, carefully placed ink blots, etc. But these were easy to catch. Most employed codes written into the text of the answer. This required some cleverness. But these men were clever. Department code readers were of the opinion that it was impossible to completely eliminate. They could look at character frequency. (The answers were large enough to be fruitful targets of this kind of analysis, but the codes themselves too small—two, at most four characters. So their effect on the text as a whole was not significant enough to allow an analyst to say—"This one is dirty.") Brush style analysis. Other methods. Nothing worked well. The problem remained. The addendum conclusion: manageable, and kept to a minimum, but not solved.

Gett returned to the planning reports. At dawn, the Examination papers would be collected. If no anomalies were recorded, the candidates would be escorted back to their dormitories. Now, surveillance had to bifurcate because there were two points of attack: the candidates themselves, but also the answer papers. But, because they'd already completed the examination, surveillance would be much reduced on the candidates. The grading always began immediately.

The candidates could sleep until lunch. Assuming no anomalies, they would be escorted to a dining hall, served food, given enough time to eat. Then escorted back to their dormitories where new clothes waited. Examination surveillance was mandated to end here.

So Gett was stumped. This was a report that both explained the structure of the security arrangements around the candidates— and it was very good—and also detailed how well those procedures had performed this time. And again, the answer was: they'd performed very well.

It took Gett reading through the *Examination* plans three times before he finally saw it.

The candidates were scheduled for a series of study groups— mostly more detailed lectures to teach them how to behave properly in the Palace. These lasted about two hours. The candidates would be given time to change then split into groups and sent out for these lectures, about fifty to each.

Near the end of the day there would be a transfer of jurisdiction from the Examination Bureau to the sub-bureau of Palace Candidate Protocol. Which for someone reading the reports looked reasonable, and also blurred itself into the mind-numbing background of bureaucratic nomenclature. But Gett, on the third reading, noticed this was *different* from the sub-bureau listed in the index *before* the Examination, and when he checked that against the master list of Palace bureaus, this second bureau existed but the one before the Examination *didn't*.

Immediately after the original transfer had occurred, between during the Hour of the Dog, and in the transition before a harvest ritual and another primer on Palace etiquette, there were two overlapping security and surveillance reports. It was recorded by the Bureau of Etiquette that the candidates had been sent to the Palace Chefs for a fruit dissection ceremony but by the Chefs that they had been sent for an etiquette primer. Both reports were filed separately. An hour later, jurisdiction was transferred back to the testing bureau.

Gett sat back to think about this. The candidates themselves were almost without question unaware of a transfer of jurisdiction. How in actual fact had it occurred? It was possible (but unlikely) that there had been a physical sign-over — literally two people standing there signing documents. More likely it was an *ex post facto* artifact in the records. And since there was no listing for the bureau in the Palace records, it wasn't clear even who to ask. Most of the people involved in the testing were gone. And monitoring had become chaotic. A full hour during which the candidates were, in essence, under *no one's* jurisdiction because whoever *was* managing them obscured his existence in the records.

THE EUNUCH

Gett checked the time of the Diao Ju's absence and flight back to the antechamber. Hour of the Dog. They matched. So:

Someone could arrange this. If he were Chief of the Bureau of Examinations. The entire test was his responsibility. Every single candidate under his jurisdiction, every single candidate whose whereabouts were unknown for a full hour during which time the concubine Diao Ju had been murdered. Not someone Gett could accuse.

The Imperial Mother then.

Because he didn't want to be noticed, Gett took the servant corridor. It led across the whole Palace and today would see very little traffic. Gett came to the main corner. He stopped, listened. Nothing. Nothing loud anyway, loud protesters had mostly been arrested. He looked behind him, just dark tapestries on the wall. Around the corner. Again, empty. And because it was the beginning of the servant corridor proper, no tapestries, just bare painted walls. He looked down the other way. Empty. He moved quickly.

Soon he was outside the courtyard of the Imperial Mother's section of the Palace.

The courtyard was also the only place on the route where Gett was exposed, could be seen by other people from more than a few arm spans away. So it displeased him to have to cross it. He looked across. The guards were standing. Rigid. They looked scared. That made sense. Although Gett wondered specifically what they were scared of (just scared in a random way — strange dangerous things happening and they felt no control over whether it would crush them? Or something concrete? Tasked to protect the dormitories to be executed if they failed?) If they had been here a while they were probably scared of a mistake. Gett gave himself a bit more time in the shadows.

Finally he stepped into the courtyard.

They hit him in the next heartbeat, came from his left, banged him down onto the ground and stuffed a gag over his mouth. Hands pulled back and tied, blindfolded. Through the moving feet around him, and just before the blind came down, he saw Sulo standing off to the side of the courtyard.

The air became immediately colder underground as the wind found its way into the holding pen tunnels. Very little light, but if he twisted he could see Sulo following behind at a distance engaged in discussion with an underling. If Sulo was doing it for his own reasons there was nothing Gett could say that would change his mind, at least not on the walk to the holding pen. If Sulo had been forced into it, then the worst Gett could do was discuss it with him. Sulo might still be motivated to release him but Gett could only make it more difficult, not easier.

So, silence as they moved down the dark stone hallway. They came to a cage. The guard opened it. Gett thrown in. He landed badly and his arm went numb. The door shut. Footsteps disappeared down the corridor. Now alone, nothing to be done except wait. The best thing to do, Gett decided was to treat it as an opportunity to sleep. So he did.

Awoke. A sound. Of what? He blinked. Complete darkness, no difference eyes shut and open. Listened. Quiet. His breathing the loudest thing. Stopped. Still nothing. He sat carefully up on the cot, worried that the unfamiliarity of the room would cause him to knock his head in the dark. Listened again. Nothing. He stood, slipped on his sandals. Then hands out in front of him.

THE EUNUCH

The thing that most worried him was assassination. They had him, would execute him if they wanted. But often easier to suicide him.

He reached back, pulled the thin blanket off the cot. If it came, a garrote. Hunched over and edged along the wall. His destination, the cage door. If someone entered, he was from the moment of entry, at his back. Forward a few steps, held his breath, listened again. Still nothing. His heart pounding hard now. Darkness was never empty. Instead, populated with horror, evil reaching out with cold hands. He continued around the wall.

Another few heartbeats and he reached out, searching for the cage door. Smooth bars. The angle wrong. Open.

So, assassination.

His body wound down, shut off motion, slowed his breathing. Everything, all experience distilled to complete silence. Before complete immobility, shift the blanket forward. If someone came, a quick wrap around the neck, fall backwards and pull until the eyes bulged.

He waited, closed up, anchored like a shellfish. It wasn't hot. On balance, good. No sweat to make him sneeze or blink. The cold, though, would get him eventually. Immobility made it worse.

Who had ordered this? He ran through a mental list. Nothing new. Unknowable. But the arrest and now this, meant he was probably close.

Soon, though, he was stiffening. He couldn't physically do it much longer. But, ears straining out into the teeming darkness, he began to think this was something else. Experience taught him to wait—most people didn't or couldn't. But it was unlikely they'd sent a pro to do this easy thing, strangle a prisoner in his sleep. So either the guy was better (unlikely) or there was no guy.

He held himself for another half of an hour then finally

couldn't. Braced himself. Moved loudly then scuttled sideways to intercept. Stopped, nothing.

Gett stood up. Felt his way along the wall. Open door, felt along the outside. He was having trouble controlling his body now he was so cold, shaking. Not just jaw chattering but full body spasms, waves of muscles trying to warm him. He felt around the door to the other side. Could see in his mind the corridor — rough wall straight ahead, guard to the left, past that a long corridor and then out to the garrison gates.

Gett stooped down. Wet ground. Smell. Blood. So a dead guard. He made his way down the corridor by feel, quiet feet on cold stone. About a hundred paces down the corridor were the prison stables with the first weak light. The stables were small, but with an angled shaft for carts to bring prisoners in and out from above. Waiting in the stable was a saddled horse. And a coat. Gett put it on, allowed himself a solitary moment to shudder his way back into warmth.

He considered his options. All excess soaked away, he had three.

He could return to the cell. There was a non-zero value attached to that. He couldn't tell exactly when it was, but the Examination had probably already begun. That and the chaos meant it was possibly safer in the immediate sense than the outside. And there was the chance he would be judged to have not been at fault in, well, whatever reason had been given for his arrest. But it was unknowable and in any case was like waiting for weather.

The second, also simple, was to go home. Again, the lockdown during the exams would make it easier. The order to arrest him had been given and carried out. So, done. What happened after was the province of another department, one that surely felt overburdened and unfairly put-upon. They wouldn't have the time, and almost certainly didn't have the desire, to track him down just to put him back in the holding cells. They might put in a request to the same bureau that had originally arrested him but it would go to the bottom of a big stack. So, he could simply walk out, go to his villa and wait out the storm. Not unattractive. And possibly his best choice in the short term. However, it would put him in a weak position in any inquiry that followed: Why did you not continue your investigation? After being released from your unlawful incarceration by a loyal hero, why did you not investigate as mandated? As usual, a question of outcome. Gett was not naturally inclined to such choices and his experience in the court had repeatedly confirmed him in his preference.

The third choice, was the Imperial Mother. She had a big gown and Gett had hidden under it before. She needed him (or somebody) to understand what had happened. A culprit for the murder could be assigned. But an investigation into a murder near the Emperor was literally the only time that wasn't an option—especially for her. A question of survival. How much realistically could she do, though? He had been arrested. It could mean she had withdrawn her protection. Or she didn't know. Or she herself was being held. Not a choice with any certainty attached to it.

The saddled horse. The coat. He considered this. Not a mistake probably. So, a fourth choice.

He approached the city gate. Earlier it had been day and busy. Now, at night, still a hole, but a dark one. A quiet but steady stream of Chinese people still nervously exiting. Extra guards at the gate watched the crowds carefully. Not focused on the entry and exit of people but on signs of chaos. This confirmed it for Gett. He had been in the cell longer than he'd calculated. The

Examination was already well under way—scholars huddled in their cubicles, those outside carefully waiting to align with those who succeeded and to abandon those who failed, oppressive watchful silence hanging over the city.

He rode the horse into the gate, swallowed up by the stone. Horse hooves echoing, then the end, papers, doors open, out of the city onto the silent ground beyond the city.

The horse walked through the night.

To a person accustomed to candles, moonlight is strange. If the landscape is large and you can see a lot of it, it is like an odd inverted sunlight—covers everything, sharp shadows. But without color and dimly; every detail can be made out, but not in the same swift way daylight allows. Things resolve themselves only as you peer at them.

At dawn, Gett, very cold, dismounted and had a bit of breakfast. Around him was grey flat farmland. The dusty road that ran through it curved away until it was lost in a low rise. Wind-bent poplars drew huge squares around the plots of each farm. Gett chewed the roll he had found. Another two hours maybe. He looked back along the road. Quiet dark as he was traveling into the sunrise. But nothing, and there hadn't been the entire night. So no immediate danger.

He thought about his options now. About the things he had not done. Interrogation of his assassins? A transfer of jurisdiction to the Dowager? Identification of the corpse that had purchased the poison? All of these avenues were now closed off to him. He had only one thin and final path that led to a possible way out. That path, stretching out in front of him, led to the town from which, Diao Ju, this ambitious and now dead concubine, had come, and where, contrary to all evidence, she must have known, and almost certainly known intimately, her murderer. Gett had been a spy. He had been an investigator. Briefly, a long

THE EUNUCH

time ago, he had been fully a man. Old scars remind us of things.

He arrived in the town two days later around noon. Or roughly arrived. It was always a sort of gentle smearing as one approached a town. Nothing but farms and isolated shacks leaning against posts or just air, then, the farms slowly got smaller, and off in the distance, a slightly larger collection. A village? Or just a larger collection of houses? It was often unclear. Finally though, he saw down a gentle grade, about two *li* away, a much larger grouping, next to a river, maybe four hundred buildings, some with second storeys. By his reckoning. This was it. He stopped. He would have been seen by now. And his clothes would mean that the sighting would have been reported.

He started down the low slope and into the town.

Grey and brown. This distinguished small places — this lack of color. Clothing — brown and grey, buildings — brown chalk, ground — grey. None of the real or attempted beauty that defines cities. People romanticized this, some version of "but they see what is functional, stripped clean of all falseness and decoration, what remains is a purer more clean more basic thing, existing only for the purpose of a task." Gett found this almost never true. The things they used had been given to them and remained unchanged essentially forever. Not only out of apathy but out of stupid resistance to change.

They weren't born that way. But country life was horrible. Backbreaking work all day, no heat, everything ugly, horrible monotony, no anonymity. A city dweller forced to live here would kill himself. Those with value left. Pretty? Gone to the nearest city. Smart? Off to the provincial center. Pretty, smart and ambitious? The Capital. Left were children, grandparents and the occasional cripple. Towns weren't even safe. Nothing went on that didn't get reported in minutes. So the moment he came within a *li* of this one, a lone man, obviously an Imperial eunuch, his time began to slip away. He had a day for them to discuss. Maybe another day for someone to report his presence to the local yamen. Maybe at best another for the message to be couriered to the Capital, and then...well, someone would come.

So, time was short.

He stepped along the dirt track that in a haphazard way became the main town road. Villagers stared at him as he passed — stared for good reason. This close to the Palace, they were not strangers to the encoded language of uniforms — and his was clearly high-ranking. A Eunuch of Standing in the Capital. And this brought with it, without fail, a list of attached privilege — a bodyguard of at least five men. A carriage wheeled or carried. An announcement a day in advance and orders for protocol as the caravan passed through the town. The men of these towns were used to a foot on the neck. And if a Palace official appeared and no foot had descended, they knew Something Was Wrong. Why was he here? To shelter him meant what? To anger him carried what dangers? So they stared, calculating.

He made his way through wind and dust-eroded streets, to the yamen. He had been through this town before (it was on the main road out to the provincial Capital). The yamen building, like all government buildings, no matter how small and decrepit the town in which it sat, was very large. A display of power. Be poor, I am rich and can crush you.

He stepped inside.

It was a courtyard. Ringed by offices, smoke drifting out of pipes set high in the walls. Two clerks were walking from one office to another when they saw him. They froze for a moment, registering his uniform. Then rushed over frightened. They dropped and kowtowed.

THE EUNUCH

"Honored official of the Imperial Palace, the lowly servants of Grain Sequester Village Yamen are here and await any requests that yourself or the Palace might have!"

Gett let them stay on the ground. Harshness would get him a few extra hours.

"I am here on a record collection. I will give you a list. It must be done in the next few hours."

"Of course, Honorable Sir! May I stand to get the records requisition form?"

"You may not, I have not finished."

"Of course, Honorable Sir!"

"I will require housing as I will be staying here for six days as I review records. I will require food and drink. The list of prescribed foods will be transmitted to you."

"Yes sir!"

"And I require a heated office in which to review the records."

"We can arrange that, sir."

"And warm clothes. Your town is cold."

"Yes, we apologize! We will bring them!"

"You may stand."

They lifted themselves off the ground.

"Go now."

They rushed off. Gett stood in the frozen air of the courtyard. A few hours of breathing space. Time to visit the dead concubine's mother.

Diao Ju's mother sat in the receiving room of her house peering down at Gett. She seemed as Gett had suspected she would — a mother whose daughter had achieved success. Self satisfied. A bit fat. Too much jewelry. The house itself. Money but no taste.

There was a real question. Did she know her daughter

was dead? There was no mandate to inform the family. The investigation, by the definition of Gett's presence, had only reached the town today. The information would be passed on in a careful way with the political goal foremost: how to manage the information, thus to manage the local grain producing relationship.

Gett was relatively certain, on balance, that she didn't know; a mother whose child has been murdered instantly betrays herself. So, a few possible reactions. The first and most likely was she didn't believe him. Either (if she was naive) thought it was a mistake. Or (if she wasn't) thought it was part of some larger conspiracy to extract information from her. The second had probably already happened since her daughter had been plucked out of the town and into the Palace. But if she did believe him, it would be a day at least before Gett could get anything useful out of her. She would be shattered—facing the double catastrophe of losing this thing she loved so much and losing the family position in the town. Really, the worst news she could possibly get. So, a day at least, probably more before she would be coherently answering questions. A lie then.

"Your daughter is pregnant."

Gett awaited a reaction.

"Oh, I just knew she would get chosen! How could the Emperor not fall in love with her!"

"Yes, I'm sure that is true."

"She is so wonderful, you see. When she was chosen to be a concubine I knew that she would be the one to give him a child!"

"Yes."

"For how long?"

"It was confirmed three days ago so we believe that the pregnancy has existed for three months."

"It is so wonderful, what are the preparations for celebration?

THE EUNUCH

Are we to go to the Capital?"

"I do not know."

"Oh?"

"I am not part of the celebration bureau."

"Oh, which bureau are you from?"

"From the harem office of lineage protection."

"Oh."

She was silent.

"It is our duty to confirm that all pregnancies are the result of impregnation by the Emperor."

"But you have procedures to assure that."

"Procedures exist; this is the final one. We perform an investigation—usually perfunctory as in this case—because our other procedures are very good."

"My daughter would never do anything like that."

"Of course not. But we still do the investigation."

"Of course."

"And it is very thorough."

"How do you do it?"

"Over the course of this month we will investigate the town and interview anyone she came in contact with."

"But just family!"

"Nonetheless, she makes a yearly trip home. The latest one was five months ago. Our calculations are not reliably accurate enough to completely rule out a pregnancy that began during that time, so we still have to do the investigation. You do not need to be overly concerned. It is routine and we will not inconvenience you. We understand that in any normal situation this would be an insult and we apologize, but it is the Emperor and we are tasked to do it."

"I understand, Chief Eunuch, we will do what we can to assist you."

Quickly the interview was done. Gett exited the house. He would have to wait for night.

Gett stood in darkness. He had embedded himself in the shadows created by the eaves of two fishsellers. And the vantage point gave him a clear view of both the main and side doors of the Diao household. He assumed that it would be a long wait so he had dressed warmly. And appreciating that an important stranger in a small village would be noticed, he had taken off his uniform and was wedged up so not noticeable unless you got pretty close. A good spot.

He sat there watching the street and the two doors for most of the night. No one noticed him. And it was only after the middle of the night, maybe two hours before sunrise, that Diao Ju's mother finally came out. She exited from the servants door, dressed in a dark shawl, meant to cover her identity. She looked up and down the street. But not carefully and not in the right places. And most importantly, she looked before she moved. So obviously not used to such things. Still though, the streets were very empty, she would be checking behind her, following would be difficult.

Gett watched her from his crevice. She moved off down the street then looked again behind her before she turned the corner. Gett decided he had even odds to follow successfully. He moved out of his corner quickly and quietly to the street where she had turned. He got down low, about shin height, looked around the edge. She was moving down the street purposefully.

She looked back quickly, but at head height, so didn't see Gett crouched down.

Again she came to a turning, looked behind her, scurried around, he followed. This was repeated several times along the dark streets until she came to a large high wall surrounding

THE EUNUCH

what was presumably a large house. There was a whispered conversation at the gate then, again turning to confirm she had not been followed, she entered. Gett waited in the dark. He thought about whether he would have to wait long. Not, he decided. Sure enough, before sunrise, she came out again and walked back the way she had come, turned a corner and was gone. Gett thought about following her but decided to stay.

He waited a bit but nobody else came out. So he slid back into the shadows and then back down and along the dark cold roads to his room. His eunuch-of-standing robe was folded on the bed—an excuse for the yamen officers to examine it carefully for information about him. He put it on.

So, Diao Ju had an affair before entering the Palace. It happened. It was usually discovered. This time not. It meant more people would die: her mother, certainly, the family she had foolishly tried to warn as well. But especially the boy. And his would be a bad death.

He had known her intimately, and for a long time.

But no one from this town had taken the Imperial Examination. And the records, as maddening as they might be, were accurate.

As a case neared its end, Gett always felt the same thing, a sense he had learnt to trust. He could feel it now, almost a physical sensation in his fingers—as if they were finally uncoiling, reaching out, so close to the object they would grasp that they could feel its heat.

An hour later, when it was fully light, Gett stepped to the door and called for one of the yamen officers. The thin small one who had met him at the gate came.

Gett said, "What is the name of the street that runs from the stables north of here to the well?"

"Sparkling Harmony," he said in his high nasal voice. What a handicap to have a voice like that, Gett thought.

"And if you follow that then turn right at the medicine store and then again at the narrow street half a *li* down what street is that?"

"The narrow street that is paved or the one that is not?"

"The paved one."

"That is the Street of Excellent Eight. Where our best families live!"

"Halfway down is an estate house, dark red door with tortoise step stones."

"Yes."

"Who lives there?"

"The Xu family."

"And?"

"And what?"

"And who are they?"

"They grow sorghum for wine."

"The storing kind?"

"Yes."

"Money?"

"Yes, big property and grow sorghum."

"Who they sell to?"

"What you mean?"

"Wholesale or Capital?"

"Capital."

"How many kids?"

"Two."

"Sons or daughters?"

"Two sons."

"What the kids do?"

"They study to take Palace Examination."

THE EUNUCH

"When do they take it?"
"Maybe next time, two years from now, the second oldest."
"Why not the oldest?"
"Oldest died."
"So there's only one."
"No, there used to be three. The oldest died."
"When?"
"Three years ago."
"How?"
"He drowned."
"How?"
"Swimming and drowned."
"Accident?"
"Yes."
"How do you know?"
"They said it was an accident."
"The investigation?"
"Yes."
"Who did the investigation?"
"Our yamen office."
"So you did the investigation?"
"I was only a small part of it."
"So."
"People said he went down to the river to swim. The currents are bad there. And then he didn't come back."
"How long until his body was found?"
"His body?"
"Yes, how long until someone found his body. Who found it?"
"It wasn't."
"Nobody found the body?"
"No."
"Then how did you know he was dead?"

"Because the currents are bad there and he didn't come back."
"Do you keep records of deaths in the village?"
"Of course we do!"
"And his death was recorded?"
"Yes!"
"Cause?"
"He drowned."
"I mean do you record the cause?"
"Of course."
"And do you share those records with neighboring villages?"
"There is a census every two years of the provinces surrounding the Capital and every six of those in the rest of the empire."
"And then?"
"We record births and deaths."
"And you have the information on record still?"
"Only our own."
"Not of neighboring villages?"
"Of course not."
"But they all keep their own records?"
"They're supposed to. How can I know?"
"Do they or don't they?"
"Probably."
"How many villages in a two-hundred *li* radius?"
He paused, thinking about it.
"That's difficult to know."
"No it's not."
"It's hard to say exactly."
"Roughly."
"Fifteen."
"I need the lineage records going back six years for each of them."

THE EUNUCH

"That will take several days. We are not staffed at full capacity here. It's very unfair, we are so close to the Capital."

"I will pay for extra staff. I need them in one day."

"It will be so expensive."

"I will pay what it costs and pay you for organizing it."

"We are very busy here."

"I'll pay you this."

Gett wrote a very large number on a scrap of paper.

"It is not appropriate."

"It is alright. Think about whether you can take the time off. And you may consider it a bonus pay from the Capital as it is in the service of an Imperial Examination."

"Then it would be in accordance with propriety and an appropriate extension of my duties."

GETT WAS SLEEPY. The cold two nights ago had kept him awake as he waited for, then followed, Diao Ju's mother. Now, in the room, with the *kang* sending out waves of dry silent heat, drowsiness overtook him. He struggled through the reports, a numbing combination; dull and factual, but also confusing as each village clerk kept the records in a personalized fashion. His mind wandered. A survey of the record keeping methods would be valuable. Take best practices and synthesize them into a standardized template. It would allow people to know what information would be available and also make the process he was engaged in easier. More efficient.

He forced his mind back to his task, drowsiness kept at bay by urgency.

In the surrounding villages within a two-hundred *li* radius there had been one hundred and seventeen deaths of men aged fifteen to twenty-five in the last ten years. For most, the cause of death had been recorded. It took a few hours to go through them. And in the end only three stuck out. One was a murder and one was a death for which no cause had been recorded. But the third, and most interesting, was recorded as an error. A death had been reported of a twenty-two-year-old man, son of a local rice family in a village about a hundred and fifty *li* away. Cause was a fall from a roof. But this had been scratched out and changed.

So. Finally. There it was. Written between the inefficient

THE EUNUCH

lines of these sloppy reports. His family had hidden him. Faked his death. Sent him far away to be adopted by the father of a dead boy. To be a new son. Followed by enough money to buy acquiescence and silence. It had worked. Almost. It took Gett only a few moments to cross reference the name of the village with the Kob Family list of Examination Candidates (which had been left with him even when he was arrested). The answer, though, when he finally saw it, brushed out on the list, was the very last name he had expected.

Gett began to pack for a three-day journey.

Gett approached the village, and here finally, the journey that had begun in a small anteroom of the Palace was reaching its end because he heard the village before he saw it. Gongs and symbols and firecrackers and *pipas* floated across the rice fields. He came over a rise and the road led down into the town, sitting next to a river. Down the main street marched a dragon parade and banners, hard to make out but still readable even at this distance, so big were the characters. Third Lamb Village congratulates honored scholar Wu of the Wu Clan. *Jinshi*. Apex of the Imperial Examination.

Mostly it was important that Gett be noticed as he rode into the village. The two yamen servants walked behind his horse. He wore his full eunuch robe including tassels. And so, as his horse made its way past poplars that edged the hill leading down into the village, two village peasants came running up. They stopped, out of breath, dropped to the ground and kowtowed.

"Honored Imperial Eunuch. Member of the superior Jurchen race. Please order your slaves."

"Announce Enchenkei Gett, Palace Eunuch of Standing."
"Yes Master! May we rise?"
"Yes, you are dismissed."

The two peasants ran back down the hill and into the village about half a *li* away. Gett, even at the careful leisurely pace at which his horse walked, soon arrived in the village. It was as he expected, a mud-and-board collection of hovels. Down the cold dusty street, a few much bigger buildings.

But today, draped across all this ugliness were streamers and paper and the name of the scholar who had placed first in the Imperial Examination and whose hometown this was.

The celebration of his ascension into the rarified ranks of power in the Capital meant the elevation of this village for at least the next fifty years. Gett looked down the street. There was the house of the scholar. A crowd outside, all waiting to enter, to kowtow to the new master family of the town.

The two peasants pushed out of the crowd. They stopped in the back of the pushing seething mess of people and started beating large gongs. At first to no effect, but then as people began to look behind them, they noticed Gett, a gasp rippled through the crowd — a real eunuch! Here! Times are different now! This is our future! We are part of the Palace!

Gett dismounted with the help of his yamen servants. He walked forward. The crowd parted, letting him pass. Knowledge of the murder, or at least inaccurate rumors of it had certainly reached them, and now belatedly probably reached Diao Ju's mother as well — enough time had now past. But they were swamped out by the good news. He stepped through the courtyard gates and into the crush of supplicants. The two servants still beating the gongs pulled people out of the way with enough vigor that quickly a path opened. Watched by all, he carefully made his way across the courtyard, under the etched-

THE EUNUCH

on-sky trees, up the short stairs and into the receiving hall of the scholar's family home.

The scholar's *adopted* father and mother sat in their opposite chairs, a good day, a day of receiving obeisance. They had already stood to see what had caused the shift in the mood of the crowd.

When they saw Gett, they too bowed and bobbed their heads and smiled and wondered, terrified, why he was here. The father, fat, short and sweating even in the cold with the weight of all the brocade on him, spoke.

"Honored Imperial Eunuch, sir!"

"Honored father of the Palace examination *Jinshi*."

"We are a humble home and not fit for an Imperial Eunuch visit."

"No, this is impressive and does your son real honor."

The father and mother bobbed and bowed more, waiting for Gett to tell them why he was there.

"Please clear your reception hall," said Gett.

The father looked up, shocked. This had been, up until Gett had arrived, probably the best day of his life.

"But..."

"Clear it now. I have a matter of Imperial fiat to discuss with you."

He hesitated for a moment, looked at the Yamen officials for guidence who were also at a loss. So he tilted his head at the servants, telling them to do it. In very little time they had pushed the entire noisy curious crowd out into the primary courtyard and Gett was left alone with the scholar's father, his mother and their servants.

"*Everyone* except you," Gett said to the father.

His wife looked at him, and still terrified, he shooed her out. The servants left and shut all the doors behind them, ears pressed hard against, straining to hear.

Gett walked over to the two receiving chairs. He indicated that the father should sit. And once he had, Gett did as well. The truth, again, an impossibility.

"There has been an error in the testing procedure," Gett said.

"That can't be possible."

"It happens."

"No."

"Well, it has happened in the past and it happened this time."

"Then it must be fixed, yes?"

"It must, but I come here because it concerns your son."

"I hope not."

"Had the scores been tabulated correctly, he would not be the *Jinshi*."

"Are you sure."

"It is not me who is sure, it is the tabulators."

"But the test is done, the result is announced, this must stand."

"Yes, it must."

"So it…some one must go to do this."

"This is why I am here. I must discuss with your son the proper answers."

"Here?"

"Yes."

"But he is in the Palace."

"He is not."

"Where is he?"

Gett just waited.

Dim, back room. No windows so no one could see in. Gett could sense the tense, terrified bustle beyond the wall, far away in the large residence—He is here! From the Palace! The eunuch! But the threat to Gett was small. Wishful thinking would bring them

THE EUNUCH

back. Gett heard footsteps approaching, listening carefully, two sets. They stopped outside the door. It opened. In walked a boy.

So, finally.

The boy, about twenty, thin like Gett but short, stood in the doorway for a moment studying him. Then he walked across the room and sat on the cushioned platform across the room. A small mouth, smaller eyes almost like slits, the single eyelid fold common to southerners, thin neck, thin body. Good at thinking but, like so many others with this skill, un-beautiful. And the birthmark, reaching its way across his neck like a thin, unsteady hand.

If he was nervous, Gett couldn't see it. And Gett, though not incredibly skilled at spotting it, was very familiar with this moment: when he sat down for the first time with a murderer. They were always—except the very calm ones, the ones with the feeling disease—on edge. This boy was not. He was—Gett searched for the word in his mind—anticipatory.

He smiled at Gett.

"I wish to tell you. It is a great honor to sit in my home with a eunuch from the Palace," the boy said.

"The honor is mine. You are the *Jinshi* of the Imperial Examination."

"It is true, yet it is a recent honor."

"You outrank me by several levels, do you wish me to kowtow?"

The boy thought about this.

"I don't wish it, but I believe it is required by protocol and I do not wish to make a mistake of etiquette or in anyway disturb the balance of order at the court or, by extension, here."

Gett lowered himself, and kowtowed the ritual three times, but without the important head to floor contact. As mandated—even with the vast disparity in their rank. Gett sat back down.

"Thank you."

Gett nodded.

The boy said. "I assume you know my name, but I do not know yours."

"My name is Enchenkei Gett."

"And you are from the Bureau of Examinations?"

"No."

"I see. My father had told me this, but I wondered if it was true. I thought it probably wasn't."

"Why?"

"I thought it was more likely you were from another bureau."

"Which one is that?"

"Well, you know, the one you are from."

"I will have to take you back to the Palace."

"I understand that you wish to. Do you gain from it?"

"It is protocol, and long-standing investigatory practice, that you stand in front of the Emperor and the Imperial Mother and make a formal confession of guilt."

"If I refuse to go, how can you force me?"

"I cannot."

"But you will return with men who can."

"Of course."

"My father has discussed this with me. He believes you are here alone."

"He is correct."

"And so he believes that this means you somehow are not protected, that somehow this investigation has resulted in your exclusion. We have heard things about the Palace in the last few days."

"And what do you think?"

"I think he wishes this to be true. Maybe it is true. Probably, in fact. But in the end it is irrelevant. You are here. More will follow.

THE EUNUCH

Your presence is not you, it is the embodiment of the Palace, so the Palace has arrived here, you are just a grain of sand in a windstorm that is coming."

"That is correct."

"He wishes to kill you but is afraid."

"And you?"

The scholar shrugged. "It is irrelevant."

They sat for a bit.

"I really am genuinely curious though. How did you figure it out?"

"It was long process. I probably should have understood more quickly."

"But what was it that I did to reveal myself? I studied the problem for a long time. As I began, I felt my preparation was adequate. Perfect even. Even though at the time I knew that wasn't really possible. So, again, I am curious."

"It was obvious, very early on, that whoever killed her understood her deeply and loved her."

"Really? Why was that obvious?"

"Think about it."

The scholar, the sort of person who took a suggestion like that seriously, who waited for people to say such things, became quiet. Finally he said, "I knew she would make it back, or close anyway."

"Yes."

"Yes, that's true. Do you know where her determination came from?"

"You may tell me if you wish."

"She was curious. Not a person who was forced to learn things but someone who was really curious about all things. She studied with me. She knew everything I knew. She had experienced so much before she was taken away. And that is why she agreed to be taken. She could have refused. But she didn't *want* to refuse. She wanted to go. Not because she did not love me but because she was curious about life, about the Palace. She wanted to know how such a person lives. She was given an opportunity. She took it. But that is also why I knew she would make it back. You are right. I knew."

He was silent for a moment before continuing.

"Still, though, even if you can get me out of this village — and I believe you can — there is the journey. And then there is the Palace. I don't think you'll survive it. I don't think you will be allowed to survive it."

"Why do you think so?"

"As you say, I will be tortured. I don't see myself holding up well to that. Anyone really, but certainly me."

"What will you say?"

"I will say what I know, I'm sure."

"What do you know?"

"In the context of what you are curious about, I know who helped me do it."

"Helped you kill her or arranged for your sexual liaison?"

"Does it matter?"

"Yes. One is the killing of a person, the other is not."

"From a moral standpoint?"

"Also from a procedural one," said Gett.

"Helped me arrange the liaison. Did not help me in the killing. He would have been horrified if he knew this was my purpose."

"We know who arranged it," said Gett carefully.

"Do you?"

"Yes."

"Head of Harem Gogoro Shen," said the scholar calmly watching Gett.

"Yes, that is correct."

THE EUNUCH

"It is true," said the scholar, finally arriving at the point Gett had been avoiding from the moment he walked into the antechamber and saw the body. "But you do not know who made the offer to my family, who makes this offer to families."

"To your adopted family."

"Yes, to my adopted family."

"They paid?"

"They did."

"For the advantage it would give you?"

"That is what they paid for."

"Your adopted parents spoke with him?"

"Of course not. It was through intermediaries. I assume those intermediaries are dead. Possibly they are not. But I'm sure they are gone."

"You spoke with that person?"

"About this matter or ever, in the natural course of my time at the Palace?"

"Ever."

"Yes."

"About this?"

"No."

"Then how do you know who it was?" asked Gett. "You would have spoken with many people in a position to communicate with Gogoro."

"I deduced it. Studied it. Study is something I am good at."

"Do you wish to identify this person to the Palace?"

"No."

"No?"

"Exactly."

Gett now had one final consideration to address. Not what he knew. But instead, what others believed he would do with that knowledge. This young unrealistic boy had killed Concubine Third Class Diao Ju. Head of Harem Gogoro Shen had arranged their liaison. But the Head of the Imperial Harem could only be introduced by someone with power. There were only four people in the Palace with that kind of power. And thus, one of them was waiting.

The return to the Capital, because he was careful, took five nights. The boy, the murderer, was not with him.

The entrance to the tunnel was about two *li* from the city walls, in the shadow of the Iron Pagoda. It was in the middle of a dull grey pig farm, behind one of the slop tubs. The mud was frozen. Good in that he wouldn't leave any footprints, but he was worried the tunnel was watched, and nothing on the ground told him either way. He squatted behind a line of poplars, thinking. There was only so much he could do. He could sit and watch for a long freezing afternoon. But he decided getting to it and in before a watcher could grab him was doable.

So he stood up from his crouch, walked quickly down, hopped the low fence and across the frozen mud to the slop tub. He kicked it to the side, brought the back of his boot down hard on the mud, cracking it and revealing a thick pull ring. He grabbed that, yanked it and the door in the ground opened up, late afternoon daylight illuminating a wood stairway into the ground.

Someone could be down there. Not likely — the tunnels were well-guarded, even in chaotic periods like this — but not impossible. He stepped in, eyes closed to adjust faster. Pulled the trap door closed over his head, as it banged shut, under cover of the sound and the sudden darkness he jumped off the staircase and took two big jumps down the tunnel arms outstretched. The second time he landed, he crouched, stopped breathing and listened.

Another long pause for listening, nothing, then he moved down the tunnel. He frequently stopped, sped up, slowed down, anything to be unpredictable. But by the time he reached the other end he was sure it was empty. He felt his way up another rickety stairway and knocked on the trap door above him. Then backed halfway down the steps into the darkness. Waited. The trapdoor was opened by a eunuch who squinted down into the darkness.

"Come up."

"You come down first."

"Gett?"

"Yes."

"There's no one up here."

"Come down anyway."

Gett saw him straighten, sigh, make his way down the stairs. Halfway down, Gett stood and they walked back up together. An implied threat — if someone is there, you will die first. But the man was a survivor; if he went up with Gett, no one was there.

They came up into the house. Dark, luxurious, warm. The eunuch went off to find Gett some clothes and food.

The eunuch, Gett knew. Another old spy, a quiet methodical man who had been a mole in the Song secretariat for twenty years. His quietness, attention to detail and great patience made him perfect also for this job; tending the tunnel entrance. It was a job of waiting, and then, very very occasionally of being instantly ready.

This time was no different. Quickly he came back to Gett with a robe, food, water and then retreated back into his room. Gett bunched his Palace uniform into a dark bag.

He stepped out of the compound carefully. It was a small house on a small alley at the edge of the city. Twilight, both heat and light ebbing away like a tide. Around him the high walls, the dark empty narrow street, an exposed beach of shadow and cold. He hurried away.

Gett banged on Curdeger's door. No answer. And the sound was loud in the dark street outside his villa. Gett banged again, then again for a long time. Finally a very old servant opened the door a finger's width. One bloodshot drooping eye looked out at Gett.

"Who are you and what do you want?"

Gett, who knew better, looked past him and whispered, "Chief Curdeger. Let me in. It is important that we talk."

And then Gett waited, almost able to hear Curdeger's quiet breathing behind the door as he pondered what to do, stooped, curled up on himself, calculating. Finally the door opened and Gett slipped in.

The dark alley remained empty for a full hour, then a servant slipped out and ran in the shadows away and into darkness. Another hour of nothing. Then Gett reemerged.

The hiding spot Gett chose was a good one. From where he crouched, high under the eaves on a rare third storey, shadowed by a water catcher and a set of hanging sheets, he could watch not only the streets that led to the Palace but also both sides of the intersection. The streets were all narrow, cramped things, houses leaning over them like trees bent by wind, hard walls, cold, stark and shadowed even from moonlight. They were mostly empty except for bodies. Gett could see at least twenty lying in the street, frozen blood reaching away from them like thin dark fingers. Chinese, from their clothing. But no one living. Cold, darkness and fear had driven them inside. So, a cull, really begun in earnest now. It meant whoever came, Gett would have some warning.

THE EUNUCH

As expected, they didn't come directly from the Palace. Instead, slowly, Gett began to make out a flickering weak light far down the street to his right. So torches, which meant a hurried unorganized departure. That was fine, it was probably the safest way. He squinted out into the darkness and soon saw them. Three on horses and the rest infantry. Some spears, no bows. A force of about forty men. Armored. Not in battle formation and swords not drawn but ready, loose in the way a patrol is loose. Hard to see but it looked like they had prisoners, not peasants but city people, Chinese, tied together in a wretched group.

Gett watched carefully. The torches were bright and it was difficult to see past them to the soldiers. Gett curled up his hand and looked through the small opening, cutting out the flames. Enforcement Bureau tasseling. But still too dark to make out faces. The group moved slowly down the street, pausing to check doorways and step around bodies. They finally arrived at the intersection below Gett. He waited. They spread out, down all four streets and secured the entrances. Gett squinted through his hand again and finally saw clearly. Sulo on a horse. Dark beard silhouetted briefly by a torch.

Gett backed away from his perch, down the stairs and exited onto the street about ten compounds away from the intersection. He walked towards them, around two more Chinese bodies, crystallized blood reflecting moonlight. When he got within speaking distance, one of the guards noticed him.

"Stop right there, fucker."

"I am Chief Investigator Enchenkei Gett. I wish to speak to The Bureau Chief of Enforcement."

The guard, briefed to expect this, escorted Gett back up the dark street and into the torchlit intersection. Sulo came down from his horse, handed the reins to a soldier, gestured for them all to step back. They did, all the soldiers retreating to posts along the outer edges of the intersection, leaving Gett and Sulo alone in the center of it.

Gett watched, right in front of his eyes, a change come over Sulo. He had seen it before in interrogations, not often but not never. As if Sulo dropped down into another state of being. Colder, calmer, more silent. He stopped moving as if slowly freezing. And those strange blue eyes opened up like an abyss, information pouring into them.

"You're not in the jail."

"No."

"How come? Why?"

"I was let out."

"By who?"

"By you."

"Somebody came and opened door, let you out and you think it is me?"

"Whoever did it killed the guard then left before I came out. I was worried someone had come to kill me so I waited before coming out. So thank you."

"Could happen. So why you here? Want me to arrest you again?"

"I know who did it."

"Great. Who did?"

Gett walked him through it.

"One of those test boys?"

"Yes."

"He is the boy, the *Jinshi*?"

"Yes."

"How'd he do it?"

"We've gone through it."

"No, I mean who helped him, who transfer the money. Who says: 'you can fuck a concubine!' Don't be a stupid cunt."

THE EUNUCH

"I don't know."
"Why you don't know?"
"I didn't ask."
"So give me the *Jinshi*."
"No."
"Why?"
"You know why."
"He's safe with me. Safe safe."
"He's safer with nobody. I'm safer."
"Everybody's safe now. You caught the bad man."
"I need an escort."
"You always need a mother's cunt escort."
"Only sometimes."
"You're done. Investigation done. Go home. Don't need an escort."
"The investigation is done, the report is not."
"You don't give me the *Jinshi*, why the dog cock I give you escort?"
"You get a completed investigation."

Now in his full robes, Ministry of Investigation red with eunuch tasseling and the two feathers indicating a Eunuch of Standing, Gett was, as he meant to be, especially as he was taller than every other person he might encounter, frightening, an embodiment of Imperial power, striding down the hallways on long legs, an escort of twenty Enforcement soldiers surrounding him. They were loud, he was quiet, and so to someone watching, crouching in the shadows or behind the cracks of doors, Gett walked through the hallways like a wraith, a demon of Imperial skin the color of blood and with the horrifying power to *notice you*. And so, in a very short time, and without a single molestation, they arrived at the Office of Interrogation. Gett's escort guard entered first, two at the door, two at the secretary's desk. Two with Gett, the rest spreading out in the courtyard and in the small office.

Gett, slipped in. Two guards and the Harug clan kid stood frightened. Gett gestured for one to come over.

The Harug Clan kid did, quickly. A sign of changing times.

"Questioner Arigh."

The kid, scared and obedient, ran off. Soon, Arigh stuck his head out from behind one of the screens and motioned for Gett to come. They walked through the interrogation corridors, screams slicing out through the thin doors, but then down to the lower underground cells. Here the walls were stone and the screams were different, not just pain, but like animal slaughter, long, high ceaseless agony and degradation. They stopped near the loudest. Arigh smiled.

"Alright Gett, buddy, what the fuck do you want?"

"Why the secrecy?"

"Why not?"

"I've got him."

"Who?"

"You know who."

"Great! So what are you going to do?"

"Present him to the Emperor and Imperial Mother."

"Why come tell me?"

"You are a part of the custody chain for the interrogations."

"Yep."

"But the reportage of the investigation is accelerated."

"So?"

"It's possible you could request that he be brought here for interrogation."

"It is possible."

Gett just waited, chewing his betel nut. The screaming and

sobbing around him intermittently louder and quieter, almost as if it were music and directed. In a way it was, thought Gett, but not in any coordinated sense. Finally Arigh got tired of waiting.

"It is possible, but we are very full with the book interrogations."

"The diary?"

"Yes."

"How is that going?" asked Gett.

"Like you would expect."

"Have you discovered anything?"

"We've discovered lots of things!"

"Anything related to the case?"

"Of course not."

Gett again waited, chewing, waiting as the screams washed over him.

"You know Gett, I'm not a curious person."

"That seems unlikely given your job."

"No, I'm not. It's a technical job in the final analysis. The curious ones, they don't last here. That's why I'm good at it. The information is in there. People need to speak it out. And that speaking needs to be true. It's just a question of how specifically to do that. A set of appropriate tools. But the ones who are curious, those guys for example headed up the departments that the book came through. And look where they are now. Here, all around us. This one is having the skin of his testicles pulled up and we are putting a combination of island pepper and bitter rock dust in the wounds. Now it doesn't hurt until we add water, see, technical. The one screaming right now. Stop, did you hear that? We are inserting a small bamboo splinter into his eye! It doesn't do any permanent damage! But it is very frightening! You see, different techniques for different people."

"And they could have avoided it if they didn't open the

book."

"Exactly! It should have stayed closed! But they didn't know that. It's a mistake many people make. Much of what goes on down here occurs because people made that mistake."

"It's bad for them. Unlucky."

"Unlucky. Stupid. Evil. Whatever."

"But it is a testament to you that you do your job with such selflessness."

"I thank you for saying that, Chief Investigator Gett. I hope when this is finished you might write such a commendation into your final report."

Gett stood in the large courtyard transition into the Ministry of Espionage and wondered if his escort was big enough. They stood on the stone steps edging the courtyard. Next to them in screened-off doorways were Espionage guards. All told, about a hundred of them, so if it came to it, a significant fight. A definite escalation from the smaller scrums that had been occurring for the last three days.

It took less than an hour of waiting. The message returned. Chief Investigator may enter escorted. The movement of men in armor is not quiet. A long clanking shuffle followed Gett out, echoing oddly and sharply in the empty stone courtyard.

After waiting another hour inside the walls of the Ministry, Gett was finally called in. Han Zongcheng sat in his chair. The table next to it was beautiful, inlaid. And the painting of his ancestors above it had been done by Li Weishi. Perfect and exquisite. Gett walked to the chair on the other side of the table. The chair was turned away in the Chinese style, so he pivoted and looked out over the enormous courtyard that led up to this room. It was impressive, steps leading down in to the paved vast space. In the far distance, the other side of the courtyard, Gett's escorts, hands on swords, slouched quiet and still, watching, heavily armored. Waiting. Han's bodyguard, more dispersed, watched them.

Gett settled himself carefully and slowly into the chair.

"Investigator Gett. You are a man of action."

"Thank you."

"No, I do not mean it as a compliment. For me, it is a neutral attribute. You are arrested. You are incarcerated. Someone lets you out. You disappear for three days. You return. This is what I mean."

Gett waited.

"So you are here now, at great personal risk. You must want something. What is it?"

"Am I at risk?"

"Probably."

Gett thought about this, about why Han would tell him. "This is something you know or you suspect?"

"Where would you draw the line between those, Investigator Gett?"

"Well, you have this information or you have intuited it?"

"Gett, I used to make those distinctions, but I no longer do. They seem, when you are young, to be important and have meaning. As you advance in age and after many decades doing what I do, I simply feel it. And this means I know it."

"There will be a report to the Emperor and Imperial Mother. I will make it. It will conclude my part in the investigation. As a matter of Imperial fiat, I am required to discuss the findings of the investigation with you. As you requested. But also I do this as a professional courtesy to allow you to know what it is that I will report."

"I see, Chief Investigator Gett. In your days of absence, what have you discovered?"

"I know who did it."

"And who was it?"

Gett went through the details.

"And where is the *Jinshi*?"

"He is in a safe place."

"What does that mean, Chief Investigator Gett?"

"It means he is in a place where people cannot find him. It makes him safe. And to a certain extent it makes me safe."

"Why?"

"He had help, clearly."

"He said so?"

"Yes, but even if he had not, it would be clear that he had."

"Yes, he was helped by the harem eunuch, Gogoro Shen."

"True."

"But you feel also by someone else?"

"Yes."

"He told you this?"

"No."

"He told you who?"

"No. He did not wish to tell me that."

"Did you ask?"

"I didn't."

"Why?"

Gett again slowed down. He had rehearsed this but he did not want to make a mistake.

"He was under your jurisdiction when he killed her."

"Yes."

"Does that worry you?"

"What do you think, Chief Investigator Gett?"

"The Imperial Mother could assume that there was only one way that he could have moved around so freely."

"They could assume that. They certainly already have

considered it."

"Yet you're still here, attached to the case."

"That is correct."

"And you controlled the entire scholar housing and examination area during the examination period."

"Yes, I did. What do you think of that?"

"I think it would be easy to hold you responsible, either through negligence or through active help to the scholar who murdered Diao Ju. Not originally, but now."

"I agree with that assessment."

"So here we are."

"That is true, here we are."

"We must—you, I and Enforcer Sulo—return to the Palace and jointly articulate the details of this case and the conclusions of the investigation to the Imperial Mother and the Emperor."

"And what are those conclusions?"

"Concubine Third Class Diao Ju was killed by a former jealous lover during a liaison arranged with a corrupt Harem eunuch."

"Chief Investigator Gett, the murderer has been discovered. He almost certainly did it. You have done an admirable job of figuring it out. But I feel that the other questions, the ones to which you have alluded—how was the money transferred? Who transferred it? Who arranged, within the Palace, to allow this man access to the restricted areas through which he had to pass? Was there a liaison between harem eunuch Gogoro Shen and the *Jinshi*? These will be questions the Emperor, the Imperial Mother and those charged with their security will ask."

"Yes."

"And how will you answer them?"

"I won't."

"And why is that?"

"They are not, do not fall, within the purview of my mandate."

"Which is?"

"To investigate and determine who killed the concubine Diao Ju."

"Those questions would seem to be relevant."

"They are, but only tangentially and importantly they fall within the purview of another department."

"Which, in your opinion?"

"Most likely security and auditing. The auditors will look at the money trail and the security review will focus on the systemic flaws that allowed it—now it has become a security issue, not 'who killed her' but 'how was security breached'. It is not my area of expertise."

"You envision yourself to not be involved?"

"I will be consulted, but it will not be, in the very strictest sense, a homicide investigation any longer and so I will not be the lead investigator."

"And how do you view your part in all of this, this investigation that will follow? What do you hope to achieve?"

"An investigator will do the following: he will investigate the family. There must be a middleman accepting the money. If he's still alive, he can be found. Second: it's an enormous amount of money to transfer. It was either transferred physically, in which case there will be a record of a large volume movement of gold into the Capital, you simply can't hide a physical transfer that large. How did the family get the gold? They must have sold property, we would even have a record of that. How was the gold transferred, from where to where by whom? All of those questions will have answers. Or it was transferred as a debt bond. There are only three financial houses that could handle one that big. An investigator will know who they are and they will cooperate with an Imperial edict hanging over their heads. Whichever it was, both of those will lead him back to the

THE EUNUCH

organizer. And if he took a cut—and he must have—then that too is a significant sum of money, and the same rules apply. This is what I would suggest, but I will not need to because they will assign a competent investigator."

"If the Emperor judges it to be necessary."

"Correct."

"If he believes that the boy had help beyond the harem eunuch Gogoro Shen."

"Correct. This leads me to an issue I wished to discuss with you."

"What is that, Investigator Gett?"

"It regards the investigation. Not mine so much as the one to come."

"The one you will not be involved in."

"I will not be the lead investigator but I will be consulted."

"Of course."

"And such a position allows me a certain distance from things."

"I too have experienced this."

"Yes, and so it allows me to be detached about it. On one level, my job is done. But on another, there are the larger philosophical issues that are touched on."

"For example?"

"For example we know there is balance in the cosmic order, and when that balance is disrupted, it manifests itself in violent natural events. It is also thus in the relationships into which humans engage themselves. Including of course our Imperial Court; this underlies the present violence. You are of the Chinese race. These things you implicitly understand. I and my race have learned these truths from yours."

Gett paused, slowing down and speaking the words he had constructed on the long lonely ride back from the village.

"There will always be minor ebbs and flows in this balance. That is natural and safe and stable. But when something—or someone—is destroyed, there is an emptiness. Something must fill it. This causes chaos. Having completed the investigation to which I was assigned, I see no incentive for me to dis-balance an existing order."

"As a servant of the Emperor, I must exhort you to continue in your investigation, leaving no unearthed fact unreported. You must pursue this matter to its logical end."

"I honor and understand the filial duty to the Emperor that causes you to exhort me in such an honorable and dutiful way. But unless the Emperor himself rearranges the structure of our investigative bureaucracy, I must regretfully withdraw myself from this investigation as my mandated role—the discovery of the perpetrator of the homicide—defines that role as having come to a successful conclusion."

"Your honorable service will be entered into the security and the secretariat records."

"I am humbled that the simple fulfilling of my duty would bestow upon me such honor."

"When is the audience with the Emperor?"

"At midnight."

"That is in two hours."

"It is."

"No time for anything else, then."

"No. There is no more time."

Gett walked down a long torch-lit corridor, trying to stay quiet. He had no escort; he had left them, armor clanking in an open courtyard, freezing. This final meeting would be alone.

His breath trailed behind him, glowing in the firelight, like a

THE EUNUCH

trail of his fears.

He arrived at a huge red door. He waited, knowing he was watched. His heart-beat slowed. The fog from his breath began to settle and dissipate. The door finally opened. He stepped in.

"Any news?"

"There is."

"Tell me."

In the dim silence of the audience hall, torches flickering, and the Imperial Mother silent behind her beads, it took Gett almost an hour to carefully retrace his steps through the investigation, leaving no fact out. When those steps finally ended she was quiet for a moment.

"Your investigation has done credit to you and your bureau."

"It is simply my job, an honor bestowed upon me by the Palace. I am ashamed that I did not complete it more quickly."

"You will be rewarded for your competence and your loyalty."

He waited for her to say more. But she did not.

Gett knew that in life there are sometimes moments—decisions—that split the path forward. Often, while we stand at these crossroads, we are unaware that we are making a momentous decision. But occasionally, as Gett was now, we are.

Gett saw himself in the hall. It was as if the entire investigation was now quickly condensing and pouring down into this hall and filling the space, all of it, every part of the investigation, the entire enormous thing, solidifying into a block, heavy in the room, and balanced on an edge, to be tipped, one way or the other by the thing Gett knew, finally, he must ask.

"It is possible the scholar, the murderer, will attempt to convince the court of…things about the Emperor that are incorrect."

For the first time ever, the Imperial Mother pushed aside the beads and leaned forward, light falling on her face, and she looked at Gett, examining his face. Eyes hard. Finally she spoke.

"Is he the Emperor?"

"Yes."

"Is the Emperor a normal human?"

"No."

"Is he the source of all law?"

"Yes."

"Do the normal rules of social etiquette apply to him?"

"They do not."

"Is a dragon bothered by the opinions of beetles?"

"He is not."

"Does he even notice them?"

"He does not."

"Then you have answered your own question."

Her hand pulled back, the beads fell shut, shifting restlessly.

He waited for her to say more. The firelight continued to flicker on the beads that, again, hid her. The cold of the floor continued to creep slowly into Gett. The silence continued.

Then he heard her stand up, and with a slight rustle, she was gone.

And now, truly, he was out of time.

GETT STOOD IN the small anteroom in which it had all started. Not because he had come here to reflect but because it was the waiting room for meetings with the Emperor. It was now clean and quiet. The carpets which had been stained with the girl's blood had been removed. New ones placed. They were jarring in that their newness clashed with the older faded carpets. But mostly, as if nothing had happened.

Gett wondered if this was purposeful, putting him in this room to wait. Probably not, just bureaucratic blindness. Sulo arrived accompanied by his bodyguards, quiet. Han Zongcheng walked in. Silence for several minutes.

During that several minutes, a new tile cleaner was scrubbing the floor. She was careful, both to do the job correctly of course, but also to be *unobtrusive*. Her predecessor, the unlucky one who had found the body, had been executed. So seeing these men, she backed out silently and shuffled down the hallway, away from that room as fast as she could. On her way back to her quarters, she passed two bodies. Little blood, but in the last few frightening days she had found that in the cold there often wasn't.

Back in her dormitory, she whispered that the great men were waiting to see the Emperor. They came to a conclusion. One listener backed out of the room, ran through the dark, picked up a lantern, made his way to the highest point in the Palace, flashed his light several times, then quickly disappeared back down the stairs. That light flashed across an empty city. Bodies pecked by birds. Dark soldiers and their twisting torch-cast shadows. A dense gridwork of moonlit streets.

From behind locked shutters, barred doors and dark shadows, people who watched for such a light felt themselves relax just a little. Not because it necessarily presaged an immediate end to the chaos that gutted the city, but it at least suggested the worst had passed. The smart and careful would survive or — thought the bitter and defeated Chinese who considered these things in longer and more dangerous ways — possibly more?

And then again, back through the dirty streets full of death, children in muddy corners, past the called-up provincial soldiers at the Palace gate, through the silent hallways passing locked doors and hiding terrified men, we return to the three men standing in the still anteroom. Gett the quiet eunuch. Han the Chinese traitor. Sulo the strange foreigner.

Then a eunuch called and they were escorted into the presence of the Emperor.

Gett watched him — how he moved, how he sat. Watched his mind.

And where he sat was up on the raised shrine, unmoving, looking out at the assembled officials.

His stillness was not the kind that comes from calm but instead from rigidity. He was furious.

The bead curtain behind him was also still and unmoving, and even squinting into the darkness behind it, Gett saw nothing. So the Emperor was alone, without guidance on this very — possibly the most — important night of his short reign. Five days ago, when the murder had occurred, he had been curious. Excited. It was a fascinating and invigorating interval. Real life had opened

THE EUNUCH

up before him! And he had been entranced. Now, though, he was learning what that meant and he did not like it.

So he sat there, hands vibrating with fury. Concealing it.

Gett carefully glanced around. Who noticed? Sulo was looking at the ground, dark beard indistinguishable from dark stone. He certainly had. Han, knees probably tired already, didn't need to tire them farther by looking. He would have guessed before they walked in the doors. Curdeger. Also a veteran. But he didn't know this Emperor. Questioner Arigh. He was much farther back in the room. Probably couldn't see the Emperor clearly. Gett also couldn't see him well enough to judge.

The last of them entered and kowtowed. Now they waited. Probably for the Emperor to gain control of his voice. He wouldn't want to sound shrill and weak. But even for this, they waited a particularly long time. The entire Throne Room completely silent, the torches flickering on the walls. A sea of robed backs spreading out from the throne, hundreds of ephemeral wisps of fog as their breath froze in the cold. Firelight on roiled ink.

Finally the Emperor spoke. His voice was tight. Higher than normal, but he controlled it well.

"The Imperial I has called you here to complete the report into the investigation of the murder of Concubine Diao Ju. Homicide Investigator Enchenkei Gett. Approach."

Gett crawled forward. He had been on his little patch of the room for so long he had warmed it up. Now crawling away, the cold again bit into him. Not so much into his knees, which were calloused from years of this, but into his hands. He knocked his head three times on the stone. Then waited.

"The Imperial I wishes you to present evidence."

And Gett did—watching the Emperor's reaction—walking carefully and methodically through the path he had taken; the likelihood that the murder occurred not in the small antechamber, but elsewhere, the analysis of how, the mental leap to the goal, and finally to the small dark room in the scholar's village.

"Upon return to the city, Exalted Emperor, I immediately sought out Bureau Chief Curdeger Aran. Such an important prisoner had to be kept safe for interrogation and punishment. The Sub Bureau of Evidence Analysis is one of seven departments that has the right to accept prisoner custody. So I sought his house of residence and transferred custody there."

"The Imperial I asks if you have the papers of transfer."

"Your August Majesty, I do."

"The Imperial I orders you to present them."

A scribe crawled forward. Gett pulled the small chopped scroll out of his robe. Handed it over.

The Emperor squinted at it.

"The murderer is still in the custody of Chief Analyst Curdeger Aran?"

"Honored Emperor, I do not know. After the transfer of custody I no longer had the right or the bureaucratic means to monitor his location or state."

The Emperor handed off the scroll.

"The Imperial I asks if the full report has been prepared."

"It has, Honored Emperor."

"Present it."

Gett pulled a much larger scroll out of his robe. Handed it to a crawling scribe.

"The Imperial I asks if it has been chopped by Enforcement Bureau Chief Sulo and Examination and Bureau Chief of Examinations and Minister of Espionage Han Zongcheng."

"It has, Honored Emperor."

The Emperor sat for a long time. Not speaking. Reading carefully through the scroll—the poison, the chase, the energy, Gogoro, the village, the Scholar. The room waited. Gett prostrate

THE EUNUCH

in front of him.

"The Imperial I declares the investigation of the murder of Concubine Diao Ju to be concluded. Investigator Enchenkei Gett is recognized to have achieved distinction. He is released from responsibility."

"Great Emperor I am deeply honored. I do not deserve such a distinction. It is only with guidance from a sage Emperor that I was able to achieve such a result."

"Investigator Gett is dismissed."

Gett crawled backwards, not returning to the section reserved for the reporting, instead now to the rearmost point in the room, mandated for observation. And when there, he pushed up against the wall, pulled in on himself, became small, and slowed his breathing. He was close.

"The Imperial I calls Chief Analyst Curdeger Aran."

Curdeger crawled forward—slid maybe more accurate as his belly never left the ground. He kowtowed.

"Honored Emperor, equal to the forbearers, to the original sage himself. Greater theorist than Mozi and greater Emperor of Action than the First Emperor himself. Greater than Forest Ogoth, defeater of all men, smighter of cavalry. Lowly Analyst Curdeger lies prostrate in front of your radiance and awaits your glorious orders."

"The Imperial I asks if you have the murderer in your custody."

" His custodianship is managed by the bureau which I head."

"He is here?"

"He is in a holding cell in our bureau, Imperial Emperor."

"Does your evidence agree with that presented by Investigator Gett?"

"It does."

"What if there is other evidence?"

"All of the physical evidence that has been examined by my bureau and myself personally supports the conclusions of Eunuch of Standing, Investigator Enchenkei Gett."

"Of course, we can all see this Scholar is a beggar and a criminal."

"Yes, Exalted Emperor, it is obvious."

"And his lies and act of murder have attempted to slander the Imperial I. But of course, how could he succeed!?!?"

"The Exalted Emperor is correct."

"Bring him forward. The Imperial I will hear the beggar's confession."

"I cannot."

A silence. Finally the Emperor asked.

"Why can you not?"

"Exalted Emperor, I will not."

This engendered a much longer and more astonished silence.

"Analyst Curdeger, the Imperial I has wished it."

"I will explain to the Great Emperor why I will not."

"Do you wish to die? To be complicit in the slander of the Imperial I? You will obey the Imperial!"

"I believe the murderer has slandered the Emperor. I believe his crime is so great as to warrant the mandated fifty-two days of torture before execution with the extra excruciation through prolongation of life by the Imperial doctors. I believe there is no need — if we need only to establish his guilt — to hear the murderer speak."

"The murderer will admit his crimes and will cry out to the Imperial I for a merciful shortening of his torture!" The Emperor's voice was rising. "He will admit that his crime was motivated by lust and evil."

"Exalted Emperor, I believe he will not do this. He is evil-hearted."

THE EUNUCH

"You will bring him to speak or you will share with him the penalty of torture for fifty-two days and execution."

For the first time, the Emperor was beginning to lose control of his voice, it was steadily spiraling upward.

"I accept this, Exalted Emperor. If I can protect your Exalted Self from his evil words and can protect the ears of all present, my life is worth ending, and the torture is worth enduring."

The Emperor motioned the guards to take Curdeger. Regular guards would have hesitated before grabbing a high official, Imperial bodyguards did not. They took hold of his arms and hair, ripped him sideways and dragged him to the back of the room where they slammed him down to the stone and yanked his head up with knees on his back. Curdeger calmly took it, waiting. He too was close.

"Who is seconding analyst Curdeger in the Bureau of Analysis?" shouted the Emperor.

There was a moment of silence. The Bureau vice chief hesitated, torn between his requirement to speak and the knowledge that Curdeger had done what he'd done *for a reason*. And in that short important silence, it happened.

From the other side of the room.

"Exalted Emperor, let me, as a representative of the Harug clan, present the murderer to you. I beg and entreat your Imperial holiness to allow me the great honor of conducting the interrogation. I promise on my own life and the lives of my family that I will excruciate the truth from him. That I will cause him more agony than any man has ever experienced in the history of our exalted Jurchen race."

Gett looked over, trying to place the voice. It was one he knew. Not well, but he had heard it before. He strained through the torchlight flitting over black robes, across the room to see.

"The Imperial I orders you forward."

A young kid, tasseling from the Bureau of Interrogations, crawled forward. Familiar. Gett raced back through a catalogue of faces.

"You are from the Bureau of Interrogations."

"Yes, Exalted Emperor. I have the honor of serving under Questioner Arigh."

Gett looked over at Arigh, who had gone still. His mouth half open to say something. Horrified. The kid continued. I am Ech Un of the Harug Clan. Third Banner of the Left. "I am honored to have been assigned and chosen from my clan. I am capable of the excruciation, I have been trained and I have studied at a master's table. Master Arigh is a master even among torturers!"

The kid. The fucking kid from Arigh's bureau. Gett finally placed him. That fucking idiot kid with the smirk. Gett had given him even odds of surviving.

"You are granted custody by the Imperial I. Order your bureau to arrange it."

Gett watched Arigh cycle through every possible solution. He watched the terror blanche out onto his face—something Gett had never, in twenty years of service, seen occur in a high-level official. In private, often. But no one, not a single person made it to this level who would ever show that on his face in this hall. But there it was on Arigh's panicking face.

Guards were sent to bring the murderer to the Throne Room. Very quickly, in under a quarter of an hour, he was dragged in.

Interrogation Enforcers stepped over to the scholar, pushed him forward and slammed him down onto the stone tiles in front of the Emperor. Blood started to slip out from a slice on his head. The Harug Clan kid stepped back and knelt again. Head touching the stone. The entire hall, silent. Curdeger, far back, face forward and expressionless, as two Enforcement guards held him. And then, the scholar raised his head, exposing the birthmark on his

THE EUNUCH

neck. Form the Emperor, came a cruel smile of triumph.

"Speak, murderer."

The scholar waited a moment to compose himself. Then began, in the same quiet voice he had used in his house. He addressed everyone present.

"I am a Chinese. The knowledge gathered by my ancestors, under our Emperors, over thousands of years, I have accumulated in my mind. I am worthy. And your people. You have done great things. Amazing things. You have pulled yourselves out of the forests and ascended to the highest plane of civilization. To rule us. To rule Chinese! It is an achievement. And you have recognized our culture. You have learned it. I am the product of that. You have learned it so well that it allows someone like myself, someone who has absorbed the thousand of years of our knowledge to compete in a competition of merit—your duplication of our Imperial Examination. It is a tradition that carries back thousands of years to the founders of our Empire. We should be grateful. We should see this for the epochal compliment it is. But..."

Gett made himself smaller.

"As our great general Yue Fue has said, the Mandate of Heaven descends only upon a civilized human. You are barbarians. You pretend there has been a coup? You initiate an investigation to find a murderer who doesn't exist? All to cover up your own inability, a frightened child's inability to fuck a woman. And then you seek to place blame on one of your natural masters. YOU murdered the concubine Diao Ju because she laughed at your impotence. I know because she told me when I fucked her."

The Emperor rose from his throne, an oddly calm expression on his face. He stepped down towards the scholar. He took the sword of the guard to the scholar's left. He swung it.

The blow struck the scholar on the shoulder. It cut deep, two hand-widths in, and his shoulder peeled away from his body as a pig's does on a butcher stall. But he kept his eyes locked on the Emperor's. The Emperor reared back with the bloody sword and then stabbed the scholar through the stomach. The sword exited through his back and must have cut the rear-bones of control because the scholar fell, finally breaking his gaze. The Emperor hacked at him as he fell but he was likely unconscious before his head hit the floor.

There was an almost imperceptible movement of the bead curtain behind the throne.

Gett remained on the ground. Head pressed against the freezing stone. His mouth just a fingers-width from it. His breath condensed on the stone, made a small dark warm patch. It was in this dark warmth that he quietly waited. He allowed himself to step into the Emperor's robes, to see through his eyes, to look out at the faces, to look out at the whole Empire, and know they knew. To be less than a man. To find himself separate and mocked. And to know there was no way back in.

The scholar had won. The Emperor would be an object of ridicule for the remainder of his life. Not in an obvious way, he would never hear it directly, but his impotence would define him.

In this moment, Gett felt, after all that had happened, and even with the great gulf of power that separated them, a kinship with the young boy.

Gett's job was finished. The speech assured that the murder would be assigned to the scholar, and in fairness, he had, with almost perfect certainty, committed it. But in the end, and this was the fundamental truth, it did not matter who had introduced him. Sulo had been warned, Arigh had been assured, Han had been been made aware of the boundaries of the possible, and the Imperial Mother had regained control over her son. All of

THE EUNUCH

them owed the restitution of this balance to Gett. And all of them wished for that balance, however unstable, to be preserved. As it has always been in all palaces.

Thus, case closed.

And finally, in his tiny dark place of warmth, surrounded by the frozen hatred of others, Gett was safe.

About The Author

Jonathan Kos-Read grew up in Los Angeles. He studied acting in high school, then molecular biology in university. He has lived in Beijing for the last 25 years working in the Chinese entertainment industry. He now lives in Barcelona with his wife and two daughters. This is his first novel.

www.ingramcontent.com/pod-product-compliance
Ingram Content Group UK Ltd.
Pitfield, Milton Keynes, MK11 3LW, UK
UKHW040238250426
12048UKWH00043B/1573